A. Mary Sharp

The History of Ufton Court

Of the parish of Ufton, in the County of Berks, and of the Perkins family

A. Mary Sharp

The History of Ufton Court
Of the parish of Ufton, in the County of Berks, and of the Perkins family

ISBN/EAN: 9783337429195

Printed in Europe, USA, Canada, Australia, Japan

Cover: Foto ©ninafisch / pixelio.de

More available books at **www.hansebooks.com**

The History of Ufton Court.

UFTON COURT.
WEST FRONT SHOWING THE TERRACE WALL AND OLD GARDEN STEPS.

The

History of Ufton Court,

of the Parish of Ufton, in the County of Berks,
and of the Perkins Family:

compiled

from Ancient Records

BY

A. MARY SHARP.

"Rassemblons les faits pour avoir des idées."
BUFFON.

LONDON:
ELLIOT STOCK, 62, PATERNOSTER ROW.
READING: MISS LANGLEY.   NEWBURY: J. W. BLACKET.

1892.

Preface.

THERE is a feeling experienced probably by most people in connection with an old house, more especially should that old house chance to be one's home, namely, a curiosity about its past—a wish to know as much as can be learnt about those who have inhabited it in past generations, whether they lived sadly or happily in the midst of these scenes now familiar to ourselves, what they looked like & what were their occupations, their interests & their characters; all these are questions to which we would fain seek a fuller answer than can be found in the histories of the country at large.

It seems very sad that men's & women's lives should pass away from their homes almost as do those of the dumb cattle, forgotten & unrecorded except for a line in the parish register, & a half-obliterated & seldom read inscription on the church floor. For if the good that a man does is not always interred with his bones, yet, alas! it often happens that he himself is not at all remembered in connection with it—so, at least, was the case at Ufton.

A certain Lady Marvyn, who lived three hundred years ago, left an endowment for a charitable bequest to be distributed yearly among the poor people of the parish, which is still duly received every Mid-Lent on a Friday afternoon; & yet when inquiry was made concerning her, no one in the place knew who she was, or cared anything whatever about her. It was because it seemed to the writer wrong that such things should be, that this book was begun. Like all other such tasks, the field of inquiry grew wider, & the interest greater as the work went on; & as deeds, grants, wills & other old parchment records each told its bit of the story, there came to light something, if not all, of what one would like to know about those who lived in former days at Ufton, & also, in addition, a great deal more of the history of the place as connected with our wider national interests, than could ever have been expected to exist.

It may be objected that after all the history of one small parish of not much more than two thousand acres cannot be of very general interest, & that the lives & fortunes of one family of English squires, in no way distinguished above their neighbours by talent, wealth or influence, can be scarcely worth chronicling. Yet surely the very fact that this is a tale so like many others which could be written, but are not, gives it a representative character. As the family at Ufton Court lived, so did, for the most part, our ancestors throughout the country. As the Ufton lands passed from the possession of the Saxon Thane to that of the Norman Baron, then to the wealthy Abbey in the neighbourhood, & finally to the English country gentleman, so it happened in other places also.

Thus the story of one small parish is a key to that of the County. It is to be hoped that this much more extended task may before long be efficiently undertaken, for a new & thorough County history of Berkshire is very much needed. So many more sources of original information are now at the disposal of the student than in the days when Lysons compiled his "Magna Britannica," that it is not surprising if many of the statements made in his short notices of the various parishes have been proved inaccurate. The first task of a county historian will be to refute & correct many errors & misstatements which have been, till now repeated & reprinted through a whole library of local histories.

With regard to the following pages, a word of explanation seems needed on one point: that of the spelling of proper names & places. Anyone at all familiar with ancient records is aware how various is the orthography; even on the same page the name of the same place or person is sometimes to be found in different passages, differently spelt; how, then, is one to know which spelling to adopt? In actually quoting the words of a contemporary record, I have tried to adhere to the spelling therein given; and if, in the text of this history also, the orthography is sometimes varied, I must crave the indulgence of the reader.

In collecting information for this book, I have been much indebted to the kindness of Mr. Maxwell Lyte, the Deputy-Keeper of the Record Office, also to the zeal & good nature of many other friends who have not grudged time or trouble in supplying to me various odds & ends of facts which have all contributed to fill in the outline of the story. Chiefly I must thank Mr. Mansfield Parkyns, not only for the materials which he has so liberally contributed out of his abundant store of genealogical & antiquarian knowledge, but also for his help in interpreting these materials, without which, I may fairly say, the following history could not have been written at all. I have also to thank Miss Alice Fowler for two of the principal illustrations, & Mr. C. Buckler for so kindly allowing me to reproduce many of his father's early drawings of Ufton Court. To Mr. Henry Hill I am indebted for the architectural ground-plans of the house.

A. MARY SHARP.

UFTON COURT,
1892.

The Contents of this Book.

PREFACE VII

CHAPTER I.

Of Domesday Book.—Measurement of land—Villeins—Bordars—Serfs—Free sub-tenants—Knight's fee—Socage—No right of alienation—Complaint in Saxon chronicle—The two paragraphs—Ghilo's estate—Estate of William FitzAnsculf—The two parishes—Ufton Richard or Nervet—Ufton Robert—Pole Manor . . . 1

CHAPTER II.

Of Ufton Richard or Nervet.—The family of Pinchegni—Richard Neyrvut—Grants to Reading Abbey—John Neyrvut sells the manor to the abbey—Contested possession—Henry de Pinkney surrenders his lordship to Edward I.—Tythe granted to Edward I. . 7

Of Reading Abbey.—Founded by Henry I.—Rights and privileges—Suppression of monastery—Abbot Hugh executed—Building granted to Sir Francis Knollys—The Book of Charters—The manor of Ufton Richard granted to Sir John Williams—Created Lord Williams of Thame—Daughter married Sir Henry Norreys . 10

Of the Norreys Family.—Sir Henry Norreys executed by Henry VIII.—Mortgage of Berks estates—Sir John Norreys—Monument in Westminster Abbey—Sir Edward Norreys buried at Englefield—Disputed succession—Frances Norreys—Created Earl of Berkshire—Death—Descendants—Earl of Abingdon—Sale of Manor of Ufton Nervet to Francis Perkins in 1709 16

CHAPTER III.

Of Ufton Robert.—Tenants in capite—William FitzAnsculf—Fulke Paganel—Ralph—Gervase—Marriage of heiress to John de Somery—John de Sutton—Estate seized by Hugh Despencer—Bradfield Manor sold to Nicholas de la Beche—Langford family—Ufton Robert transferred to Tidmarsh Manor—Thomas Englefield—Sir Francis Englefield—Estate forfeited—Transaction of the gold ring—Death—Sir Peter Vanlore—Monument in Tilehurst Church—Extinction of feudal claims · · · · 23

Of the Sub-tenants of Ufton Robert.—Ralf de Offinton—Grant to Reading Abbey—William de Offinton—Robert de Offinton—William de Uffinton—Patron of the living—License to hear Divine service in his own house · · · · · 27

Of the Pagnels of Ufton Robert.—Richard Pagnel—Pagnel's Manor in Borwardescote—License to enclose a park—Thomas Pagnel—Agreement with the Abbot of Reading—Lawsuit concerning John Pagnel—Dame Constance Pagnel · · · · 30

CHAPTER IV.

Of the Family of Parkyns.—Peter Morley, *alias* Perkins, *servus* to Lord Despencer—Spelling of the name—Mention of Parkyns in the manor rolls of Madresfield—Despencer estates—Hugh Despencer—John Parkyns, (1398)—Thomas Despencer, Earl of Gloucester—William Parkyns, (1411)—Patron of Ufton Robert—*Ballivus* to Humfry Plantagenet, Duke of Gloucester—Accounts of Corporation of Reading—Agreement between John and Elizabeth Collee and William and Margaret Parkyns—Ecclesiastical union of the two parishes—Thomas Parkyns, (1451)—Agreement between Earl of Warwick and John Montague and Thomas Parkyns with Bernard Brocas—Inq. P. M. of Thomas Parkyns—Ancestor of Nottinghamshire family—Visitation of county of Worcester—Thomas Parkyns of Mattisfield—John Parkyns, (1478)—Margaret Collee—Thomas Parkyns, (1518)—His various estates—Peter Cowdray—Sir George Foster—Richard Parkyns, (1524)—Assault of Sir Humfrey Forster—Richard Parkyns' will—His settlement of Ufton Robert on Francis Parkyns—The sepulchre—His monument—The coats of arms—A display of pedigree—Fate of the monument—William Parkyns' will—Margaret, Countess of Salisbury—Cardinal Pole—Death of William Parkyns—Fever in 1558 · · · 35

CHAPTER V.

Of Pole Manor.—Elizabeth, Lady Marvyn—Sir John Marvyn's will—Pole Manor a sub-division of Ufton Robert—Sir Thomas Ipre, (1396)—Lord Lovel, (1408)—Francis, Lord Lovel, (1483)—Created viscount—Conspiracies—Battle of Stoke—Discovery of skeleton at Minster Lovel—Pole Manor granted to Richard Weston—Sold to Lady Marvyn, (1568)—Complicated tenure—Locality of Pole Manor—Will of Lady Marvyn · · · · 66

CHAPTER VI.

Of the Recusants.—Francis Perkins (1st, 1581)—Disputed succession—Sergeant Plowden—Wardship of Francis Englefield—Effects of the Reformation—Repressive legislation—Provocations—Elizabeth's justification—Father Bluet's declaration—Information of Roger Plumpton against Francis Perkins—George Lingam—List of Recusants—Subscription to the defence fund—Fines—Search of Ufton Court—Lawsuit—Sir Francis Knollys—Death of Francis Perkins—His monument—His widow Anne—Her will—Edmond Perkins—Francis Perkins (2nd, 1616)—Forfeiture of two-thirds of rents—Petition for permission to leave his home—Civil wars—Skirmish at Padworth—Petition of parishioners concerning certain charitable gifts—Answer to petition—Inscription on the tomb of Margaret Perkins—Katherine Tattersall—First deed of settlement Second deed—Death of Francis—Inscription of his tomb—Inscription on the tomb of his eldest son . . . 85

CHAPTER VII.

Of Later Times.—Francis Perkins (3rd, 1661)—His mother, Frances Winchcomb—Jack of Newbury—Epitaph on her tomb—First wife, Katherine Belson—Her epitaph—Second wife, Ann Perkins—Death of Francis Perkins—His epitaph—Francis Perkins (4th, 1694)—John Berrington's accounts—Purchase of Ufton Nervet—Marriage with Arabella Fermor—Portraits—Poem of Parnell—The Rape of the Lock—Pope's dedication—His letter on her marriage—Settlement on Arabella—Francis (5th, 1736)—Lord Kingston—Aldermaston Bowling Club—James Perkins—Charles Perkins—John Perkins—His will—Death, 1769—Francis Prior—Father Madew's note—Relaxation of laws against Papists—William Perkins executed—Visit of Prince Charles Edward to Ufton—Father Price—Father Madew's further notes—Bishop Chaloner—Father Baynham—Ufton estates inherited by Mr. Jones, of Llanarth—Sold to Mr. Congreve—Purchased by Mr. Benyon de Beauvoir . . . 115

CHAPTER VIII.

Of the Court.—Situation—East front—Construction—The kitchen—The central porch—The hall—The dining-room—The library—Copy of Shakespeare—The oratory—The priest's room—Little cupboard—The chapel—The hiding-places—The upper story—Ghostly appearances—The drawing-rooms—Inventory of furniture—Terraced garden—The fish ponds—Fish sauce—The park . . . 137

CHAPTER IX.

Of the Parish.—Soil—Boundaries—The Bath road—The Kennet and Avon Canal—The common fields—Enclosure Act—Grimmer's bank—The chapel of St. John the Baptist, Ufton Nervet—Act of union of the parishes—Granted by Henry VIII. to R. Andrews and Leonard Chamberlayne—Sold to Thomas Burgoyne—Resold to Richard Bartlet—Sold to Sir Humfrey Foster—Sold to Thomas

Wylder—Ruined chapel—The church of St. Peter—Old church—Stained glass—Inventory of church goods—Monuments—Present church—Windows—Benefactions—Yew tree—Registers—Rectors—Suit with Abbot of Reading—Master Thomas Abberbury—Nomination by the Venerable Robert Wright—Marmaduke Goode—Appointment of lay registrar—Act of Parliament—Thomas Wilson—Sale of advowson to Oriel College—Dr. Beke—William Bishop—Dr. Fraser—The Rectory—Gibbet piece—Murder of William Billimore—Hail storm—Letters patent—Feast after the battle of Waterloo—Prince of Wales's wedding—Queen's jubilee—Parish accounts—Increased prosperity of the parish in recent times . 169

APPENDIX.

A full table of Descent of the family of Perkins of Ufton . 201

Section 1.—Paragraphs from Domesday Book—Note on manors of Finchampstead, Padworth and Suthamstead—Pedigrees of Perkins of Ufton, from Herald's Visitation—Note on the same—List of institutions to livings of Ufton Nervet and Ufton Robert—Extracts from Ufton Parish Registers—Ditto from Beenham—Notes by Father Madew—Inventory of Church ornaments in 1889—Inscriptions in parish church, Ufton—Note on wild flowers in Ufton—Recipes by F. Madew 203

Section 2.—Notes concerning the families of Perkins of Beenham, Co. Berks—Perkins of Wokingham, Co. Berks—Perkins of Winkton, Co. Hants—Parkyns of Madresfield and Nottinghamshire—Sir Christopher Parkyns—Pedigrees of Parkins of Ashby, Co. Lincoln—Parkins of Grantham, Co. Lincoln—Perkins of Llandogo, Co. Monmouth—Perkins of Norfolk—Parkins of Sheffield—Parkins of Marston Jabet, Co. Warwick 219

Section 3.—A roll of the pioneers of New England of the name of Perkins, compiled by Mr. D. W. Perkins of New York . 247

INDEX 263

List of Illustrations.

OUTER COVER—View of Ufton Court.

FRONTISPIECE.—View of the west front, showing the terrace wall and old garden steps.

TITLE-PAGE.—Well in Shootersbrook Lane.

CHAPTER I.
	PAGE
Norman knights	1
A caruca with team of oxen, *from an ancient MS.*	6

CHAPTER II.
Arms of the lords in chief of Ufton Nervet	7
Illuminated letter from the book of the charters of Reading Abbey	10
Ruins of Reading Abbey in 1805	12
Anathema from the book of charters	14
Statue of Sir Edward Norreys	18
Seal of Reading Abbey	21

CHAPTER III.
Arms of the lords in chief of Ufton Robert	23
Monument of Sir Peter Vanlore, *Mr. J. Buckler, F.S.A.*	32

CHAPTER IV.
Mompesson coats of arms	35
Facsimile of MS. *Elias Ashmole*	56
Monument restored	57
Frieze from Hall	65

CHAPTER V.
East view of Ufton Court	66
Ruins of Minster Lovell	71
Panel from oratory	81

CHAPTER VI.

	PAGE
Panel from oratory	83
Sir Francis Knollys' party carrying away the chests. *Miss Alice Fowler*	101
Effigies of Francis and Anna Perkins	104
Plowden Arms	113

CHAPTER VII.

Distant view of Ufton Court	115
Portrait of Arabella Fermor as a child	120
Portraits of Mr. and Mrs. Perkins	121
Portrait of Arabella Perkins	123
Seal, 1709	134

CHAPTER VIII.

Ground-plan of Court. *Mr. Henry Hill*	136
Hall ceiling	137
Stables	138
Triangular shield	139
Kitchen roof	141
View of outbuildings now pulled down. *Mr. J. Buckler, F.S.A.*	142
Porch	143
Lozenge ornament	144
Interior of hall as in 1838. *Mr. J. Buckler, F.S.A.*	145
Carved shield	146
View of Ufton Court as in 1820	147
Doorway	148
Scratched inscription	148
First floor plan. *Mr. Henry Hill*	149
Staircase	150
Chimneypiece of library	151
Details of chimneypiece	152
Window in south wing	152
Oratory	154
Newell staircase	155
Plan of attic floor. *Mr. Henry Hill*	156
Wooden lock	157
Statuette	158
Garden steps	163
Prospect of situation of Ufton Court	165
Old gateway	166
Pollard oak	167

List of Illustrations. xvii

CHAPTER IX.

Map of Parish	168
Bath road	169
Travelling in olden days. *Miss Alice Fowler*	172
Ruins of chapel	181
Old church. *Mr. J. Buckler, F.S.A.*	182
Ipre Arms	183
Perkins chapel	184
Brass of William Smith	186
Church porch	187
Old fonts	198

The History of the Parish of Ufton.

Chapter j.

Of Domesday Book.

HE history of Ufton begins in Domesday Book; it is there called Offetone, and is named among the manors in Berkshire belonging to William FitzAnsculf. The passage has been translated as follows:

A.D. 1083.

The same William holds in Offetone, & For original see Appendix *a certain knight of him. Herling held it of King Edward. It then answered for five hides, now for four and a half. There is land for five ploughs, there is one in demesne, & eight villeins & five bordars with five ploughs; there is one bondsman & forty acres of meadow & wood for one hog. Another knight holds three virgates of this land, & has one plough there; the whole was in King Edward's time worth one hundred shillings, & afterwards & now sixty shillings.*

And again, in the list of the possessions of Ghilo:

GHILO, the brother of Ansculf, holds Offetone. Saulf held it of King Edward; then it answered for five hides, now for three hides & a half. There is land for five ploughs; there are eight villeins & five bordars with three ploughs & thirty-six acres of meadow. It was worth a hundred shillings, now sixty.

<small>CHAP. I.
A.D. 1085.
———
DOMESDAY BOOK.

Eyton, Key to Domesday Book, p. 13.</small>

The term *hide* originally expressed a homestead, with whatever land was attached to it ; later on it practically came to imply a certain extent of land which could be ploughed with one team of oxen, and it was in consequence also often called a carucate, from *caruca* a plough ; hence the coincidence between the number of hides and ploughs mentioned. A drawing of a caruca and team of oxen, with peasants ploughing, taken from an early MS., will be found at the end of the chapter. The hide varied in extent in different districts ; its average measurement is generally considered to have been about 120 acres; it was divided into four virgates : thus the two estates of five hides taken together would have contained about 1,200 acres of arable land, besides 76 acres of meadow land and woodlands, the extent of which is not specified. The *one hog* ought, perhaps, rather to be translated one head of swine. The parish now contains 2,122 acres.

The different measurements and values at the time of the Survey and previously, which are so specially mentioned, may be accounted for by the consideration that, owing to the disturbed state of the country and the change of masters, less land was probably under cultivation than during the reign of King Edward the Confessor.

<small>F. Seebohm.
Village Communities p. 76</small>

Mr. Seebohm has described the vill, or manor, as divided into two parts. The lord's demesne, or, as we should now say, the home farm, was distinct from the rest of the estate, which was held in villeinage ; that is, let out to villeins and cottars for fixed services. Each villein held, usually, one virgate of land, with a messuage or dwelling in the village ; his thirty acres, however, did not lie in one plot together, but were distributed in acre and half-acre strips through the open fields of the parish. This custom was not one of those introduced by the Norman conquerors, but had prevailed in the country from very early times. It seems to have been a very widespread arrangement, and is common to this day in some parts of Germany and also in India. The probable explanation of it is, that in this way each landholder enjoys equal advantages with regard to water and soil, and has an equal interest in guarding the village lands from the depredations of wild beasts that may haunt the unenclosed woods beyond; and in the early days of English history, when wolves abounded and foxes and hawks were more numerous than at present, this last reason may have been of considerable force.

CHAP. i.
A.D. 1085.

The villein, so called from the *vill*, or manor to which he was attached, was by no means a serf; he was a person of some responsibility, as is proved by the fact that it was from information given by six villeins in each manor that the returns for Domesday Book were framed. But he was not a freeman; he was bound to certain services to his lord, and these varied according to the customs of each particular manor; usually he had to give a portion of the produce of the land he held to his lord, and besides which he must *reap and mow on his lord's land, hew the deer hedge, make new roads to the farm, pay church-shot and almsfee and must hold head-ward and horse-ward;* that is, keep watch at his lord's tent and guard his horses. *He must also go errands far and near whithersoever he was directed.* But for these services he could sometimes pay as relief *the best animal he had, whether it be an ox or a horse,* and must have been in that case a man of some means. He was sometimes called the customary tenant, as holding by the *customs* of the manor; later on he became the copyholder.

VILLEINS.

Thorpe's Ancient Laws.

Below the villeins were the bordars, or cottars. These had smaller holdings than the villeins, or none at all; they worked as farm-labourers on their lord's land, being housed, fed, and directed by the steward or bailiff of the estate. Lower still in the social scale came the bondsmen or domestic serfs, of whom there appears to have been only one at Ufton.

BORDARS OR COTTARS.

When the lord held the demesne in his own hands he visited it from time to time, staying, perhaps, as long as the food supply, sufficient for the maintenance of his crowd of retainers, lasted, and then moving on to another of his estates.

LORD'S DEMESNE.

1—2

In the absence of the owner the estate was managed by a resident bailiff or steward, or it was sometimes granted to a free sub-tenant, who held it of the liege lord in fee; that is, for feudal service, being bound to supply one fully-equipped knight whenever required, for a certain-sized tract of land. This tenure was known as a *Knight's fee;* or the land was held on *socage;* that is, for some conventional service other than military.

In theory it was not in the power of any landlord to sell or alienate even a single acre of land, the whole country belonged absolutely to the King; but in practice these grants from the tenant in capite, as the original receiver of land was called, to his sub-tenant were often made for money payments instead of service. At the death of the sub-tenant they descended to his heirs, and he became, in fact, as he was generally called, the lord of the manor. In his turn he often regranted his land in part or in whole to other tenants holding under him. But in case of failure of heirs the land always reverted to the superior lord, or to the King, if it was the tenant in capite whose family had died out.

Owing to the legal difficulties which in early times impeded the direct transfer of land from one owner to another, all sorts of indirect methods, such as fines and recoveries, etc., were made use of in transactions which were virtually sales; the King, however, constantly reasserted his rights by the exaction of money payments whenever a case of alienation came before him, and it was not till very much later in English history that the complications in legal procedure arising out of this theory concerning the ownership of land were entirely cleared away. The poor Saxon landowners after the Norman Conquest lost all their rights. Everyone who wished to acquire land was obliged to purchase or to receive it as a grant from the King, and the unfortunate thane had but little chance in competition with a Norman baron. Sometimes he was fain to take his own land as a sub-tenant under the Norman usurper, or even to become a villein or a serf where once he had been master. In the Domesday survey of Buckinghamshire there is mention of one Ailric, who held four hides of land of that same William FitzAnsculf, lord of

Ufton, and, it is added, *the same held it of King Edward, who now holds it at farm of William. Graviter et miserabiliter.* Of Saulf and Herling, the Saxon owners of Ufton, we know nothing at all.

CHAP. I.
A.D. 1085.

The minuteness of detail with which the survey of the conquered land was made seems to have been especially irritating to the Saxons. It provoked from their historian, the old Saxon chronicler, the following piteous lament:

So narrowly did he (the King) cause the survey to be made that there was not a single hide nor rood of land, nor, it is shameful to relate, that which he thought no shame to do, was there an ox or a cow or a pig passed by, that was not set down in the account & then all these writings were brought to him.

And here something must be said of the existence of two paragraphs in Domesday Book, both referring to Offetone. There is sufficient resemblance between the two to have suggested the idea that they might possibly be repetitions, and might both refer to the same estate; but when they are carefully considered, that view seems hardly probable, and it is more reasonable to suppose that they refer to the two separate manors which existed from early times in Ufton. The two estates together, considering them as separate holdings, correspond very fairly in extent with the size of the present parish. Moreover, the differences in the descriptions are more marked even than the points of resemblance. The owners, both Saxon and Norman, are different, and so also are the conditions of the land.

In Ghilo's estate there is no mention of a demesne, and it was probably all held in villeinage; while that which came to the share of William FitzAnsculf contained a lord's demesne, and the rest was divided and held under him by two separate knights, or free sub-tenants. These conditions correspond with tolerable accuracy to what is found to have been the case during the later history of Ufton. It was divided into two separate manors and parishes, taking their names from two of the early sub-tenants. That which corresponds to Ghilo's estate was called Ufton Richard or Nervet. In this, as has

UFTON RICHARD OR NERVET.

been said, there was no demesne, and it is noticeable that there is no record of there ever having been a manor-house in this parish, nor is there any existing trace of one now to be seen.

The parish of Ufton Robert would seem to be the same as the estate of William FitzAnsculf. It was subdivided into two manors. The larger was called, like the parish, Ufton Robert, while the smaller of the two was known by the name of Pole Manor or Ufton Pole. I am aware that in giving the names of the two parishes as above I am not following the account which has long been accepted from the statements of Lysons in his "Magna Britannica." According to him, the estate granted to Ghilo was afterwards called Ufton Greyshall, and the name of Nervet was given to the manor which belonged to FitzAnsculf.

But for the nomenclature that I have adopted I have, among other authorities, that of the Sarum Diocesan Register, a contemporary record dating from 1297, where the two parishes are entered as Ufton Robert and Ufton Richard or Nervet respectively.

They are also so called in all the early deeds and charters which I have seen, in which, as will be shown in the sequel, the manor called Ufton Robert is repeatedly mentioned as being in the lordship of the successors of FitzAnsculf, while the sub-tenants of Ufton Nervet are said to have held under the family of Pinqueni, to which family Ghilo belonged.

I have therefore thought it right to keep to the original names of the parishes as I have found them in early records. It will be more convenient to relate the subsequent history of these two estates and parishes separately.

Chapter ij.

Of Ufton Nervet or Richard.

HILO held eighteen other manors in different parts of the country besides his estate in Ufton, the principal being that of Weedon, in Northamptonshire. He was of the family of Pinchegni, or Pinkeneye, and was uncle to William FitzAnsculf. His son Ghilo founded Weedon Priory in the time of Henry I.; his grandson, Ralph, was living in 1140. After him came Gilbert de Pinkeneye, living in 1167; then Henry, who died about 1209; then Robert and two other Henrys, the first of whom died in 1253. It must have been of him that it is recorded in the Testa de Nevill that *Richard Neyrvut held in Uffinton one Knight's fee of Henry de Pinkeny.* From Richard Neyrvut the parish subsequently took its names.

A.D. 1085;

Ghilo de Pinchegni.

Richard Neyrvut. Testa de Nevill, i. 443.

Holding the manor himself of the tenant in capite, he in his turn had another tenant under him. Among the charters of Reading Abbey is one recording a gift to the monastery by Simon, son of Nicholas (elsewhere called of Bradefield), and Isabella, his wife, of land in Ufton which they had received from Thomas, son of Alan, who had held it of Richard Neyrvut:

Know present & future that I, Simon, son of Nicholas, & Isabella my wife, have given & granted, & by this my

CHAP. ii.
A.D. 1250.

present charter have confirmed, for the safety of our souls & for the souls of our ancestors & successors, to God & the Blessed Mary & to the Abbot of Rading & to the monks, in free alms, all that land, with the appurtenances, which Thomas, son of Alan, at one time gave to us, in the vill of Huffinton, & confirmed by his charter; to have & to hold all the aforesaid land with the appurtenances to the aforesaid Abbot & monks forever, freely & quietly, wholly & fully, in wood & plain, in meadows & pastures, in ways & paths, with all easements & liberties pertaining to the aforesaid land. The aforesaid Abbot & monks rendering therefore annually to the aforesaid Thomas & his heirs 1d. at Easter, & to Richer Nervut lord of the fee & his heirs 7s. sterling at the Feast of St. Michael the Archangel, for all custom, demand, suit & secular service except foreign service, namely, as much as pertains to the aforesaid tenement which the said Abbot & monks shall acquit; & we & our heirs will warrant all the aforesaid land with the appurtenances as our free alms to the aforesaid Abbot & monks against all men & women forever.

Charters of Reading Abbey.

In another deed *Isabella de Rushel*, as she is now called, who was the wife of Simon, son of Nicholas, in her widowhood & lawful power, for the safety of the soul of Simon, formerly her husband, repeats the gift; and by a third charter Richard Neyrvut himself confirms to the Abbot and monks of Reading the same gift and grant already received.

Notwithstanding all these charters, however, there seems, later on, to have been some dispute about the property. In Trinity Term 32 Henry III. (1248), Nicholas de Ingepenne, the nephew of Simon, son of Nicholas, made some claim upon the land; but decision was given against him, and the Church remained in possession.

Assize Roll, M. 1. 7, 2 m. 18.

JOHN NEYRVUT.
Hundred Rolls, Berks, vol. i., p. 17.

In 1275 John Neyrvut, perhaps the son of Richard, sold all his rights in *the manor of Uffinton Richer to the Abbot of Reading*, and it was then stated *that the Abbot held Offinton Richer of Henry Pinkeneye, rendering for it annually to the ward of Windsor* 20s., *and the same Henry holds the manor of the lord the King in chief.*

But neither did this transaction pass undisputed. After the death of John Neyrvut in 1284, his sister, Juliana, the wife of John Rymbaud, and his three nephews, Nicholas, Richard, and Nicholas, demanded of the Abbot the restitution of the lands that had been given, on the plea that they were the heirs to John Neyrvut, and that *he was not sound of his mind* when he demised them. The Abbot thereupon answered that, in his opinion, John was of very sound mind and good memory. For that, on the day when he made the grant, he was *coroner of the liberty of the Abbot & for two years afterwards*, and that he took from the Abbot for the said lands *the livery of four monks & ten marks & four robes by the year for seven years after that he had demised to him the said land.*

Chap. ii.
A.D. 1284.
John Neyrvut.
Assize Roll,
M. 1, 8, 1 m. 15.

Whatever may have been the nature of these privileges enjoyed by the defunct John, the Abbot's plea was successful, and the manor continued to be then, and for many years afterwards, the property of the monastery of Reading.

In the year 1291 another Henry de Pinkeny finally *granted and surrendered to the magnificent Prince Edward* (the first) *King of England, the homage and whole service of John Nereuit & of his heirs for one Knight's fee, which the same John had held of him in Offinton in the County of Berks.*

Exchequer Q.R., Miscell. books, vol. ii., Book of the Exchequer, fol. 3.

John had already made over all his rights to the monks of Reading, who thus henceforth held their land as tenants *in capite* directly of the King.

Some uncertainty exists as to the original form of the name which has been given here as *Neyrvut*; according to the old MSS. where it is found, it may also be read *Neyrvnt* or *Neyrunt*, or even *Neyrmit*. The fact, however, that it has come down to modern times in connection with Ufton as Nervet seems to suggest the probability that it was intended to be pronounced according to the spelling here chosen.

One more incident may be noticed concerning the abbey property. In 1288, by permission of Pope Nicholas IV., King Edward was granted a tithe of all ecclesiastical benefices throughout the country, including the possessions of Reading Abbey in Ufton Richard, for six years, for carrying on the war against the infidel in the Holy Land.

Taxation of Pope Nicholas p. 192.

CHAP. ii.
A.D. 1539.

There seems no reason to suppose that there was ever any branch establishment of monks at Ufton. They were the landlords and proprietors of the farms and messuages, and as such they continued to hold the property till the dissolution of the monastery in 1539. They certainly did not own the advowson of the living, which, till the union of the two parishes in 1434, formed part of the endowment of the preceptory of the Knights of St. John of Jerusalem at Greenham.

Of Reading Abbey.

A.D. 1121.

HERE it may not seem out of place to give some short account of the Abbey of St. Mary, Reading, occupying as it does so important a place in the history of Ufton, and, indeed, of that of the whole neighbouring district.

It was a Benedictine monastery, one of the oldest and wealthiest in the country, founded by Henry I. in the year 1121. Its church had been consecrated by Archbishop Becket in person, and within its walls were buried Henry I., the founder, his wife, Queen Matilda, and their daughter, the Empress Maud, besides various other princesses of royal blood, and a host of noble knights and barons, including, later on, the Earl of Warwick, the King-maker, and his brother John, Lord Montague. By royal charter the abbey enjoyed freedom from all taxation whatever, and its mitred Abbot was a peer of the realm with the right of administering justice and of coining money. Till the reign of Henry VIII. it continued to receive grants and endowments from successive monarchs as well as from private individuals. The valuable library of books which it possessed, the numberless relics in their costly shrines of gold and jewels, the magnificent buildings, including the church, the palace of the Abbot, and the spacious cloisters, refectories, and dormitories—all these have been described to us in the reports of the greedy spoilers bent on its destruction.

The story of its fall is a sad one. Though the wholesale suppression of monastic houses throughout the land did not take place till 1539, yet the idea of such a suppression was by no means a new one. Wolsey's high-handed act in seizing upon the revenues of St. Frideswide's College for the endowment of his projected school at Ipswich and his new college at Oxford no doubt led the way to the later and wider confiscations, and suggested to King Henry an easy source of wealth, as well as a weapon of retaliation against the Pope for his opposition to the divorce of Queen Katherine and the marriage with Anna Boleyn. But even Henry needed a cloak for a deed so unrighteous. Accordingly, in 1539 a Royal Commission was appointed, with the minister Cromwell for its director, ostensibly to inquire into the morals of all the monasteries, convents, and priories throughout the kingdom.

What amount of guilt or innocence was found elsewhere is not here to the purpose. Reading Abbey was visited among the rest, and the report, at any rate in this instance, of the Commissioner, John Loudon, does not justify its terrible consequences. He says, writing to Cromwell: *I have requyred of my Lord Abbott the relyks of hys house, wich he schewyd unto me w^t gudd will. I have taken an inventary of them, & have lokkyd them up behynd ther high Awlter & haue the key in my keping, & they be always redy at yor Lordeschips commandment. They have a gudde lecture in Scripture dayly redde in their Chapiter House both in Inglisch & Laten, to the wiche is gudde resort, & the Abbott ys at yt hymself.* In another letter he says: *My servant shall bring you a tokyn in parchment under the Convent seale from the Abbott & Convent here. He desyrith oonly yor favour & no other thing, & I know so moch that my lord schall find him as conformable a man as any in thys realm, as more at largh I will tell you at the begynning of the term by the Grace of Godd.*

If this parchment token was in any sense an act of submission, as seems probable, it was of no avail; it was not submission, but spoliation, that was required.

On the strength of such reports as these an obsequious

CHAP. ii.
───
A.D. 1539.
───
READING
ABBEY.

Gasquet, Suppression of Monasteries.

Parliament passed an Act declaring that for the better observance of morality and religion in the country all monastic establishments whose yearly incomes were less in value than £200 were to be suppressed, and their revenues ceded to the King; but this Act did not condemn the Abbey of Reading, seeing that its revenues far exceeded the limit fixed. A fresh expedient, therefore, was resorted to; the oath of royal supremacy was imposed upon the heads of the larger monasteries, and when they refused it, as contrary to their religious allegiance to the Pope, they were tried and condemned for high treason, and afterwards hung, drawn, and quartered before their own abbey gates. Such was the fate that befell Hugh, the last Abbot of Reading. Three of his monks suffered with him, and then the corporate property of the abbey, of which no surrender had been obtained, was, against every received principle of law or justice, treated as if it had been the private property of the Abbot, and confiscated to the Crown on his attainder.

The beautiful abbey survived its uses for some little time, during which it occasionally served as a resting-place for royal personages who chanced to pass through Reading. Then it was granted by Queen Elizabeth to Sir Francis Knollys, her Treasurer of the Household and Privy Counsellor. In 1650 it was partly in ruins, and shortly afterwards it was sold and demolished for building materials, and now nothing remains of it but shapeless masses of rubble and brickwork where once were the lofty cathedral aisles and the delicate tracery of vaulted cloisters. Only the gateway is still standing which

witnessed that last terrible catastrophe, that crowning act of injustice and cruelty, the execution of the last Abbot of Reading.

CHAP. ii.
A.D. 1539.

The various charters and deeds of grant which have been quoted above, as also the initial letter at the beginning of this section, are to be found in a MS. volume of the Charters of Reading which has been preserved to the present day in a curious manner.

CHARTERS OF READING ABBEY.

The book is the property of the Earl of Fingall, who has most kindly allowed me to copy from it. On a fly-leaf is written the following story:

THIS book of the Charters of Reading Abbey was found secreted in a very concealed & unknown corner in my Lord Fingall's house at Shinfield, near Reading; it was brought to Woolhampton great house, now Mrs. Crew's, by Gul. Corderoy, the steward, with several other books, found by a bricklayer necessitated to pull some part of the house, or, rather, part of a wall, down in order to repair thoroughly a chimney in Shinfield House. This account I had from the forementioned Mr. Corderoy on Wednesday, the twentieth of June, 1792, who likewise supposes the bricklayer, who is now living at Reading, found no small sum of money, or something valuable, as shortly after that time he advanced much in the world by means of money which no one knows how he could be worth.

Wrote this account on June 23rd, 1792.

N.B.—Mr. Corderoy told me that in this concealed place there was convenient room for three persons, there being three seats.

Though this memorandum is not signed, yet there is every reason to believe that it is genuine, and that the book was found at Shinfield in the manner described. It may be supposed that when the hour of danger came upon them the monks took the precaution of hiding away their deeds and books of charters, or committing them to the charge of faithful friends who would keep them till the hoped-for return of better times. Such times never came, and for more than two hundred years this book and its hiding-place were forgotten.

On the first page is an adjuration of anathema, not

14 *The History of Ufton.*

CHAP. ii.
A.D. 1539.

CHARTERS OF READING ABBEY.

uncommon in old MSS., against anyone who should sacrilegiously tamper with, or misrepresent, the record; a facsimile

[facsimile of manuscript inscription]

of it is here given, which may be translated as follows: *This is the Book of the Monastery of St. Mary of Reading: whoever conceals or perverts the true meaning of it, let him be anathema. Signed, Wyanynghtoun.*

The book contains copies of the various grants made to the abbey by Henry I., its founder, and also by private individuals. These have been written out by the secretaries of the monastery in varying handwriting, as one scribe succeeded another in the task, but always with great beauty and clearness. There is also a catalogue of the books belonging to the abbey. They were mostly copies of the Gospels or the works of the Fathers; but at the end of the list come a few classics—Aristotle; the odes, poetry, satires, and letters of Horace; the Bucolics and Georgics of Virgil, and a book of Juvenal.

There is besides a long list of relics kept in the abbey church, including the famous hand of St. James the Apostle, which was given to Henry I. by his daughter, the Empress Maude, to be by him bestowed on the abbey.

This valued possession is the subject of a special charter which is given in the body of the volume as follows:

(Translated).—A CHARTER OF THE SAME (KING HENRY I.) AS TO THE GIFT OF THE HAND OF ST. JAMES.

HENRY, King of England & Duke of Normandy, to the Abbot & Convent of Reading, greeting. Know ye that I transmit to you, according to her petition, the glorious hand of St. James the Apostle, which Matilda my daughter, the Empress, on her return from Germany, gave to me, & I give it for ever to the Church of Reading. Wherefore, I command you that you receive it with all veneration; & as well you, as your successors, take care to exhibit it in the Church of Reading with as much honour & reverence as you can, or as is due to the relics of so great an Apostle. Witness, William, Archbishop of Canterbury, Matilda, Empress, my daughter, Simon, Bishop of Worcester, Rannulf, Chancellor, Roger Bigot, my food-bearer [dapifero], *William de Crevequer, & others.*

<small>CHAP. II.
A.D. 1539.</small>

When the vast possessions of the abbey had fallen into the hands of the Crown, its affairs were administered, the rents were received and leases granted, by the Commissioners of the Augmentation Fund, the name given to the proceeds of the spoliation of the church goods. These transactions are all entered in the Minister's accounts, and the rolls containing them are kept in the Record Office. From them we learn that the estate of Ufton Richard was retained in the King's hands till the year 1545, when, by special patent, and for the sum of £746 5s. 10d., Henry VIII. granted *to John Doylye, and to our very dear Counsellor, Sir John Williams, Kt., Treasurer of our Court aforesaid* (the Court of Augmentation), *all that our manor of Ufton, in the county of Berks, with its rights, once belonging to the late monastery of Reading, to have and to hold of us in chief by the service of the twentieth part of one Knight's fee.* <small>Patent Roll. 35 Hen. VIII.</small>

John Doylye was distinguished as a soldier, and was brother-in-law to Sir John Williams, the two having married the daughters and coheirs of Richard More of Burghfield. Though his name is here introduced as a co-grantee, Sir John Williams eventually appears to have been alone in possession. <small>JOHN DOYLYE.</small>

This man acted a conspicuous part in the history of his time. He began his career with John Doylye ten years before, when they were both employed in Wolsey's service in the suppression of St. Frideswide's College at Oxford. After the great Minister's fall Williams still continued in favour with the King, and held the appointments of Keeper of the Royal Jewels and Treasurer of the Augmentation Court, in which capacity he received and had charge of <small>SIR JOHN WILLIAMS.</small>

Chap. ii.
A.D. 1553.
Lord Williams of Thame.

all the plate and other valuables, the plunder of the monastic churches. He was also a considerable receiver of the confiscated lands. He must have possessed to a great extent the gift of being all things to all men; for, in spite of the active part he had taken in the suppression of religious houses, he was as much favoured by Queen Mary as by her father. In 1553 he was by her created Lord Williams of Thame, and, together with Sir Henry Bedingfield, he was entrusted with the keeping of the Princess, afterwards Queen, Elizabeth. Here, again, his adaptability to circumstances stood him in good stead, for while Sir Henry Bedingfield was so harsh and discourteous in his treatment that Elizabeth always spoke of him as her gaoler, Lord Williams gained her sincere gratitude by the kindness of his behaviour towards her. Fuller writes of him as *a noble person from whom the Queen had received more than ordinary observance*, and says that he gave her a noble entertainment in his house at Rycote. He died in 1559. While his guest Elizabeth had contracted a life-long friendship for his daughter Margery, whom she used playfully to call *her own crow*, alluding to her dark complexion.

Fuller's Worthies.

On her father's death this Margery, who had married Sir Henry Norreys, inherited both Rycote and the Berkshire estates, including the manor of Ufton Richard or Nervet.

The Norreys Family.

Sir Henry Norreys.

Sir Henry Norreys had also a claim on the Queen's favour on his father's account. He was the son of that ill-fated Henry Norreys who fell a victim to Henry VIII.'s jealousy in regard to Anna Boleyn, and was beheaded in the year 1536. It was said that the King had sent for him and promised him his life if he would bear witness to the Queen's guilt, but that he answered that in his conscience he believed her guiltless, and that he would die a thousand deaths rather than ruin an innocent person. Elizabeth, among whose faults ingratitude was not numbered, never forgot this act of chivalry towards her mother.

In the fourteenth year of her reign she sent Henry, the husband of Margery, as Ambassador to France, when he acquitted himself so much to her satisfaction that on his return she created him Baron Norreys of Rycote. He and his wife must have been some short time afterwards in money difficulties, for he seems to have mortgaged his estate in Berkshire to the Crown for the sum of £3,000. The money was not paid when due, and the estate was forfeited; but the Queen refused to take advantage of the forfeiture, and declared by letters patent that, *wishing to do & show to Henry, Lord Norreys, & to Margery his wife, our grace & munificence more abundantly in this behalf, & also in consideration of the good & laudable service in our wars, to us many times formerly done & bestowed upon us, & in future to be done & bestowed by Sir John Norreys, Kt., son & heir apparent of the same Lord Norreys & Margery his wife, & wishing to give & to grant a greater length of time to the aforesaid Lord Norreys for the payment of the sum by these present*, she would renew the mortgage; and the estates, including the manors of Burfield, Greyshall, Amors Court, Arbor, Sulhamstead, Sheffield, and Ufton, were left in pledge for a still longer period in the hands of her ministers Lord Burghley and John Fortescue.

Sir John Norreys here mentioned was the second son, but the eldest surviving at the time. He had distinguished himself much in the wars in the Netherlands, and was afterwards made President of Munster and General of the Queen's forces in Ulster. He died in Ireland before his father in 1597, and is buried at Yattenden in Berkshire, where he had a property. On the occasion of his death Queen Elizabeth wrote with her own hand an affectionate consolatory letter to the Lady Margery, his mother. Lord Henry and his wife survived five of their six sons: they were all knights. Naunton describes them as *men of haughty courage & great experience in the conduct of military affairs, & to speak on the character of their merit, they were persons of such renown & worth as future times must out of duty owe them the debt of honourable memory*. Fuller is enthusiastic in their praise, and says of Baron Norreys: *It is hard to say whether this tree of honour was more remarkable for the root from whence it sprang, or the branches that sprung from him. If the truth must be told,*

18   *The History of Ufton.*

Chap. ii.
———
A.D. 1597.
———
Norrey's
Monument.

however, they seem to have been rather difficult people to get on with. Sir John, at all events, in the Netherlands, according to Motley, made himself very disagreeable by his overbearing insolence and his jealousy of Leicester, and, moreover, hindered considerably the action of the war.

A magnificent monument stands to this day to the honour of the family in Westminster Abbey. The statues of Lord

Norreys and his wife lie under a canopy supported by eight marble columns, and between the columns on either side life-sized effigies represent the six sons kneeling below. The sixth and youngest son, Sir Edward Norreys, is figured in a different attitude to the rest, whose hands are all clasped in prayer; he has also a lively expression, which seems to point him out as the survivor. He, too, had won military fame, having fought valiantly at the siege of Ostend, where he received a severe wound in his head. Afterwards, with Sir Francis Drake, he made an expedition against Spain and Portugal, when they attacked Corunna (called in the history of the time Grogné), burnt the town, and captured four ships.

Sir Edward inherited the estates in Berkshire from his father and mother. He married late in life the daughter and heiress of a certain Sir John Norris, and settled at Englefield. The house in which he lived was probably the old manor-house, purchased some time ago by Mr. Benyon de Beauvoir, and presented to the living as a rectory; it has since been pulled down. If so, it was there he had the honour of entertaining Queen Elizabeth at dinner at the time of her visit to Reading, on which occasion she knighted his father-in-law, and also Reade Stafford of Bradfield. He died at Englefield, and is buried in the churchyard. In the collection of Talbot letters his death is thus mentioned by Thomas Edmonds, writing to the Earl of Shrewsbury: *Date, Oct.* 9*ᵗʰ* 1603. *We have lost of in these few days a worthie gentleman, Sir Edward Norreys, whom all who knewe his noble disposition have greatlie cause to lament. The discontent between him & his wyfe overthrewe his mynde & consequently his health.* Knowing something of the family dispositions from other sources, we may guess that poor Lady Norreys may not have been altogether to blame for this unhappy termination of their married life.

After Sir Edward's death a dispute occurred concerning the disposition of his Berkshire property, which had been settled by entail on the son of his eldest brother. The sister of Margery, Lady Norreys, had married Sir Richard Wenman, and had inherited from her father, Lord Williams, of Thame, the property of Thame Park in Oxfordshire. Either this Richard Wenman or his son of the same name, and John Norris of Heywood (perhaps the father of Sir Edward Norreys' wife), and William Boulton of Englefield, claimed that the late Sir Edward had made a will leaving the manor of Ufton, with the rest of his neighbouring estate, to them.

Chap. ii.
A.D. 1620.

Francis Earl of Berkshire.

As there were three of them, it may have been that their claim was made as trustees for the widow, particularly if, as seems likely, she was the daughter of one of the parties. But however that may be, the claim was set aside. Francis, son of Edward's eldest brother William, pleaded that he was *verylie persuaded that if Sir Edward Norreys did cut off the original entail, it was not with any purpose of his disherison, or to defraud the true meaning of his progenitors,* and he was declared the lawful heir. He was then twenty-four years of age, and had succeeded to his grandfather's title as Baron Norreys of Rycote. In 1620 he was created Earl of Berkshire, but he did not enjoy his honours long. In 1623, in consequence of a disorderly broil in which he was engaged with Lord Scrope in the lobby of the House of Lords, he was sent to the Fleet prison. The indignity so preyed on his mind that he shortly afterwards committed suicide, wounding himself with a crossbow. At his death his earldom became extinct. He left one daughter, Elizabeth, who inherited all his estates and the barony, which descended, again through the female line, to her grandson, who in 1682 was created also Earl of Abingdon. His descendant still retains, as his second title, that of Baron Norreys of Rycote.

The following table will explain the descent:

Francis, Baron Norreys of Rycote, created Earl of Berkshire in 1620.
|
Elizabeth = Edward Wray.
|
Bridget = Montague Bertie of Lindsay.
|
Francis, Baron Norreys of Rycote, created Earl of Abingdon in 1682.
|
Montague, second Earl of Abingdon.

In this way the estate of Ufton Nervet passed to the Bertie family. In 1709 Montague, Earl of Abingdon, sold his manor of Ufton, including Marrige Farm and various

other farms and messuages, to trustees on behalf of Francis Chap. ii.
Perkins, Esq., of Ufton Court, by which sale both the manors
of Ufton Richard or Nervet and Ufton Robert were united A.D. 1769.
under one and the same ownership.

Seal of Reading Abbey.

SUCCESSION OF TENANTS IN CAPITE OF UFTON ROBERT.

William FitzAnsculf.

Fulke Paganel.

Ralph Paganel.

Gervase.   Haweis═John de Somery.

John Ralph de Somery, died 1210.

Roger de Somery, died 1235.

Roger de Somery, died 1272.

Roger de Somery, died 1290.

John de Somery,   Margaret═John de Sutton, as of   Joan   Thomas
died 1322.   Bradfield.   Botetourte.

Nicholas de la Beche, 1342.

Sir Thomas Langford, 1364.

William Langford, 1410.

Edward Langford, 1470.

Thomas Langford, 1475.

Sir John Langford, died about 1509.

Sir Thomas Englefield, as of Tidmarsh, 1528.

Sir Francis Englefield, died 1592.

Sir Peter Vanlore, died 1627.

Chapter iij.

Of the Tenants in Capite of Ufton Robert.

IT has been said that the parish afterwards called Ufton Robert appears to correspond with that manor in Ufton which, at the time of the Domesday survey, was held by William FitzAnsculf as tenant in capite under the King.

A.D. 1083.

William, as well as his uncle Ghilo, was of the family of Pinchengi or Pinkeny. Dugdale says of him that he *was a great man in the time of the Conqueror, as may be seen by the extent of those lands he possessed.* He own'd a castle at Dudley, one of the very few then existing. He was lord of twenty manors in Staffordshire, fourteen in Worcestershire, and seven in Warwickshire, all lying within five miles of Dudley; he also held twenty manors in Buckinghamshire, fifteen others in various parts of the country, and eleven in Berkshire, namely, Englefield, Bradfield, Hartridge, Ufton, Hodcote, Ilsley, Eddington, Stanford, Inkpen, Compton, and Kingston. In fact, he received a larger share of the conquered lands than anyone else not connected with the Royal Family. But why he was so favoured is not known, nor, indeed, much more about him. Dugdale confesses that *whether he had any issue or not, or what became of him, I never could discover.*

Dudley Castle and his vast estates passed eventually to one Fulke Paganel. Fulke was succeeded by Ralph Paganel, who defended his castle of Dudley against King Stephen for Empress Maud, and was by her made Governor of Nottingham; he was living in 1139.

Gervase Paganel, the son of Ralph, was present at the coronation of Richard I. (1189). He left no sons, and his inheritance passed by the marriage of his sister Haweis to John de Somery. It will be seen, by a reference to the illustration at the head of this chapter, that the Somery family adopted the shield of Gervase Paganel, changing only the ground from *or* to *argent*; this was frequently the practice in cases of inheritance.

The estates remained in the Somery family till 1322, when, at the death of another John de Somery, the last male heir, they were divided between his two sisters, Margaret, wife of John de Sutton, and Joan, who had married Thomas Botetourte. This was during the troubled reign of Edward II. The Berkshire estates, with the castle of Dudley, fell to the share of Margaret Sutton and her husband, but they did not long enjoy them undisturbed. Their manor of Bradfield, to which was attached the lordship of Ufton Robert, was in 1326 forcibly seized by the King's arrogant favourite, Hugh Le Despencer the younger; and though in the same year, by a turn of fortune, the Queen and Mortimer got the upper hand, and Hugh was hanged at Bristol, yet the Suttons did not immediately fare much better for the change. The property was then treated as having belonged to Despencer, and in consequence of his attainder it lapsed to the Crown. However, at the accession of Edward III. John de Sutton and his wife seem to have regained possession of their estate.

Their son and heir, also called John de Sutton, sold Bradfield and its dependencies for an annuity of fifty marks to Nicholas de la Beche, probably of Aldworth, and the same who was summoned to Parliament in 1343. The De la Beche family is now extinct, but a series of remarkable tombs in Aldworth Parish Church still preserves their memory. Nicholas de la Beche presented to the living of Bradfield in 1342. When he died in 1346, it was stated in the Inquisition that he had held the manor of Bradfield *as of the honour of Dudley*; that is, that he did not hold it of the King direct, as tenant in capite, but as sub-tenant from the lord of Dudley, which lordship then still remained in the Sutton family. Nicholas de la Beche left no son, and Bradfield, with the lordship of Ufton Robert, passed after his death, perhaps by the marriage of a daughter, to Sir Thomas Langford.

From this time successive Langfords continued to hold the manor, and with it the lordship of Ufton Robert, till, at the death of Sir John Langford about the year 1509, the family seems to have become extinct, and the property lapsed to the Crown. Bradfield Manor then came into the possession of one Thomas Stafford; the lordship of Ufton Robert, however, did not go with the rest of the estate, but was then attached to the manor of Tidmarsh, and became the property of Thomas Englefield of Englefield in the same neighbourhood.

The resemblance between the Englefield and Langford arms, with a change of colouring only (see illustration, p. 23), suggests, as in the case of Gervase Paganel, that the estates probably passed from Langford to the Englefield family by the marriage of an heiress.

Sir Francis Englefield, the son and successor of Thomas, was Sheriff of the counties of Berks and Oxon, and was knighted in the year 1547. He was one of the chief officers of the Princess Mary's (afterwards Queen Mary) household, but having been commissioned by the Lord Protector Somerset and the Council to forbid the celebration of Mass in her house, he refused to deliver the order, and was in consequence imprisoned. At Elizabeth's accession he found himself obliged to leave the country, and was indicted for high treason and outlawed, and in 1586 all his manors and possessions were declared forfeited to the Crown.

It is related that, in order to save his estate of Englefield to his family, he had before leaving England executed a deed by which he settled it on his nephew Francis, but with the power of revoking his grant if, during his natural life, he should tender to his nephew a gold ring; and that Queen Elizabeth, declaring him to be as an outlaw, legally dead,

CHAP. iii.
A.D. 1592.

took advantage of this condition, sent a gold ring to Francis Englefield, and seized the property. By this stratagem the manor of Englefield, which had been for more than 780 years in the family, was transferred to the Crown. Sir Francis ended his days in the English College at Valladolid in 1592.

SIR PETER VANLORE.

The manor of Tidmarsh and the rights over Ufton, forfeited to the Crown with the rest of Sir Francis Englefield's property, had been granted to Sir Peter Vanlore, a Dutch merchant and banker. Of this new lord in chief of Ufton the inscription on his magnificent tomb in Tilehurst Church records:

See p. 32.

> *A LONG, industrious, well-spent life has shown*
> *His worth, as far as our commerce is known;*
> *His conversation London long approved,*
> *Three English monarchs have employ'd & loved;*
> *His industry, his providence and care*
> *Let his enriched family declare;*
> *The poor his bounty speak that he was not*
> *A slave at all to what his wisdom gott;*
> *After full fourscore years to him here lent,*
> *The greatest part in one chaste wedlock spent,*
> *His soul to heaven, his earth to earth is come,*
> *Utrecht his cradle, Tilehurst loves his tomb.*

The friendship and the favours that he received from successive sovereigns were no doubt in return for pecuniary services. He was, in fact, one of the class so well described by Walter Scott in the "Fortunes of Nigel" in the person of the Scotch worthy, George Heriot.

I. P. M. 17
Hen. VIII.,
1-20, No. 33.

Sir Peter Vanlore is the last tenant in capite of whom any mention is found in connection with Ufton Robert. In his time the rights attached to this position were very small indeed—a pound of cummin paid annually to the liege lord as an acknowledgment of a feudal claim, which was then merely an anachronism. The more substantial rights formerly existing had doubtless been resigned long before, in exchange for money payment, to the sub-tenant, who now became in name, as he had been actually long ago in fact, the only real owner and lord of the manor.

Of the Sub-Tenants or Lords of the Manor of Ufton Robert.

A certain Knight is mentioned in Domesday as holding the manor of Ufton under William Fitz Ansculf, but his name is not given. The first tenant of whom any record has been found is one Ralph de Offintone. His name occurs among the charters of Reading Abbey in the following grant (translated):

Know all faithful men that I, Ralph de Offintone, give & confirm by this my charter one virgate of land in Offinton for the safety of my soul & of all my parents' souls, in free and perpetual alms to the church of Rading. These are witnesses: Elyas de Englefeld, Edmund de Benham, Turstan de Witeleia, Simon de Herwardesleia, & many others.

Further on there is another charter by William de Offinton, grandson of Ralph, confirming the previous gift:

Know, present & future, that I, William de Offinton, grant & confirm the gift which Ralph, my grandfather, made to the monks of Rading of a certain virgate of land in Offinton, with all its appurtenances, which is called Wronkeshulle, in free & perpetual alms, in quit from all secular services; & if anyone shall demand any service from the aforesaid monks for the aforesaid land, I & my heirs will acquit them against the King & against all men, & the aforesaid monks gave to me for this gift & confirmation, one mark of silver before the Lord John Marescalle & Ogger, son of Ogger, & Master Siefridus, Treasurer of Cirestreusis, & the Master Thomas de Husseburne, then Justices of the Peace to the Lord the King in Berscir [Berkshire]. *These are witnesses: Stephen Martel, Baldwin Cuserugge, Gurden Basset, & many others.*

No dates are given to these charters, but we know that Reading Abbey was not founded before 1121. The mention of Thomas de Husseburn as justice of the peace fixes the time of the second charter to the reign of Henry II., when he is known to have held office. William de Offinton, then, must have been living some time during that reign—that is, between 1154 and 1189—and his grandfather some thirty years before.

As to the locality of the virgate of land called Wronkeshulle, we find, later on, that the abbey was in possession of a small property in the parish of Ufton Robert, described as Rockmore and Crondalle. This estate comprises about thirty acres of land, and therefore corresponded in size with the grant of Ralph and his grandfather William. It is mentioned, among the possessions of the monastery at the time of the suppression, as quite distinct from the manor of Ufton Richard, or Nervet, also held by the abbey. It was the subject of a separate grant from Henry VIII. to Sir John Williams, and finally, when the land held in Ufton by the descendants of the latter was eventually sold in 1709 to Francis Perkins, the then Squire of Ufton Robert, this small property of Rockmore and Crondalle was again transferred by a separate deed.

It seems, therefore, not unreasonable to suppose from its history that the name of Crondalle may be identical with Wronkeshulle, and that this plot of land was the same as that referred to in the charters as granted in the twelfth century to the monks of Reading.

In 1199 there was a final agreement between William de Offinton and a certain lady, Eva de Whitmore, concerning half a hide of land in "Ovinton," *whereof a recognisance of mort dancester was summoned between them. That is to say, that the aforesaid Eva remised & quit-claimed to the aforesaid William & his heirs the whole right & claim which she had in the aforesaid land. And for this fine the aforesaid William has given to the aforesaid Eva 100^s sterling.*

Succeeding William was Robert de Offinton, who is chiefly interesting as being the person from whom this parish of Ufton henceforth took its name. He is mentioned in the collection of documents known as Testa de Nevil; or, Liber Feodorum, which contains an account of those who held of

the King in capite. He is there said to hold *in Uffinton half*   Cusw. III.
a knight's fee of Roger de Sumery of the honour of Duddeley; ⎯⎯⎯
that is, that for the land he held as sub-tenant of the estate of A.D. 1272.
Roger de Sumery of Duddeley, he was bound to provide half
the cost of the equipment of one Knight for service, which at
that time was estimated at about 20s.

   There were no less than three Rogers de Somery lords of
Dudley; but if we may suppose that the returns in the Testa Testa de Nevil,
de Nevil of the landholders in Berkshire were all made about Berks, f. 44d.
the same time, an entry concerning the manor of Ufton Neyrvut gives a clue to the date, and to which of the three
Rogers is here intended. It states that Richard Neyrvut
held in Uffinton one Knight's fee of Henry de Pinkney. The
Roger de Somery who was the contemporary of a Henry de
Pinkney died in 1272.

   In 1305 a second William de Uffinton was lord of the WILLIAM DE
manor, and also patron of the living. In that year he UFFINTON.
presented a kinsman, one Walter de Oftone, to the rectory Sarum Regr.
of St. Peter's, Ufton Robert, as it now began to be called.

   The name of this William occurs in several documents of Harl. MSS.
the time. He is entered in the Nomina Villarum of 1316 as Brit. Mus.
one of the two lords of the manors in Ufton, the other being
the Abbot of Reading in right of his lordship of Ufton
Richard, or Nervet. In 1322, at the death of the tenant in
capite, John de Somery, he is mentioned among the other sub-
tenants as holding of the same John *the manor of Ofton, in the
county of Berks*. And three years later, when, in consequence
of the failure of male heirs, and possibly a disputed succession,
the Somery estates would seem to have been temporarily
alienated, he is again mentioned as the lord of the manor of
Ofton Robert, holding under a certain Walter de Encroys.
The Sheriff of Berks was then ordered to inquire if William
de Ofton had not *granted to John de la Beche & Isabella, his* Inq. ad quod
wife, a certain meadow in Ofton Robert, with one pike to hold Damnum, 18
for their life, rendering annually to the same William & to Ed. II., No.
his heirs one rose at the feast of St. John the Baptist for ten 182.
*years, & after the end of the same ten years ten marks
annually*.

   The ten years had then elapsed, and the King now laid

claim to the meadow *by reason of the forfeiture of the same John.* (He had been dead three years.)

Lastly, in probably extreme old age, in 1333, William received a license from the Bishop of the diocese (Salisbury) to enable him to have divine service performed in his own house of Ufton Robert. The old manor house has now disappeared, but it probably occupied a moated site still to be recognised not far from the parish church. Such licenses were then legally necessary, and were not unfrequently granted in cases of sickness or infirmity.

A few years later—1338—another lord of the manor, Richard Pagnel, reigned in his stead.

Of the Pagnels of Ufton Robert.

There were several more or less important families of Pagnels, or Paganels, all assumed to have been descended from William Paganel, lord of Pakinton, and brother to Fulke Paganel, the successor of William FitzAnsculf.

The Richard Pagnel who succeeded to the property of Ufton Robert had previously, since 1326, held an estate called Pagnel's Manor in Borwardescote, or Buscot, also in Berkshire; that is, during William de Ufton's lifetime. The first mention of him as lord of Ufton is in a grant which he received from King Edward III. in the year 1338, to the following effect:

The King to the Archbishops, &c., greeting. Know ye, that we of our special grace & by this our charter have confirmed to our very dear Richard Pagnel that he & his heirs forever may have free warren in all their demesne lands of the manors of Oftone Robert & Borwardescote, in Co. Berks. . . . we have granted, moreover, of our special grace to the same Richard that he can enclose 300 acres of pasture & wood in his said manor of Oftone Robert, & make a park thereof. Given by our hand at Westminster on the 22ᵈ day of April. By writ of Privy Seal.

It is interesting to note that the rights of the chase did not then by any means belong as a matter of course to owners of landed property, but were reserved by the Norman and Angevin Sovereigns in their own hands or bestowed on the tenant by special license.

In 1339 Richard Pagnel, as patron of the living of Ufton Robert, presented Thomas de Ofton, the son of William, his predecessor, as Rector, an appointment which leads one to suppose that there may have been some relationship between the two families.

In 1348 Thomas Pagnel, son of Richard, had succeeded his father. An agreement exists, dated on the Saturday next after the feast of St. Leonard, between him and *Henry, by the Grace of God Abbot of Radyng, concerning a certain piece of land & moor which is parcel of the manor of Oftone Nevent, called le Carpenteres lond, containing 9 acres of land lying next the Park of the said Thomas in Oftone Robert, between the moor which is called clarissemore on the one part and land which is called Hethlond on the other part,* which piece of land Thomas Pagnel and his heirs were to rent of the abbey for sixty years, for the annual payment of 3s. The agreement is witnessed by Sir Philip Englefield, Sir Michael Beleth, Knts., Roger Atte More, John Banastre, Nicholas Kenetwode, and others. Unfortunately, not one of these local names has survived to help us to fix the boundaries of the two parishes of Ufton, or to know the locality of the originally enclosed park.

In 1379 Thomas Pagnel was accused at the Reading Assizes of having *unjustly disseised John, son of John Pagnel, of his free tenement in Ufton Robert.* But here again the historian is at fault, for no sooner was the inquiry begun, and just when one might have hoped to have gathered from the proceedings some interesting family details, when *thereupon came the Abbot of Redyngesby, Reginald de Sheffield, his attorney, to challenge, prosecute, & defend all his liberties. And he says that the manor put in view & the parties of the assize aforesaid are within the Bailiwick of the same abbot, & therefore he demands his Court*—that is, the hearing of the case; and *we* hear no more of it.

In the diocesan register, in which his presentations to the living of Ufton Robert are recorded, Thomas is styled

CHAP. iii.
A.D. 1406.

I. P. M., 16 Hen. VI., No. 9.

I. P. M., 9 Hen. IV. No. 29, m. 19, and 33 Hen. VI., No. 28, m. 30.

CONSTANCE PAGNEL.

Donzell, an equivalent title to Esquire, and signifying a man of good birth, but not knighted. He lived to be an old man. If he was already of age when he came into his inheritance in 1348, he must have been nearly eighty in 1406, the date of his last presentation to the living.

In 1410 his name drops out of the list, and one Alice Pagnel acts as patron. She may have been his widow. There was an Alice, widow of a Thomas Pagnel, who died in 1437. But there was also, at this time, another widow in the family, who is named in more than one deed as holding rights over lands in Ufton. In 1408, and again in 1455, it was stated in Inquisitions that Sir John Lovell, and after him his son William, held certain lands in Ufton and the neighbourhood of *Dame Constance Pagnell, lady of Ufton*. Where nothing further is recorded one can only conjecture. These rights may have been of the nature of a jointure, and Dame Constance may have been the widow of John or of some other member of the family who was knighted. Thomas, as we have seen, is only called Donzell. He had no son to succeed him, and his manors and estates passed to William Parkyns, the first of his name of Ufton.

Monument of Sir Peter Vanlore, 2nd
1627

J. Buckler, F.S.A.
28 June 1816

EARLY DESCENT OF THE FAMILY OF PARKYNS OF UFTON.

Peter Morley, *alias* Perkins,* of co. Salop, *servus* = Agnes Taylor.
to Lord Hugh Despencer, Lord of Shipton,
co. Oxon; living 1380 and 1381.

|

Henry Perkins.*

|

John Parkyns, seneschal to Thomas Despencer, Earl of Gloucester;
living 1397 and 1400.

|

William Parkyns, Lord of Ufton   Robert, bailiff   Margaret,
to Humphrey Plantagenet, Duke of Gloucester;   daughter
living 1411 and 1447.   of ....

|

Thomas Parkyns, living 1452 and 1479.

|

John Parkyns, living 1495. = Margaret Collee.

|

Thomas Parkyns, living 1495 and 1524 = Dorothy More

* The names of the founder of the family and of his son are here spelt in the modern way, for the reason that they are so given in the Visitation Pedigree, 1623, the only document in which mention of them has been found. The names of their descendants are spelt as in contemporary records.

Chapter iv.

Of the Family of Perkins.

N the Heralds' Visitation for Berkshire of 1623 this family is said to have been descended from a certain Peter Morley, *alias* Perkins, of Shropshire, "servus" to Hugh Despencer, Lord of Shipton in Oxfordshire, who was living in the year 1380, and who married Agnes Taylor. The word "servus" is considered to mean bailiff, and its use here seems to imply that Peter Morley was the bailiff, or manager, of the estates belonging to Lord Despencer at Shipton. "Perkin" was an old English form for the Christian name of Peter, familiar to everyone in the instance of Perkin Warbeck. Perkin, Wilkin, Jenkin, etc., are all frequently found in early times as diminutives and synonyms of Peter, John, and William, etc., the "kin" being of Flemish origin.

A.D. 1380.

See Appendix

The addition of the *s* seems to be a characteristic common in Wales. In England, when the patronymic was used, the word *son* was usually affixed, as *John Adamson*. In Wales, on the contrary, no affix was used, but the paternal name was put in the genitive, as *Griffith William's* or *David John's*, which have become *Williams* and *Jones*. *Perkins* is, therefore, merely a Welsh or western county form for *Perkin's son*; in England, Perkinson or Parkinson. Perkin Morley,

A.D. 1380
Chap. iv.

as it has been seen, came from Shropshire, on the borders of Wales. It is, therefore, natural to find that his son was called Henry Perkins.

The name of the Berkshire family, however, though so spelt in the Visitation pedigree, is in other and earlier deeds generally found written thus—*Pkyns*, and the abbreviation, when extended at any date before 1600, was *Parkyns* or *Parkynnes*. It was only from the time of James I.—that is, shortly before the date of the Visitation, when the influence of classical literature made itself felt even in the orthography of proper names—that the *y*, unknown in Latin, was changed for *i*, and *Per* substituted for *Par*. The very same pedigree referred to, where the name is given as *Perkins* in the official copy, is signed on behalf of the then representative of the family, *ffrauncis Parkyns*. In the following pages the name will be given as far as possible as spelt in records contemporary with the history.

Excerpta Scrinio Maneriali de Madresfield in Com. Vigorni, 1873.

It has been ascertained that within a not very extended district, including the adjoining parts of Shropshire, Worcestershire, and Herefordshire, many families of the name of Perkins or Parkyns were settled from early times. In particular, the manor rolls of Madresfield, in Worcestershire, record that one John Parkyns held some land there called Parkynscroft, conjointly with a Richard More. The names of More and Perkins here occur very constantly together, while Morley is not to be found at all, suggesting the idea that it was More, not Morley, which should have been written in the pedigree.

In these rolls, in 1388, Agnes, daughter of John Tyler, is mentioned as one of the smaller tenants. It will be remembered that Agnes Taylor was the name of the wife of Peter, or Perkin, the founder of the family.

In the immediate vicinity of Madresfield, in Worcestershire, were the estates of Hanley Castle and Malvern Chase, which, about the year 1340 became the property of Hugh Le Despencer, the third of that name, by his marriage with Elizabeth, daughter and heir of William Montacute, Earl of Salisbury. It is not, therefore, surprising to find that there existed the connection of master and servant between the great lord and his humble neighbour, a connection which, as will be seen in the sequel, was continued through several generations.

This Hugh was the son of Hugh Despencer, commonly called the Younger, who had been executed at Bristol in the same year as his father, known as Hugh the Elder, when their vast estates had been forfeited to the Crown. Alianore, the widow of Hugh Despencer the younger, was the eldest sister and coheir of Gilbert de Clare, Earl of Clare, Hertford and Gloucester. She had inherited the estates of Hanley Castle, Malvern Chase, in Worcestershire, and the manors of Bisley, Tewkesbury, and Fairford, etc., in Gloucestershire, and she married secondly William La Zouche of Mortimer. She died in 1337, leaving her property to her son by her first husband, Hugh Le Despencer (the third of the name), then twenty-nine years of age.

He was at the time in disfavour with the King and kept in prison at Bristol, in the custody of Roger Mortimer. However, after the death of his mother, as Dugdale says : "*the beams of the King's favour beginning to shine upon him, he did homage, and had livery of the lands of her inheritance,*" and betook himself to the King's service in the wars in Gascony and Scotland. He behaved himself so well during these campaigns that the King bestowed upon him a discharge of all the debts he then owed or should owe to the Exchequer to the ensuing Michaelmas. He was summoned to Parliament from 12 Edward III. till 22 Edward III. inclusive, and died February 8, 23 Edward III. (1349), being seised of the manors of Great Marlow, in the county of Buckingham; Maple Durwell and Ashleigh, in the county of Southampton (Hampshire); Caversham, Shipton, Burford, and Chadlington, in Oxfordshire, and many others. He was buried at Tewkesbury, near the high altar.

If Peter Morley, or Perkins, was living in 1380, he must have been quite a young man when in the service of Hugh Le Despencer.

The following slightly sketched table of descent will help to explain the further connection of the Despencers and their descendants with this story :

A.D. 1398.
CHAP. iv.

| Hugh Despencer (3rd), died without issue, 1349. *Peter Morley, bailiff.* | Elizabeth, dau. of William, Earl of Salisbury. | Edward Despencer, died 1342. | Anne, dau. of Lord Ferrers, died 1367-68. |

Edward Despencer, died 1375 = Elizabeth, Baroness Burgersh, died 1411.

Thomas Despencer, created Earl of = Constance, dau. of Edmund, Duke of
Gloucester; killed 1400.   York, fifth son of Edward III.
John Parkyns, seneschal.   buried in Reading Abbey 1420.

| 1st husband, Richard Beauchamp, Earl of Worcester. | Isabel, heir to her father; died 1439. | 2nd husband, Richard Beauchamp, Earl of Warwick; died 1439. |

| Elizabeth, co-heir with half-sister. | Henry Beauchamp, died without issue 1445. | Anne, co-heir of Despencer and Beauchamp estates; died 1470. | Richard Neville, Earl of Salisbury and Warwick, the "King-maker." *Thomas Parkyns co-trustee.* |

JOHN PARKYNS.

The grandson of *Peter Morley, alias Perkins*, John Parkyns, was, according to the Visitation pedigree, seneschal to Thomas Despencer, and was living in 1398 and 1399. This Lord Despencer, by the favour of Richard II., whose kinswoman he had married, obtained a revocation of the judgment of exile which had been passed against his great-grandfather Hugh, and also repayment of the value of the possessions of various kinds which he asserted to have then been forfeited to the Crown. The list gives one an idea of the manner of life of the great barons of the time and in what their wealth consisted. From it we learn that Hugh was

Rot. Parl., 21 R. II., n. 35.

possessed of no less than 59 lordships in various counties, 28,000 sheep, 1,000 oxen and steers, 1,200 kine and their calves, 40 mares with their colts of two years, 160 draught

Cart. de Ann. 21, 22, 23 Rich. II., n. 21.

horses, 2,000 hogs, 3,000 bullocks, 40 tuns of wine, 600 bacons, fourscore carcases of martinmass beef, and 600 muttons in his larder (all this meat being probably salted); 10 tons of cider, armour-plate, jewels, and ready money better than £10,000; 36 sacks of wool and a library of books. For all this Thomas Despencer received compensation, and he was, moreover, in 1398 created Earl of Gloucester. But in the course of the very next year he was one of the chief of those peers who formally deposed his unfortunate master in favour of Henry IV. He did not live long after his act of treachery. Before many months were passed he fell into disgrace, was degraded from his earldom, taken prisoner to Bristol, and there in the market-place beheaded by the mob on January 5, 1400.

The two dates mentioned in connection with John Parkyns coincide with his patron's installation as Earl and with his disgrace, from which it may be supposed that he was in some way connected with both events.

On February 23, in the year 1400—that is to say, a few weeks only after the death of the Earl of Gloucester, John Parkyns, with one Thomas More, received from King Henry IV. *the custody of one Water-Mill & one carucate of land in Shipton under Wichewode, in the County of Oxford, which Anne, late Queen of England, deceased, held for the term of her life as parcel of her dower . . . so that the aforesaid Thomas & John may always have sufficiency of Timber for the construction, repairing, & sustaining of the Mill aforesaid, as often & where it shall be necessary.* This small property must have been adjoining or very near to the property of John Parkyns' late master, but whether the grant had any connection with the forfeiture of the estates of the Earl of Gloucester does not appear.

In 1390 John Parkyns, as we learn from the Madresfield court roll before referred to, had held one messuage and eighteen acres of land there, for which he did homage to the lady of the manor, Johanna Bracey, showing that he had then only recently acquired the property.

William Parkyns, the son of John, was the first of the family who was lord of Ufton Robert. From 1411 he is named in the diocesan registry as patron of that living, and is styled variously *Lord of Ufton, Donzell*, and *True Patron*.

He was attached to the service of Humphry Plantagenet, Duke of Gloucester, as *bailtious*, or agent, and it was probably in that capacity that he was concerned in an agreement by which one William Leyre confirmed the lordship of Child's Manor, East Barsham, Norfolk, to Humphry, Duke of Gloucester, Alianore his wife, and William Parkyns, Esq.; for immediately afterwards, in another deed, he released his right therein to the Duke. He sealed this deed with the arms, or, a fesse dancetté between eight billets ermines. This is the first time in which the armorial bearings of the family appear. They differ from the later shield in the number of the billets, which were afterwards increased to ten. Humfrey, Duke of Gloucester, was brother to Henry V., and uncle and guardian to the young Henry VI. during his minority—"the good Duke Humfrey," as he was called, whose disgrace and tragic death suggested to Shakespeare the lament which he puts into the mouth of Henry:

For in the shades of death I shall find joy, in life but double death, now Gloster's dead.

William Parkyns is said in the Visitation pedigree to have been living in the year 1419; that is, during the French wars. On May 29 of that year, soon after Rouen had capitulated to the English, a meeting took place at Menlau between the French Queen, accompanied by the Duke of Burgundy and Henry V., to arrange conditions of peace, the most important of which was to be the marriage of the King with the French Princess Catherine. Henry was on that occasion accompanied by his brother, the Duke of Gloucester, and from the special mention of the date in connection with William Parkyns it may have been that he also was present in attendance on his patron.

In 1426 and the two succeeding years his name appears in the accounts of the Corporation of Reading as follows (translated):

For payment at games given before the Mayor at William Parkyns', 6s. 8d. For ale given at the same, 2d. To the minstrels of the Duke of Gloucester at the Mayor's breakfast at Parkyns', 20d.

Whether the Mayor came out to Ufton is not clear, or

whether William Parkyns entertained him in Reading. One is reminded of a passage in one of Margaret Paston's letters to her husband in which she tells him that *the Mayor and Mayoress of Norwich sent their dinner this day.... they dined here. I am beholden to them, for they have sent to me divers times since ye went hence.*

In William Parkyns' case the Mayor only paid for the ale and the music and the games provided for the entertainment. William married a lady whose Christian name was Margaret, and conjointly with her, in 1424, he was party to an agreement with John Collee and Elizabeth his wife by which the manor and advowson of Ufton Robert and a moiety of lands in Borwardescote were settled on the same William and Margaret, and in case of William's death then on Margaret and her heirs male; subject to the yearly payment of eight marks of silver to Elizabeth Collee. It is certain that the manor and advowson of Ufton Robert had been already for some years past the property of William Parkyns. This deed may, therefore, perhaps be considered as of the nature of a marriage settlement on his wife. From the fact that Elizabeth Collee had a charge on the Ufton Estate, it seems probable that she was in some way a relation of William Parkyns—perhaps his own or his wife's sister. But this is only conjecture.

John Collee was the owner of a manor in the neighbouring parish of Padworth, called Hussie's Manor, and his name appears, with that of William Parkyns, in a list of gentry of the county of Berks, returned in 1434 by Robert Nevil, Bishop of Sarum, and his brother, Sir William Lovel, commissioned by Henry VI. to administer the oaths.

In 1427 and during several succeeding years William Parkyns served as escheator for the counties of Berks and Oxon. The most important event, however, in which he took part—at least, as regards the history of Ufton—was the ecclesiastical union of the two parishes of Ufton Robert and Ufton Richard or Nervet. In 1435 an agreement to this effect was sanctioned by the Lord Bishop of Salisbury, and signed respectively by William Parkyns and the Prior of the Knights of St. John of Jerusalem, who with his brethren had owned the advowson of the smaller living (see p. 10). This they now resigned, and William Parkyns and his successors henceforth for several generations held the patronage of the united living of Ufton as it now is.

In 1444 William signed his name as a witness to a deed of grant, made by Henry VI. to the Provost and College of Eton, of lands in New and Old Windsor and in Clewer.

In 1447 he is mentioned in the Court Rolls of the Manor of Bray as still holding the office of ballious to the Duke of Gloucester. The manors of Bray and Crookham had been granted to the Duke by his father, Henry V.

William must have died not very long after this date, for in 1451 his son Thomas presented to the living of Ufton as *true patron*. He continued to do so on successive occasions till 1474.

These dates include the time of the Wars of the Roses, which culminated in the final triumph of the Yorkist party in 1461, supported by Richard Nevile, the Earl of Warwick, the King-maker.

There is a deed of that date by which Thomas Parkyns, in conjunction with the Earl of Warwick and his brother John, Lord Montague, received from Bernard Brocas, of Horton, co. Bucks, a Lancastrian, certain manors in Hampshire, Buckinghamshire, and Hertfordshire, in which Thomas Parkyns probably acted merely as co-trustee. By the light of contemporary events one may guess that it was an amicable transaction, such as was frequently practised at the time by which the adherents of the conquered party saved their estates from confiscation by handing them over temporarily to some friendly opponent.

Some such arrangement was probably made in the case of Thomas Parkyns himself later on, when his patron, the Earl of Warwick, having taken arms against Edward IV., had been defeated and slain at the battle of Barnet. For though it is certain that he had inherited his father's estates, and also that his son held the same after him, yet at the inquisition taken after his death in 1478 it was declared that

THOMAS PARKYNS Armiger held no lands nor

tenements of the King in Capite; nor was seised, the day on which he died, in demesne as of fee nor in service in the county of Berks of any lands or tenements. And further, that the same Thomas Parkyns was seised & held on the day of his death in demesne as of fee, of the Abbot of Redynge, as of his manor of Foxell's Court in Sulhamsted Abbotts, one messuage & divers lands & tenements with their appurtenances in soccage. And that the said Thomas Parkyns held no other lands or tenements in Capite, nor was seised on the day of his death or any other in demesne or in service except the messuage, lands & tenements aforesaid.

His manor and other possessions had probably been made over for the time to some friend in trust for his family. It is to be noticed that the only property of which he was declared to have been possessed was the land he held of the Abbey of Reading, and the more likely to be safe from confiscation on account of being Church property.

Thomas Parkyns is a person of some interest in the family history, as he is referred to in the records of the Nottinghamshire branch as their ancestor. He is there called "Thomas Parkyns, of Ufton and Mattisfield, co. Berks." There is no such place as Mattisfield, in Berkshire. The place so named, both here and in the Worcestershire Visitation of 1569, must evidently be considered as Madresfield, where, as it will be remembered, John Parkyns, the grandfather of Thomas, had owned property which doubtless had passed to his descendants. Thomas Parkyns, of Ufton, would, therefore, be rightly described as also of Madresfield, in Worcestershire. In the Appendix will be found a further notice of the Nottinghamshire family.

John Parkyns, the son of Thomas, was 28 years of age when he inherited his father's manor of Ufton Robert. He was already married to Margaret Collee, and through her he came into possession of Hussie's Manor in Padworth and also of West Court in Finchampstead, with an alternate right to the presentation to the living. A settlement which she made of her property, dated November 6, 1519—probably after her husband's death, since no mention is made of him—is quoted in a subsequent Chancery Inquisition. In it she gave the whole over to trustees *for her use during her life, and for three years afterwards to carry out her will*, and afterwards to her son Thomas Parkyns.

The additions thus made to the landed property of the family remained for a long time in their possession; indeed, Hussie's Manor is still to this day attached to the Ufton estate, being that part of Padworth parish which adjoins the parish of Ufton. The old manor-house was still standing on the slope of the hill between Padworth Rectory and Ufton Court almost within the memory of those now living, and was then known as Pam Hall.

An account of the descent of Finchampstead Manor is given in the Appendix.

Margaret Collee's arms, argent, a cross sable wavy, are quartered with those of John Parkyns on a monument erected in 1560, which will be described later on.

John Parkyns presented to the living of Ufton three times between the years 1504 and 1511.

Thomas, the son of John Parkyns and Margaret Collee, married Dorothy, daughter of Edward More, of Wichwood, co. Hants. The Chancery Inquisition, taken six years later, in 1524, at the time of his death, gives a very full and interesting account of the property belonging to him, and incidentally of the neighbouring gentry. Thomas, it states, had held the manor and advowson of Ufton Robert and lands in Borwardescote in demesne as of fee tail. Ufton Robert held of Thomas Englefield as of his manor of Tidmarsh, by fealty and a pound of cummin, Borwardescote of Thomas Fettiplace, services not known. Then comes the settlement already quoted, made by Margaret Collee, his mother. Another deed is then quoted, dated July 13, 10th Henry VII. (1495), by which William Parkyns, Esq., and other trustees gave a certain Edward More lands, etc., in Woolhampton and Aldermaston to the use of the said Edward More for seven years, and afterwards to the use of Thomas Parkyns (as son and heir of John Parkyns) and of Dorothy, wife of the said Thomas, and their heirs. (This would be Dorothy's marriage settlement. She was living, and in actual possession of this land, at the time of the Inquisition. The land in Woolhampton was held of the Prior of St. John of Jerusalem by fealty and 4s., and that in Aldermaston of Sir George Foster.

And, further, it is stated that Thomas had held lands in Beenham and Bradfield of Thomas Stafford as of his manor of Bradfield, and also lands in Ufton of Richard Parkyns by fealty and 1s. 6d., as of his manor of Ufton.

Also, that he had held Hussie's manor of Padworth and other lands and a messuage in Padworth of Peter Cowdray, as of Cowdray's Manor in Padworth by fealty and 6s. 8d.

And, finally, that he had held a messuage and lands in Ufton Nervet called Pangbourne's land, and land in Sulhamstead Abbotts of the Abbot of Reading.

In this account of the property it is to be noted that the chief lordship of Ufton Robert had now passed away from the manor of Bradfield, and was attached to that of Tidmarsh with merely a very nominal service, namely, the yearly payment of a pound of cummin.

In these ante-Reformation days the Brotherhood of St. John of Jerusalem, with its establishment at Woolhampton and the Abbey of Reading, appear among the large landowners of the district.

The ancient family of Cowdray was still at Padworth. The parish had been divided since the time of the Conquest into the two manors afterwards known as Cowdray's and Hussie's. The latter has been already mentioned; the former was granted to Fulke de Cowdray by King Henry III. *in chief by the sergeanty of holding a rope on the Queen's ship when she shall cross over between England and Normandy.* Peter Cowdray in 1524 was the last lord of Padworth of his name. At his death his property was divided between his three daughters—Joan, who married Peter Kydwelle, Elizabeth, wife of ——— Poulet, and Margery, wife of William Hythe. The shares of Joan and Elizabeth eventually passed to the Brightwell family, and that of the third sister, Margery, was finally purchased by Sir Humfrey Foster, grandson of the Sir George Foster, of Aldermaston.

Sir George Foster was the first of his family settled at

A.D. 1524.
Chap. iv.

Thomas Parkyns.

Aldermaston, which property he had acquired by marriage with Elizabeth, daughter and heiress of John de la Mere. His is the beautifully carved alabaster monument still to be seen in Aldermaston Church, on which he is represented in armour with his wife by his side, and his very numerous family and sons and daughters standing in niches below. He died in 1532.

See Appendix.

A reference to the table of descent in the Appendix, will explain the probable identity of William Parkyns, who acted as trustee for Dorothy More's marriage settlement. Also that of Richard Parkyns, of whom Thomas held land in Ufton *as of his manor of Ufton.* He was probably the representative of the Madresfield family, still holding apparently some share of the Ufton property. Thomas Parkyns of Ufton, whose possessions have been here recapitulated, had a large family, as set out below.

Thomas Parkyns, died 1524 — Dorothy, dau. of Edward More, of Wichwood, co. Hants.

| Richard Parkyns | =Eliza- beth, dau. of Sir J. Mom- pesson. | Wil- liam | =Anne, dau. of Richard Welles. | Francis- | Anne, dau. of | Alice. | Eliza- beth Bartil- mewe. | Chris- topher. | Mar- garet. |

| Francis Perkins. | Dorothy. | Kathe- rine. | Eliza- beth. | Ger- trude. | Mary. | Susanne. | Daughters. | Daughters. |

Richard Parkyns.

Richard, the eldest son, was 24 years of age when he succeeded to the property at the time of his father's death. He had married Elizabeth, daughter and coheir with her three sisters of Sir John Mompesson, of Bathampton, in Wiltshire.

In the year 1534 the third son, Francis, was also married, and was living at Padworth, possibly in the old house belonging to Hussie's Manor before alluded to.

In that year the following incident took place, as has been found recorded among the proceedings of the Star Chamber Court. The occasion of it seems to have been a long-standing dispute between the Parkyns family and Sir Humfrey Foster of Aldermaston, as to fealty or service which he claimed as tenant in capite of the manor in Padworth, but which they refused to acknowledge. At last Sir Humfrey's irritation seems to have passed all bounds of moderation, and

A.D. 1534.

CHAP. iv.

RICHARD PARKYNS.

On the xth day of Juyn, in the xxvth yere of King Henry VIII.'s most noble Reigne (1534), betwene the houres of v & vi of the clok, did the saide Sir Humfrey with his servants, x in number, w^t Force & armes, that is, to wit, w^t bowes & arrowes, swords, Bucklers, daggers, & long Javelyns, & other wepons, come to the dwelling of Frauncis Pkyns, of Padworth, besetting & compassing the saide house w^t his s'vants aforesaide. And he, the saide Sir Humfrey, forsibly entred into the hall of the house, & thanne & there founde Frauncis sitting upon a stole in the hall bokeling of his shoes, & Sir Humfrey thanne & there made assaute & a Fr'ey upon Frauncis, saying unto hym these words: "What, thou arraunt knave! art thou there?" and w^t those words toke hym by the hed and gave hym many grete & strang blowes w^t his Fist & violently & maliciously hym cast unto the grounde & knokled & brake hys hed ageinst the harth of the heyborne. By reason of the blow grete plentye & abundaunce of blud descended from his hed & face upon his body, untill suche tyme that Anne, the wyffe of the saide Frauncis founde Sir Humfrey furiously treding her husbonde under his Fete, & further-more, wold have slayne hym yf that Anne had not piteously & lamentably kneling upon hur kues in hur Smok by a long season intreated Sir Humfrey to w'draw his malicious purpose, Ranco', & malice; & Sir Humfrey thanne & there Riotously toke the saide Frauncis w^t force & ageinst his will led hym as a prisoner & hym brought unto the dwelling-house of Richard Parkyns, his Brother, at Ufton Rob'. And Sir Humfrey Riotously entred into the house betwene the houres of vj & vij of the Clok in the mornynge of the same day, Richard his wyffe & straungers thanne being in the house at that houre & tyme, being set to Brekefast in the Chamber where Richard, hys wyffe, & children accustumably were wont to lye; the saide Sir Humfrey at his entring

Star Chamber Proceedings, 25 Hen. VIII., Bundle 21, No. 152, Parkins v. Foster and others.

A.D. 1534.
CHAP. IV.
RICHARD PARKYNS.

demaunded of one of the s'vants where his Maister was, the s'vant making answere ageyne that his M' was in his chamber, & w' those wordes the s'vant hastely reto'ned into the chamber, and or he coulde pleynly Notyfie unto his Maister the comynge of Sir Humfrey, the same Sir Humfrey, w' viij of his s'vants, sodenly entred into the chamber, having their wepons & speres in their handes assauting & making affray upon Richard; saying these wordes: "Parkyns, I cannot be in Rest for the & thy blud;" & w' that, toke Richard by the ere & by the here of the hed, the said Richard & the straungers, than there being, Holding their Cappes in their hands, supposing Sir Humfrey at his first comyng to have come theder to none evill intent, the said Richard desiring Sir Humfrey gentely to w'drawe his handes from his hed, & saying he never did unto hym any displeasure whereby he shulde thus handyll hym, & affermyng of that sayinge one Will'm More, gent, then being in the house, who saide these wordes unto Sir Humfrey: "Sir, I dare depose upón a boke that Richard Parkyns nor no'on of his s'vants, never did you displeasure;" & at these wordes, Sir Humfrey being past all reason, & w' Malice & Rauco' thrust Will'm More in the brest w' grete violence w' his Fist, & incontynent thrust hym ageyne, so that by force he was feyne to Reeale abakke upon a table borde, & w' that Sir Humfrey drew oute his sworde & wolde have stryken therw' Will'm or Richard if that Elizabeth, wyffe of Richard, had not taken Sir Humfrey by both the Armes & so helde hym w' piteous & lamentable cryinge unto such tyme Sir Humfrey commanded one of his s'vants to take his sworde. And thenne he sware by Godde's blud, his hart, & other abhomynable & terrible othes, that he wolde make Richard & his brethren that the grounde they went on shulde burne there fete & that ev'y birde that flieth oute of a busshe, he & they shulde thinke to be a Sprite, & also he swore depely that he wolde hew hym & them as small as flesshe to the pot. And thus departed thens leding & dryving Riotously Fraunces lyke a prisoner afore hym unto his manor of Aldermaston, & thus kepte & Imprisoned hym in one chamber, lokked by the space of all that day & the next nyght followinge.

This lamentable tale of assault and violence is set forth in a petition from the injured parties to the King, Henry VIII., and his most Honourable Council of the Star Chamber. The frequent repetition of the word *Riot* with a capital letter and the recapitulation of the arms of the assailants, their swords, spears, and javelins, etc., are all of them particulars which brought the offence under the cognisance of the Court. The Star Chamber had been instituted in the preceding reign for the laudable purpose of providing redress for the poorer and less influential classes against the violence of the strong and the partiality of the regular courts of law. It was, in fact, though afterwards made use of for other purposes, a criminal Court of Appeal. In this particular case Richard Parkyns, the brother, and Anne, the wife of Francis, had *compleyned unto yo' Justices of the peace, that is to say, to Sir Thome's Englefilde, Knyghte, one of yo' justices of yo' common peace, to Hew by dyvyne sufferaunce Abbot of Reding, & other moo Justices of the peace wynne yo' countie assigned, and they, according to yo' lawes & their ductye came to the quarter sessions holden at Okingh'm the xj' day of this present month of Juyn. At the whiche day the saide Sir Thomas Englefeld, etc., Inquired as well upon the premisses as also upon other Ryottes & mysbehaveors perpetrated wynne yo' saide Countie, & thereupon xv men according to yo' lawes were sworn to enquyre of the same amonge other thinges, and ij billes of Indictamente of the saide Ryotte was delivered to them, & evidence not only thereupon openly given by the others of seven sundry credable & substanciall persons proving the said Ryotte, but also the saide Sir Humfry openly knowleged & confessed the same to be true. Whereupon divers of the said Jury were fully agreed to fynde the said billes to be true, & divers of the saide Jury were so specially labored by the synester labor of the said Sir Humfrey & other his Frendes that they in no wise wolde agree to fynde the saide billes. Whereupon Sir Thomas Englefelde perseyving the parsialitie of the saide inquest caused the said xv men secretly to be examyned. And so upon their examynacion it was founde that v of them therto agreed & no moo by reason wherof the saide Sir Humfrey & his said Riotous servants for as moche as the said Sir Humfrey*

A.D. 1534.
CHAP. iv.
RICHARD PARKYNS.

is Sheriff of yo' saide countie, cannot be punysshed according to his & their condigne offences to the grete incoraging of other like offenders onles streight & dew correction the fouer be had for the premisses. In consideracion whereof & for as moche as tenne of the said inquest thenne being secretely examyned apart did not regarde nor consider the apparent evydence to them geven & the manyfest confession of the saide Sir Humfrey, but ageinst all reason conscience & ductye refused to fynde the two billes of Ryotte & offence for yo' highnes the names of the whiche tenne persons be hereunder written & are to the same Justices well knowen & unto your compleynant unknowen, it may please yo' highnes to graunt severall writtes of Subpena to be directed to the saide sir Humfrey Foster & other the said Riotous persons comaunding them to appere before yo' Highnes & yo' moost honorable Counseill in yo' Starre chamber at Westminster to answere the premisses.

One would like to know what was the final decision in the matter, and whether the ten obstinate jurymen had any reasons for thinking that Sir Humfrey Foster was not altogether in the wrong, or that the Parkyns brothers were not really as blameless and peaceable as this one-sided statement would make them appear. But if the record of the other side of the picture is not lost in common with so much forgotten history, it has at any rate not yet come to the surface of the heaped up reports of the Star Chamber still to be explored at the Record Office.

This must have been one of the last occasions when the Abbot of Reading took his place among the magistrates and county magnates of Berkshire. Hugh was abbot at the time of the dissolution of the monastery, and suffered martyrdom in the year 1539.

William More, mentioned as having been with Richard Parkyns, may have been a relative of his mother, Dorothy More. From this account Richard seems to have had children, who, with his wife and himself, had all slept in the same room, where the family afterwards breakfasted. None, however, survived him.

In 1550 Richard Parkyns is mentioned in a deed concerning the manor of Aldermaston among the *ffreesuters*, or free tenants, holding land of Sir Humfrey Foster, for which he paid yearly one *clove gelon*, possibly a clove gillyflower or pink, as a nominal acknowledgment of his feudal suzerainty; also, he is stated to have held *the half dele of the manor of ffinchampsted by knight's service*.

A.D. 1560.
———
CHAP. IV.
———
RICHARD PARKYNS.

He died in 1560, and his property descended to Francis, the son of his second brother, William, who had died before him.

Richard's will contains so much that relates to the family history, or bearing upon the manners of the times, that the greater part of it is here given verbatim.

Somerset House, Wills, 43.

*In the name of God Amen. I, Richard Parkyns, of Ufton Robert, in the Countie of Berks, Esquyer, the xxvj*th *day of Januarye in the year of oure Lorde God a thousande five hundred fiftie & eighte & in the furst yeare of the Reigne of oure sovcraigne Ladie Quene Elizabeth, quene of England &c., make this my present last will & testamente in maner & fourme following.*

First, I bequeth my soule unto almightie God & to Jesu Criste, his onely sonne, my maker & Redemer, & my bodie to be buryed in the chauncell of the parishe Churche of Ufton Robert in the place where as the sepulcre standeth.

Item, I will & bequeth unto the pariske Churche of Ufton xx^s.

Item, I bequeth to the parishe churche of Padworth vi^s *viij*^d.

Item, I bequeth to the mother Church of Sarum iiij^d.

*Also I will & bequeth to Elizabeth my wife all suche howses & howsinges. That is to saie the Scite of the manor & mansion house of Ufton Robert, w*th *all & singular arrable landes, meadowes, leasures, pastures, waters, fysshinges, commons and Feedings therto belonging whiche I nowe have & holde in myne owne occupation & custodye withe a certain pasture called Bowyers with woodes & arable landes therto belonging. And in this my last will I give to her all the premysses above wrytten during her life naturall.*

Item, my will is that if the advowson of the churche of

A.D. 1560.
CHAP. IV.
RICHARD PARKYNS.

Ufton do fall afore that Frauncis Parkyns the sonne of my brother William Parkyns come to the age of xxj yeares, then my will is that Elizabeth my wife shal have the gifte and nominacion thereof to suche persone & persones as she shall name or appoynte.

Also I will that my wife shall fynde & bringe upp honestly & competently Frauncis & Dorothe Perkins, my brother William Parkyns' children. That is to saie Frauncis Perkyns, sonne of my brother William Perkyns, untill he comme to the age of xxj yeres, & as for Dorothe Perkyns, suster unto the said Frauncis Perkyns above named, shalbe in the custodie & bringing upp of my said wife.

And I give unto the said Dorothe at the day of her marriage fourtie poundes.

Also I give & bequeth unto my Newye Harry Perkyns my manor & ferme & tenementes, &c., &c., in Woolhampton, Brympton, Aldermaston, Mygeham, & one grounde of woode & pasture called Kyst lande, now in the tenure of John Undrewood, of Shrynfelde, & one tenemente & certeyne mesuages, &c., &c., thereto belonginge in Bughulburye, to the clere yerely value of xl^{li}.

Also my will & myne entent is that never none of my heyres in tyme to comme shall take no fyne nor rent for a certen tenement & grounde late edified & buylded by me, Richarde Parkyns, in the parishe of Ufton Robert in the Countie of Barkes, now in the tenure of one Robert Newton, whiche tenement & grounde I will that my heyres shall maynteyne & kepe while the worlde endureth for a poore manne to dwell sole in & to pray for my sowle and all my Freudes sowles.

Also I will & bequeth to every one of my brother William Parkyns' daughters iiij^{li} apece. That is to saie, Katheryne, Elizabeth, Gertrude, Marye, & Suzanne, to be paide at the daie of theire severall mariages, orels at the age of xx yeres. . . .

Also I will & bequeth to my brother Frauncis Perkyns' sonnes, that is to saie, William & Frauncis, to every of theym iiij^{li} apece, & to Arthure Perkyns xl^{s}, & to be payed within two yeres after yt shall please God to call me to his mereye.

Also I will & bequeth to my brother Cristofer Perkyns

my best coate, my best doblett, & my russett gowne, garded with veleett, & a little square silver salte that I had of my suster, Margrett Perkyns.

Also I will & bequeth to every one of my brother Christofer Perkyns' doughters iiij˚ a pece, to be paide at the day of theire severall mariages, or els at their severall age of xx yeres.

Also I will & bequeth to my sister Bartelmewe doughters, that is to saie, to Elizabeth, Anne & Margarett, to every one of you x˚ a pece, to be paide to theym at the daye of their severall Mariages.

Also I will & bequeth to my sister Alice Parkyns iij˚ vj˚ viij˚, to be delyvered within one monethe after my decease.

(Then follow bequests to various servants.)

Item, I give to my Nephew Henrye Parkyns my yonge trotting colte, with the bridell & sadle that was my brother William Parkyns'.

Item, I give unto Fraunces Perkyns, my brother William Perkyns' sonne, one Rynge whiche I comenly use to seale withall, to be delyvered when he comith to the age of xxj yeres.

Item, I give to my sister Suzanne Mompesson one rynge pounced with fethers.

Also I will and bequeth all the residue of my goodes, catelles, dettes, & sommes of money not bequeathed nor given, to Elizabeth my wife, whome I do ordeyne & make my wholle executrice of this my present last will & testamente.

Also I ordeyne & make & most hartely desyre Sir Fraunces Inglefelde, knyghte, my speciall good master & frende, & my cosyn Thomas Vachell to be oversears of this my present last will & testament, desyring theym to be assistaunte unto my poore wife. And the said Sir Fraunces to have for his paynes iij˚ vj˚ viij˚, & my cosynne Vachell my crosbowe.

In witnesse wherof to this my present last will & testament I have putte my seale the date & yeare above wrytten.

Barnarde More, Edmonde Brymson, William Asshepole & John Salter.

The names of the different relatives here alluded to will be found in the full table of descent given in the Appendix.

A.D. 1560.
CHAP. iv.
RICHARD PARKYNS.
Inq. P.M., 13 James I., part II., No. 181.

In the January of the preceding year, 1559, Richard Parkins had made a settlement for the use of his nephew Francis of the manor of Ufton Robert and the advowson of the living, as well as certain property, consisting of 10 messuages, 10 tofts, 1 dovecote, 10 gardens, 300 acres of land, 100 acres of meadow, 100 acres of pasture, 10 acres of wood, 60 acres of furze and heath, 60 acres of marsh in the parishes of Ufton Robert and Ufton Nervet or Richard, as well as free fishing in the Kennet, which must be considered as exclusive of the property he here leaves to his widow for her life; that is to say, the site of the manor and mansion house of Ufton Robert and the land belonging to it, which he had held in his own hands.

By the bequest of the signet ring and the allusion to the advowson in the will he clearly recognises Francis as his heir.

The almshouse, so solemnly commended to his heirs to be kept up *while the worlde endureth*, has long since entirely disappeared. No memory of it, even, exists at the present time in the parish.

Glossary of Ecclesiastical Ornament, A. D. Pugin, 1844.

The precise directions that he gave as to the place of his burial have a significance. By the *sepulcre* that he mentions was intended the shrine which in all old churches stood against the north wall of the chancel at the extreme east end; that is, immediately by the side of the altar, but at right angles with it. Pugin says that it was a place where the Blessed Sacrament was solemnly reserved from Good Friday till Easter Sunday. Sometimes these sepulchres were merely temporary erections of framework and hangings, set up for the occasion, but frequently they were permanent, built into the north wall of the choir or chancel, and adorned with a rich canopy and appropriate imagery. Of this kind two beautiful examples may be seen at Heckington and Navenby Churches, Lincolnshire, and at Hawton Church in Nottinghamshire. "But," as Pugin goes on to say, "there are few parochial churches which are not provided with a tomb on the north side of the chancel, which served for the sepulchre, and was adorned on these occasions with hangings and other decorations. Devout persons erected these tombs with the special intention of their serving for the sepulchre, that those who came to visit it might be moved to pray for their souls." A very good instance of this latter arrangement may be seen in the Parish Church of Englefield in the neighbourhood.

Just such a tomb was the monument erected shortly after his death to the memory of Richard Parkyns by his widow—afterwards Lady Marvyn—on the spot which he had selected. It was an imposing structure, and till within a few years ago it was still to be seen *in situ* and almost in its original condition. Its history, however, is a disastrous one. Before it had been in existence a hundred years it had suffered defacement and injury at the hands of the iconoclast Puritans of the time of the Commonwealth. Elias Ashmole, who saw it sometime previous to 1660, states that then already the figures of Richard Parkyns and his wife were broken down.

His very careful description is in its wording and arrangement so important to the understanding of the full purport of the monument that a facsimile copy of the page from the MS. notes in the Bodleian Library is here given on page 56.

On the opposite page (57) an attempted restoration of the whole, partly from Ashmole's description and partly from the still existing remains, is also given.

There was never any inscription on the monument, although two ornamental panels in the stonework seem to have been intended for the purpose. The numerous shields, however, that adorn it were intended to tell their story, and require some notice.

The three shields described by Ashmole as having been *on the north side* all have reference to the wife's family, Elizabeth Mompesson. The centre shield belonged to her father, Sir John Mompesson, impaling the arms of his wife, Alice Leigh, and those on the right and left are her father's parents, Mompesson and Watkins, and her mother's, Leigh and Lucy. These are given separately at the head of this chapter. The other set of three, described as "on the fore-side," will be seen, by a glance at the illustration of the restored monument, to form a line with the two on the pedestals of the columns.

Taking them thus in order, and beginning from the left—that is, the reader's right hand, these five shields will be

27: Aug: 1666.

Ufton.

Towards the East end of this Chancell, on the North side, is raised a faire & large stone Monument, where the statues of Richard Parkins Esq & the Lady Martyn his wife, were made kneeling before a Deske, but now broken downe.

At the top of y^e Monum^t. is this Coate & Crest.

On the fore side, are these Armes.

RICHARD PARKINS.

On the two Pillars, which stand on each side y^e Monu^t.

On the North side of the Monument.

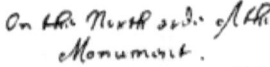

  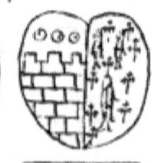

 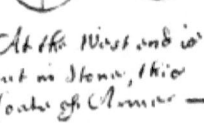 

At the West end is cut in stone, this Coate of Armes.

Of the Family of Perkins. 57

found to represent a genealogical sequence of five generations of the family.

CHAP. iv.
A.D. 1560.

RICHARD PARKYNS.

At the extreme left the shield marked No. 1 in the illustration gives the arms of Richard Parkyns himself, quartered

CHAP. IV.
A.D. 1560.

RICHARD
PARKYNS.

with those of his heiress-wife, Elizabeth Mompesson. No. 2 is the arms of his father and his father's wife, Dorothy More. No. 3 quarters the Collee arms, and represents the shield of John Parkyns, whose wife Margaret Collee brought the Padworth and Fenchampstead manors into the family (see p. 43). No. 4 impales blank. This of itself is a convincing proof of the intention with which this row of shields was arranged. Had there been no intention of describing the descent of the family, any coat of arms connected with Richard's ancestors would have been represented; but here, when Thomas, the great-grandfather's place, is reached in the sequence, his wife's arms not being known, nothing is put, and the impalement of the shield is left blank.

The father of Thomas was William Parkyns, the first of the family who was lord of Ufton, and therefore very suitably his shield, No. 5, occupies the first place in the series. His wife's Christian name was Margaret, and the deed of settlement which has been quoted (see p. 41) is fair evidence of her having been an heiress; but the arms here represented in the quarterings are borne by several families of possible connection with the Parkyns, and it is difficult to identify her family with any certainty.

The same arms, or very nearly so, were borne by Mitchells, and a family of the name owned a manor called Mitchell's Court at Borwardescote. William Parkyns, we know, owned a moiety of lands in Borwardescote, and if we may suppose this to have been the property that Margaret brought to her husband, probability seems to point to her having been a co-heiress of that name.

Above the columns, on an upper row, are two shields—Nos. 6 and 7—which from their position might be supposed to refer to early ancestors or founders of the family. From the marks of cadency, they appear to represent two brothers, and the shield of the second brother occupies the place of honour; from which one might infer that the Ufton family descended from a second son. But here we have no other record to support the hypothesis.

The last shield—No. 8—described by Ashmole as on the

west end of the monument, bears the arms of Sir Francis
Englefield, the chief lord of the fee of Ufton Robert.

There remains to be noticed the coat of arms and crest of
Richard Parkyns, with his name attached, which, as Ashmole
describes it, surmounted the whole. It is still in existence,
though without the inscription.

This was probably the first occasion on which the crest
was used by the Ufton family, for it was only on August 18,
1559—that is, the year before Richard Parkyns' death—
that the grant of the crest had been made by William
Hervey, *alias* Clarenceulx King-of-arms, to another Richard
Parkyns, who was the representative of the Madresfield
branch of the family—the same who has been already mentioned (p. 46) as having some rights over part of the Ufton
lands.

A copy of the grant and an account of the Madresfield
family are given in the Appendix.

From the fact that the crest was so soon made use of at
Ufton, it seems possible that the grant may perhaps have
been applied for, at the instigation of Richard Parkyns, of
Ufton, or of that of his widow, with the express intention of
its display on this monument. Perhaps also the unusually
elaborate genealogical arrangement of the coats of arms with
which it was decorated, may have owed something to heraldic
researches made at the time on their behalf by their relative,
Richard Parkyns, the younger, who was then a barrister,
living in London.

All this, however, has been described from Ashmole's
account of what was, but is no more. I have said that the
history of this monument is a disastrous one, nor did its
misfortunes end with the ill-treatment of the Puritans. It
probably remained much as Ashmole saw it till 1800, when
the old church was replaced by the present building. Then
the architect seems to have judged it out of keeping with his
plans for the new church, so it was pulled down and its broken
fragments were cast out. They would have utterly perished
and been lost had not Dr. Fraser, the then rector, collected
some of the carved stones and built them up again in some
sort of fashion, as an arbour in his garden; but five out of

the twelve shields have disappeared, and such as remain have in the rearrangement lost half their significance. To make the catastrophe complete the centre stone of the beautiful frieze which decorated the canopy was somehow missed, and lacking this, and in default of any inscription, the memory even of those to whom the monument had been erected was completely lost. Some time afterwards, when Mr. Erskine was rector, a visitor whose genealogical tastes led him to take an interest in the pedigree of the Perkins family, came to Ufton to hunt for their relics. After examining the church and the above-mentioned arbour, he was further told of some old bits of carved stone in a neighbouring farm, and there in the yard (to use his own words) *I found the centre stone with the initials R. E. P. in a sort of trefoil, meant for a true lover's knot, supported by two angels or cherubs. It was used to prop up one end of a pig trough, that the little pigs might feed the easier!* I inquired whether a certain *Lady Marvyn* had been heard of, & learned that she was remembered as a benefactress to the Parish, & then—I preached a sermon!! & was faithfully promised that the stone should be put in a safe & more proper place, pending the hoped-for restoration of the tomb.*

But, alas, this sermon was no more heeded than many others. Mr. Erskine's health obliged him to be a great deal away, and after his death, in 1878, the centre-stone had been again forgotten. It was found again by Mr. Fraser Cornish, the son of the present rector—not in quite so ignominious a position as before, but lying out of doors among some rubbish in the farm-garden, and unfortunately very much cracked and damaged by the frost. However, its rediscovery came, happily, in time to help to the identification of the dismembered monument. A subscription was got up, and the beautiful canopy, at all events, has been moved into the church under safe shelter, and re-erected as nearly as possible in its original place. One cannot but hope that all the remaining fragments may as soon as possible be also replaced.

Unfortunately, as has been said, a great deal is hopelessly lost, and the architectural work is so broken up that it is very difficult, if not impossible, to understand its original design.

The destruction is all the more to be deplored because the parishioners continue to this day to benefit by a charitable endowment bequeathed to them by Richard Parkyns' widow, Lady Marvyn, whose effigy was originally on the tomb; nor are they in any way disturbed in their enjoyment of her gifts by the fact that they have forgotten the donor, and that her monument has been turned out of their church.

Richard Parkyns' second brother William had probably married late in life; for his wife Anne was niece to his sister-in-law Elizabeth Mompesson, her mother being Sir John Mompesson's second daughter Mary, wife of Thomas Wells, of Bambridge. He died in 1558. In his will he describes himself as *William Parkyns, of Brympton, in the countie of Barks, gentilman.* Brimpton is about six miles distant from Ufton. As it does not appear that the Parkyns family ever had any estate there, it is probable that William had no more than a lease of the house he occupied in that parish. He says that—

Being seeke of bodie, & hole & parfite of mynde & memorie, I make this my present last will & Testament in manner & forme following. First, I bequeath my soule unto Almightie God & to Jesus, his only sonne, my Maker & Redeemer, & to the blessed Ladie the Virgin, & to all tholly company of Heaven; & my bodie to be buried in the Chauncell of the churche of Sainte Peters of Ufton Robert, in the countie aforesaide, in the left side of my mother, where as she lieth buryed. Item, I will that within one year after my decease, thatt my executours or their assignees doo buye one marble stone of the price of 53ˢ 4ᵈ, & to cause it to be laid upon my saide mother & me; & thies wourds to be graved upon him: Of your charitie pray for the soule of Dorothye Parkyns, who died the ... day of ..... in the yere of our Lorde God 1550 & fiftie; & William Parkins, her sonne, who deceased the ... day of ..... in the yere of our Lorde God 1558, sometyme gentilman Ussher to the Righthonourable Ladie Margarette Countess of Sary, & after her decease gentilman Ussher to her sonne, The Lord Cardinalles Poles grace. Item, I bequeath to the poor people 40ˢ; that is to say, 20ˢ at my buriall, & thother

CHAP. IV.
———
A.D. 1558.
———
WILLIAM
PARKYNS.

20ˢ at my monnethes mynd. *Item, I bequeath to the mother churche of Sary £4. Item, I bequeath to the hie altar of Brympton, for tithes forgotten,* 3ˢ 4ᵈ. *Item, I bequeath to the hie altar of Thatcham, for tithes forgotten,* 3ˢ 4ᵈ. *Item, I will that mine executours buye one new pall, price* 13ˢ 4ᵈ, *the whiche I give unto the parishe churche at Brympton to be laide uppon any personne or personnes that shall die within the said parishe & be broughte to the churche. Item, I bequeath to Saint Peters churche of Ufton Robert* 13ˢ 4ᵈ. *Item, I will that some honnest priest pray & say a trentall of masses for my soule immediatelie after my buriall, & another trentall after my yere's mynde, & they to be rewarded as my executours thinke meete & convenient. Item, I will that myn executours immediatelie after my buriall, & before my monnethys mynde, that they do praise & cause to be praised all my goods & cattalles, corne in the fielde, plate & housecholde stuffe, & then to content & pay all such debts as I doo owe to any personne or personnes being in the knowen & proved by honnest witnes. Item, I give & bequeath to ffrancis Parkyns, my sonne, one ringe of golde which I did comonly use to wear upon my finger to seal withal.*

Then follow small bequests to his sister *Alice Parkyns;* his brother *Christopher;* his *nevewes Harry* and *Francis;* and to his cousin *Elizabeth Hobson* he leaves *my russettes furred gowne garded with velvet.*

Also he gives and bequeaths *Thone half of my goodes, cattalles, &c., &c., unto Anne my wife, & thother half of my goodes to Katherine, Elizabeth, Gurtred, Mary, & Susanne, my five daughters, ymediatilie & after my inventary taken. . . . Also, I will thatt such goods as shall come to my daughters shall be in the custodie of my brother Richard Parkyns & my uncle Thomas Standish, to be employed for the most profite & advantage & bringing up, & to be divided amongst them the day of their marriage or else at the age of* 21 *yeires.*

* * * * * *

Also, *my will is that if any of my said daughters doo marry against the will of my wife or my executours, that thene they shall have none of my legacie.*

Item, my will is that my wife shall have thordering & bringing up of all my saide children, she being sole & unmarried. . . . & if it be fortune my saide wife to marry, & my said children not bestowed, then I will my executours to have the order & bringinge up & setting furthe my said children.

Also, I ordayne & make my brother Richarde Parkyns & my unkill Thomas Standishe my full & hole executours. Item, I give to my brother Richard Parkyns, for his paynes herein to be taken, my bay curtall gelding & a young sorrell gelding with a balde face. Item, I give unto my uncle Thomas Standish . . . a golde ringe with a dyamon in him, & my best cross bow & my best racke, a payer of Spanish blanketts, a rapyer, a dagger, a sworde, that are in my chest at Lambeith. Also, I ordain & make the Righthonourable Sir Fraunces Inglefield, Knight, who been alwaies my singuler good maister & freende, to be overseer of this my last will & testament, desiring him to be good maister in aiding & assisting my said wif & children & myn executours, as my hole trust & confidence is he will, & I give him in token of remembrance, that is to say, one ringe of golde with a turkayes in it.

The witnesses are his sister *Elizabeth Parkyns, Bernard More, John Ffisher, & John Salter.*

In 1562 both the executors, Richard Parkyns and Thomas Standishe, being dead, a commission was issued to William's widow, who had married again a Mr. George Tatershale, to administer the will. Whether the gravestone and its inscription was ever put in the church, according to William's direction, we cannot say; it was not there, at any rate, in 1660, when Ashmole made a careful description of all that he saw. But to account for its absence it must be remembered that the Rebellion and the Commonwealth had intervened, and that to Puritanical bigotry the request for prayers for the soul would probably have been enough to cause its destruction.

William Parkyns' patroness, Margaret Countess of Salisbury, the last of the Plantagenets, was also descended from the Despencers and Beauchamps through her grandmother Anne, the wife of Richard Nevile, the king-maker, as is shown in the following table, a continuation of that on page 38:

Chap. iv.
A.D. 1558.

Margaret Countess of Salisbury.

| | Richard Nevile, Earl of Warwick, = Anne Beauchamp, heiress of killed 1471. | | Despencers, died 1490. |

Isabel, died = George, Duke   Edward, Prince = Anne, died = Richard III.
1476.   of Clarence.   Wales.   1485.

Edward Plantagenet.   Margaret Plantagenet, died 1541   Sir Richard Pole.
                      Countess of Salisbury.

Henry Pole Lord Montague,   Reginald Cardinal Pole,   And others.
beheaded 1537.   died 1558.
                            Willm Parkyns,
                            Gent Ussher.

She was, therefore, a direct representative of the family of Hugh Despencer, the first patron of the Parkyns family, and also of Thomas Earl of Gloucester, whom John Parkyns had served as bailiff. Thus the connection between the noble house and the family of esquires had been handed on from one generation to another, and may almost be said to have been hereditary.

The Lady Margaret, after her brother's death, was the heiress of the house of York, and as such could not escape the suspicion and distrust of Henry VII. But she showed no signs of ambitious intentions with regard to the Crown, and married a very worthy man, Sir Richard Pole, himself a connection of the Tudor family. In the following reign she became the intimate and attached friend of Queen Katherine of Aragon, and finally some of her family possessions were restored to her, her eldest son was created Lord Montague, and she herself Countess of Salisbury. Her tragic end is well known. On the divorce of Queen Katherine she fell into the disfavour of the Court, and her sons were more than suspected of plotting on behalf of the Princess Mary. Lord Montagu was thrown into prison and executed, and Reginald Cardinal Pole escaped abroad. The venerable countess, accused of corresponding with her son and being privy to his plots, was sent to the Tower; and finally Henry VIII., being particularly irritated by a pamphlet written against him by the cardinal from abroad, ordered the execution of his mother. She was beheaded, without any trial or show of justice, on May 27, 1541, on Tower Hill, in the seventieth year of her age.

From the expression that William Parkyns makes use of, one may perhaps gather that he had stayed with his noble mistress and served her to the end, after which he may have escaped abroad and joined the cardinal during his exile. In 1553 a revival, as it no doubt seemed to them, of better things came. Mary was queen, and the old form of religion was restored, and Cardinal Pole came to Lambeth as Archbishop of Canterbury, accompanied by his gentleman usher. But the time was short. In 1558, within one week in the month of November, the queen, the cardinal, and his faithful servant all passed away.

Grafton's Chronicle relates that Mary *fell sick of a hote, burning Fever*, and died on November 17; Cardinal Pole died of the same disease on the 18th; and from the fact that William Parkyns' will is dated November 17, and was proved on the 23rd, we must suppose that his death had taken place not later than November 18 or 20, or two or three days previous to the second of these dates. The fever specially mentioned in the queen's case was a very fatal epidemic, which, as Grafton goes on to say, *was common that yere through all the realme, & consumed a marvaillous number, as well noble men as Byshops, Judges, Knightes, Gentlemen, & riche Farmours*.

With the close of Mary's reign, the final extinction of the Papal supremacy in England, and the disappearance of the house of Warwick and of the royal Plantagenets, the old order of things seems to pass away, to make room for modern history, for the glories of the Elizabethan age, the subsequent struggles of the spirit of liberty against the power of the Crown, and a wider-spread, if more prosaic, civilization.

How these changes affected the lords of the manor of Ufton Robert will be shown in the sequel.

Chapter v.

Of Pole Manor.

A.D. 1566.

LADY MARVYN.

LIZABETH, the widow of Richard Parkyns, married again very soon after his death. Her second husband was Sir John Marvyn, of Fountell Gifford, in Wiltshire, himself connected with the Mompesson family. His grandfather, Sir Walter Marvyn, had married Mary Mompesson, the sister of Drew Mompesson, Elizabeth's grandfather. They were, in fact, second cousins.

```
                         John Mompesson.
          ┌─────────────────────┴─────────────────────┐
    Drew Mompesson.                              Mary═Sir Walter
          │                                               Marvyn.
    John Mompesson═Alice Leigh.                           │
          │                                               │
   ┌──────┼──────────┬─────────┐                          │
Elizabeth═1st, Richard  Susan.  Mary═Thomas  Anne═William │
        Parkyns.                     Welles.      Wayte   │
      2nd, Sir John                                       │
        Marvyn.                                           │
          │                                               │
   ┌──────┴───────────────────┐                           │
John Marvyn═Elizabeth, dau.  Edward Marvyn═Elizabeth, dau. and co-heir
       of Lord Mor-                         of Sir Edmund Paken-
         daunt.                             ham, of Finchampstead.

    1st, Jane═John Marvyn═2nd, Elizabeth, widow of Richard Parkyns.
```

The property of Fountell, or Fonthill, has an interest as being the same which in more recent times belonged to the well-known William Beckford, author of 'Vathek' and patron of arts at the beginning of this century.

Sir John Marvyn was a man of considerable wealth and of good position, and had represented his county in Parliament in the year 1554. He died in 1566. His bequests to his wife in his will are as follows:

Item, first I give & bequeath unto Elizabeth my ladie & wife my wholl entiere manor of ffountell Stoppe & Stop fountell lyinge & beinge of the parish of Stopfountell, & in ffountell, also with all the errable landes, pastures, wooddes, feadinges, leasures & comens unto the same belonging. Also I give my manor of Compton Basset my entiere manor their unto my wief for the term of her lief without impeachment of waste. Item, I give unto my wief all the stockes of Ufton, Bathampton, Langford, Apshill, Wyley & Depford. I give unto my wief all such things as she brought with her & her ward also.

It will be seen, therefore, that at her second husband's death Elizabeth Lady Marvyn was a very wealthy woman. Besides, what she received under her two husbands' wills she had inherited from her father, Sir John Mompesson, Great Bathampton and other manors in Wiltshire, for her share as coheiress, with her three sisters, Susan Mompesson, Mary Wells and Anne Wayte.

In 1567—that is, the year after Sir John Marvyn's death —she took steps towards adding to her landed property by the purchase of a small manor in Ufton known as Pole Manor. The purchase was first made nominally by her nephew, Richard Brunynge, who the following year handed it over to Lady Marvyn herself.

Pole Manor was a subdivision of Ufton, forming part of the Manor of Ufton Robert, and held under its lord. It corresponds in that respect with the description given in Domesday Book of the subdivision of the estate of William FitzAnsculf, which, it says, was held by a certain knight, and that *another knight holds three virgates of this land, & has one plough there.*

CHAP. V.
———
A.D. 1396.

Add. Charter 9242, Brit. Mus.

The earliest mention of it by name that has been found is in a deed, dated 1396, as follows:

Know all men that I, Sir Thomas Ipre Rᵗ, have remised, released & altogether for me & my heirs have quit-claimed to John Lord Lovell of Holland, his heirs & assigns my whole right & claim which I have had, or in any manner can have, in my manor or lands & tenements of Pole, in the county of Berks. Dated at Aldeford, co. Wilts.

Of the name of Ipre only one other record is known in connection with Ufton. A fragment of stained glass in a window in the old church of Ufton Robert bore the Ipre arms—argent, a chevron between three oxen's heads caboshed gules—and seems to point to the fact that the family had once some interest in this place.

Inq. P.M., 9 Hen. IV.

In a post-mortem inquisition, dated 1408, it is stated that Lord Lovell held his property in Ufton in right of his wife, Matilda, daughter of Robert, Lord Holland.

Inq. P.M., 6 Ed. IV., No. 20.

In 1467 Pole Manor is again mentioned as having been the property of *Joan Lovell, late the wife of Sir John Lovell, Knight;* and it is added: *The manor of Pole is held of Thomas Parkyns in socage. The said Joan died on the 5th day of August last past. And that Francis Lovell is son & next heir as well of the aforesaid John Lovell, knight, as of the aforesaid Joan, & he is of the age of 10 years.*

It is clear from this statement that Pole Manor was held as a sub-tenancy under the lords of Ufton Robert.

Francis Lovell, who inherited it at his mother's death, was the last and most notorious of his family. He was still a young man when in 1483, the last year of the reign of Edward IV., he was created viscount. The following is the account of the ceremony of the creation given in an old manuscript:

Brit. Mus. add. MSS. 6113, fol. 134.

*Item, on the xii*ᵗʰ *day, the Kinge being in a redynes, the said lord was apparelled in his Parliament robes, & so brought fro the Kinge's wardrobe betweene the lord Morley & the lord Fitzhughe with the officers of armes before hym, until they came into the Kinge's Gᵗ Chamber, where his Grace stood under* his clothe of estate; where, after obeysaune made, his pattente was reade by the Kinge's secrettarye, which was to him & his heyres males; which don, & thanks given, they departed toward his chamber thorowe the halle, ledde & accompanyed, as afore, with the sound of trumpettes to his chamber, where he delivered to the officers of arms their fees, whereof, after the Kinge's largess cryed, hys was cryed in iij places in the halle as followeth: *Largesse de puissant et noble Viscomte Lovell, Seigneur de Holland, de Burwell, Deyncourte, et de Grey de Rotherfeld, &c.*

After King Edward's death Lord Lovell attached himself especially to the service of Richard, Duke of Gloucester, and shared in his fortunes and his unpopularity when he became King as Richard III. The well-known dogerel alludes to him as one of Richard's most intimate advisers:

> *The cat, the rat and Lovel the dog,*
> *Rule all England under the hog.*

By the hog was intended Richard himself in allusion to his cognisance of a white boar; the cat and the rat were Catesby and Ratcliffe. This squib cost its author, Collingwood, dear; he was hung, drawn, and quartered on Tower Hill as a warning of the danger of wit when aimed too high.

After the battle of Bosworth and the death of Richard, Lovell took refuge in a sanctuary. Catesby was not so fortunate; he was taken prisoner and beheaded.

In his will he begged, *My lords Stanley, Strange & all that blood, help & praye for my soule . . . & let my lord Lovell come to grace, then that ye shew him that he praye for me.* His intercession, as might have been expected, had not much effect, for Lovell was specially excepted from the general amnesty passed by Henry VII. on his accession. He was attainted of high treason, and all his property including the manor of Pole, was forfeited to the Crown. The statute declares that in a former bill of attainder against Lord Lincoln and others of Richard's adherents Lord Lovell had been ignorantly omitted, *to the most perilous ensample of others being of such traiterous myndes.*

CHAP. V.
A.D. 1487.

FRANCIS
LORD
LOVELL.

He retaliated by joining in plots and conspiracies. In the spring of 1486 he left his refuge, and with a handful of men surprised and almost succeeded in making the King his prisoner during a royal progress near Ripon. Then he fled to the court of Margaret, Duchess of Burgundy, who was sister of Edward IV. and a sworn foe to the House of Tudor. While there Lovell took up the cause of Lambert Simnel, a youth who was made to personate Edward Plantagenet, son of George, Duke of Clarence. Joined by the Earl of Lincoln, he landed in Ireland, and passed over to England with an army of wild Irishmen, whom they collected. They met the King's forces at Stoke, near Newark, where they were utterly defeated (1487). Lincoln was killed, and Francis Lord Lovell disappeared, and was never seen again alive. It was supposed that he had been drowned, as he was last seen trying to swim across the river Trent after the battle. Some said, however, that he had succeeded in getting away, and that he was lying hidden in some secret place. Three hundred years afterwards a strange discovery threw some light on the mystery. The story is told in a letter written by William Cowper, clerk of the Parliament, dated

Hertingfordbury, 9th August, 1737.

SIR,—I met t'other day with a mem^m I had made some years ago. You may remember that Lord Bacon in his Hist^y of Henry VII., giving an account of the Battle of Stoke, says of Lord Lovell that he fled & swam over the Trent on horseback, but was drowned. Another account says he lived long after in a cave. Apropos of this, on the 6th day of May, 1728, the present Duke of Rutland related in my hearing that about 20 years before, viz., 1708, upon occasion of new laying a chimney at Minster Lovell, there was discovered a large vault under ground, in which was the entire skeleton of a man as having been sitting at a table which was before him, with a book, paper, and pens, &c. In another part of the room lay a cap, all much mouldered & decayed, which the family & others judged to be the Lord Lovell whose exit has hitherto been so uncertain.

If this suggested explanation is correct—and it seems very

probable—the unfortunate Lovell must have made his way from the battlefield by the banks of the Trent to his own home, the principal seat of the family in Oxfordshire, knowing of this secret retreat, in which he promised himself he would be safe till pursuit slackened, and he should be able to leave the country, some friend or servant being in the secret to supply him meanwhile with food; and then perhaps the friend

was killed or proved faithless, the door locked from outside was never opened, and the slow death of starvation overtook this restless, ambitious man and cut short his career in its prime. In the village of Minster Lovell, about two miles from Witney, still stand the ruins of the Castle where this strange tragedy occurred. On the attainder of Lord Lovell the sub-tenancy of Pole Manor had lapsed to the Crown; and it was not till twenty-three years later that it was granted by Henry VIII. to Richard Weston, one of his pages, or *Esquire of our body*, as he is called in the deed, *in consideration of the true & faithful service which he has bestowed upon us, & during his life intends to bestow*. This manor and lordship of Ufton Pole (here so called for the first time) *having come into the hands of the late King, our dearest father, whom God absolve, by reason of the attainder of Francis Lord Lovell, & which by the death of Sir John Langford, K*., *are in our gift, & disposition*. Here the claims of the tenant in capite, Sir John Langford, of Bradfield, alone are noticed, and nothing is said of the rights of the Parkyns' family, from whom certainly the Lovells had formerly held the manor. After Sir Richard

<small>Chap. v.

A.D. 1546.

Sir Richard Weston.</small>

Weston's death legal proceedings were taken against his widow, Dame Anne Weston, to contest her right and to maintain the claim of Richard Parkyns, son of Thomas, which eventually seem to have been made good.

The fact was that at this time the old feudal lordships were falling into abeyance, and were often disregarded and set aside or mistaken. Moreover, the young king was apt to be rather high-handed and reckless in his gifts. To judge by an existing patent, dated 1515, only five years after he had given it to Sir Richard Weston, he bestowed this same manor of Pole on a young favourite, Sir William Compton, on the occasion of his marriage with a Lady Warburga; but as nothing more is heard either of him or his wife in connection with Ufton, it is possible that some other Pole Manor was intended, or that the mistake of the double gift was discovered and rectified.

<small>Patent Roll, 6 Hen. VIII.</small>

In 1567 Sir Henry Weston, possibly the son and heir of the former Sir Richard, made over his possession of the manor of Ufton Pole to Richard Brunynge, who in the following year paid the fine of £6 13s. 4d. due to the Crown on the transfer of the land, in consideration of which the queen *pardoned the trespass made on that behalf;* for still at that time all landed property belonged, not only in theory, but absolutely to the Crown. Any transfer was illegal which had not the direct sanction of the sovereign; and whenever such transfers did take place, the offence had invariably to be condoned by the payment of a fine, and a special license was then granted.

<small>L.T.R. Mem. Roll Hilary, 10 Elizabeth, Roll 91.</small>

Richard Brunynge, as has been shown, acted in the matter merely as agent for his relative, Lady Marvyn, who in the year 1568 purchased the manor for herself. Subsequently she settled it, after her own lifetime, on her first husband's nephew, Francis Parkyns, to be held by him *of her heirs*, the same Francis, under whom, as lord of Ufton Robert, she herself held it. This is one of the many curious instances of the complications of feudal tenure : Pole Manor was held by Sir Peter Vanlore as tenant in capite from the Crown; under him it was held by Francis Parkyns as a dependancy of Ufton Robert, of which manor he was lord; and again, as sub-

<small>L.T.R. Mem. Rolls, Hilary Roll 98. Inq. P.M., 15 James I., Part ii. No. 181.</small>

tenant, of Francis Parkyns by Lady Marvyn, who was, in fact, the real and actual owner, and who by her deed of settlement, to take effect after her death, bestowed the possession of it on the lord of the manor, under whom she held it; and he in turn was to hold it of her heirs.

But while the history of the ownership of Pole Manor, or Ufton Pole as it was latterly called, can thus be traced, one important point connected with the place still remains unascertained—namely, its locality. No name of field or lane has preserved its memory in the district; the Court Rolls of the manors are not forthcoming, and in the absence of any further evidence we can only put together what knowledge we have and—conjecture.

Pole Manor was within the boundaries of the parish of Ufton Robert. It was an addition made to the Parkyns' estate by Lady Marvyn, and consequently it was not where the manor-house of the lords of Ufton Robert originally stood. It will help towards the solution of the difficulty if we can ascertain where this manor-house actually was.

Some recent excavations have proved that there formerly existed a fortified dwelling-house on a site not far from the church of Ufton Robert. Its moat, the wooden piles of the ancient bridge, some of the masonry of the gateway above the bridge, and part of the foundation walls of the house itself have all been found. In addition to these points of evidence, the field lying beyond the moat is known to this day as the Bowling Alley. It is evident that there once stood an ancient house of some importance on this spot near the church; it is common in the neighbourhood to find the house of the lord of the manor so situated. We may therefore fairly presume that here was the manor-house of Ufton Robert of which we are in search. Now there is no doubt that long before the Elizabethan additions to Ufton Court were built, there had stood a much older house on the same site. This house was within the same parish, but at its most western extremity (see map), where it may well have been the centre of a separate property.

Summing up the results of the above evidence, then, one may say that the house that once stood within the moat, but has now disappeared, was probably the manor-house of Ufton Robert, while the present Ufton Court and its surroundings were anciently comprised in the separate estate called Pole Manor.

Favouring this conjecture is the opinion of Mr. Congreve, of Aldermaston, who, in 1838, when parting with the Ufton estate to Mr. Benyon de Beauvoir, wrote thus to him concerning it: *I think it pretty clear that Ufton Court is the same house that was called Pole Place in the time of Henry VIII., though there is no proof of it.* And he repeats the opinion further on: *I conceive Pole Place to be the old Mansion House now called Ufton Court.*

Richard Parkyns in his will bequeathed to his wife *all such howses & howsinges, that is to saie, the seite of the Manor and Mansion house of Ufton Robert.* Did he mean by that that the old manor house on the moated site was already then pulled down, and that the purchase of Pole Manor and the erection of an enlarged mansion there was then contemplated? It is impossible to say. Certain it is that a considerable part of the present Ufton Court dates from Lady Marvyn's lifetime, and that then, or very shortly afterwards, the much-enlarged house was adopted as the family residence.

Lady Marvyn died in 1581. Her will is as follows:

In the name of God, Amen. I, Dame Elizabeth Marvyn, late the wife of R^d John Marvyn, Knight, deceased, doe ordaine & make this my last will & testament in manner & forme following. First, I bequeath my Soul unto Allmightie God, hopinge by the mercy obtayned through the merits of the death, passione & precious blood-sheddinge of Jhesus Christe that the same shall enjoye everlastinge reste & joye in the Kingdome of heaven. And my bodye I will to be buried in the parish Church of Ufton, in the sepulchre there, wherein the bodye of Richard Parkins, Esq., my first husband, lyeth in suche good order as shall seeme best to myne executors & overseers. And first a touchinge the ordering & disposition of my landes tenemented & hereditaments in the Countie of Wilts, I will that my kinsmanne, Francis Parkynnes, Esq., shall have theme & enjoyne theme duringe his liefe, & after his decease to suche other persounes as be lymitted in my deede

indented bearing datte the third daie of November, in the
xiijth yeare of the raigne of our Soveraigne Ladye, Queene
Elizabeth, accordinge, to the intente & meaninge of the saydt
deeds indented, whiche deed indented is made betweene me, the
saide Dame Elizabeth of the one partie & the saide Francis
Parkyns & one Henry Parkins, gent., of the other partie.
Item, I will that the said Francis Parkyns for & duringe his
natural liefe, & after his decease his fyrst, seconde, thirde,
fowerth, fyveth, sixth & seaventhe sonne of his bodye begottenne
& the heyres males of theire bodyes begottenne that shall have
or enjoye my saide laudes, tenements & heriditaments by the
intente & meaninge of the saide deede indented shall everie
yeare yearlye after the first yeare next after my decease aboutes
the middest of Lent distribute & bestowe amongst the poore
people of the parishes of Steeple, Langforde & Wylye in the
countie of Wilts fower quarters of wheate, & amongst the poore
people of the parish of Tysburye in the saide countie of Wilts
one quarter of wheate, & amongst the poore people of the parish
of Ufton & Padworthye in the countie of Berk twentie
busshells of wheate, the same wheate to be made into good &
howshoulde breade, & so then bestowed as is aforesaide, &
shall likewise everye yeare, yearlie after the firste yeare nexte
after my decease destribute & bestowe emounge the poore people
of the parrishe of Tisburye aforesaide twentie shillinges in
moneye, & shall likewise everye yeare yearlie after the firste
yeare next after my decease destribute & bestowe amongst the
poore people of the saide parrishes of Steeple, Langforde,
Wylye, Ufton & Padworthye, fyftie ells of canvas of twelve
pence the elle to make theme shirtes & smockes, & fiftye
yardes of narrowe blewe clothe of twenty pence the yarde to
make them coates & cassockes (that is to say) twenty fyve ells
of the same canvas, & fyve & twentie yardes of the same
clothe amongest the poore people of Steeple, Langford, &
Wylye, & the other fyve & twentie ells of canvas & fyve &
twentie yardes of clothe amoungest the poore people of Ufton
& Padworthy. Item, I will & devyze that if the saide
Francis Parkyns shall dye withowte heire male of his bodye
lawfullie begotten or if the said Francis Parkyns & the heyres
males of his bodye begottenne doe not destribute and bestowe

CHAP. V.
A.D. 1581.

(after a reasonable requeste maide by anye of the Churchewardens of the sayde parrishes) the saide corne, monney, canvas, & clothe, according to the trewe intente & meaninge of this my will, & of my saide deeds indented, that then the saide Henry Parkyns & Margarett his wieffe and the heyres males of theire owne bodyes lawfullie begottenne shall have & enjoye my saide landes, tenementes & hereditaments according to the trewe intente & meaninge of my saide dede indented & shall yearlie destribute & bestowe the corne, moneye, canvas, & clothe before lymitted to be destributed & bestowed in suche manner & forme as is before expressed & sette downe. And my further meaninge & will is that if the saide Henry Parkyns & Margarett his wieffe doe dye withowte heires males of theire two bodies lawfullie begottenne or of the saide Henrie & Margarette & the heires males of theire twoe bodyes lawfullie begottenne, after my saide landes, tenementes, & hereditaments shall comme to theme or anye of theme doe not destribute & bestowe (after a reasonable requeaste made by any of the churchwardens of the saide parrishes) the corne, monneye, canvas, & clothe as is aforesaide, that then Thomas Monpesson, gentlemanne, son of John Monpesson, gentlemanne, deceased, & the heyres males of his bodye lawfullye begottenne shall have & enjoye my saide landes & tenementes to him & the heires males of his bodye lawfullie begotten & shall yearlie destribute & bestowe the corne, monneye, canvas, & clothe before lymitted to be destributed & bestowed in such manner & forme as is before expressed & sette downe. Item, I will & my further meaninge is that if the saide Thomas Mompessonne doe dye withowt heyre male of his bodye lawfullye begottenne, or if the saide Thomas Mompessonne & the heires male of his bodye lawfullye begottenne doe not destribute & bestowe (after a reasonable requeaste made by anye of the Churchwardens of the saide parrishes) the corne, monnye, canvas & clothe before lymitted, to be destributed & bestowed in such manner & forme as is before expressed & sette downe, that then the right heyres of me the said Dame Elizabeth Marvyn shall have & enjoye my said Landes & Tenements, & shall yearlie destribute & bestowe the corne, monnye, canvas, & clothe before lymitted to be destributed & bestowed in such manner & forme as is before expressed. All which myne intente & meaninge is partlie expressed & sette downe in the saide Indenture of the conveyance of my saide Laundes before expressed. And as touchinge the dispositionne of my gooddes & chattels. First, I give & bequeath unto my saide Kinsmanne, Francis Parkynnes, all the stocke of howsholde stuffe, cattell, corne, & other gooddes & chattells which I shall have at Ufton at the tyme of my death. Item, I give & bequeathe unto my lovinge sister, Suzanne Monpessone, & to my saide Kynnesmanne, Thomas Monpessone, the son of Johnne Monpessonne, deceased, my stocke of horsses, ploughes, cartes, sheepe & corne upon Deptford, to be divided into twoe parties, & my saide sister Suzanne firste to make choise of the one moytie & parte therof, & my saide cosigne Thomas to have the other parte. Item, I give & bequeathe to Rychard, Henry, Marye, & Dorothie Blanche, sonnes & daughters of my cosen, Henry Blancharde, esquire, deceased, to everie one of theme tenne poundes, to be paid in forme followinge (That is to saie) To the sayde Rycharde & Henrye when their shall accomplishe & comme to the full age of one & twentie yeares, & to the saide Marye & Dorothie at their severall ages if one & twentie yeares or at the daie of their marriages which shall first happenne. Item, I give unto my cosizne M^{res} Eŭr Brunynge all suche summes of monneye as she doeth owe unto me, & to either of her three daughters yette unmarried the somme of fortie shillings, so in the whole to theme six poundes & to be paide to them at theire sev'all ages of one & twentie yeares, or at the daie of their marriage whiche shall firste happen. Item, I give unto my cossignes Edmonde, Anthonye, Jane, & Martha Drewrye, childrenne of my cosigne Margarett Herbyn, by her firste husbande, to either of them towards theire good educacionne & bringinge uppe in vertue & learninge five poundes, thirtene shillinges, fower pence, so in the whole to them six & twentie pounde, thirtene shillinges fower pence.

Item, I give & bequeath to my Cosigne Drewe Monpessonne, the sonne of L—— Monpessonne, one annuitie or yearlie rente of fortie shillings, paiable yearlie duringe his

CHAP. V.

A.D. 1581.

WILL OF LADY MARVYN continued.

naturall liefe, at two daies & tymes in the yeare. Item, I give & bequeathe to my cosigne Elizabeth, wiefe of the saide Drewe Monpessonne, after the decease of the saide Drewe, for & duringe her naturall liefe, one annuitie or yearlie rente of five poundes, thirtene shillinges, fower pence, paible also at two tymes in the yeare. Item, I give & bequeathe to Marye Monpessonne, the daughter of Edward Monpessonne, deceased, the somme of twentie poundes. Item, I give & bequeathe to either of the three daughters of my saide cossigne Thomas Monpessonne, sonne of the saide John Monpessonne, five poundes, thirtene shillinges, fower pence, so in the whole to them three Twentie poundes, to be paide at theire severall ages of one & twentie yeares or daie of theire marriage, whiche shall first happen. Item, I give & bequeathe to my cossigne Robert Hawle & his wiefe towardes the buildinge his howse & storinge his groundes the somme of one hundred markes, so that they doe permitte & suffer my servante Thomas Towne to have, houlde, occupy, & enjoye for & during the liefe of John Bridges, father-in-lawe of the saide Thomas Towne, all that howse rome, landes, & groundes in Padworthye nowe in the tenure & occupation of the saide Thomas Towne, without payinge any yearlie rente for the same. Item, I give to the saide Thomas Towne the somme of three poundes sixe shillinges eighte pence. Item, I give & bequeathe to my cosen Margarette Parkyns, Thomas & John Parkyns, her sonnes, all that my farme or tenemente wilbe Th' appurten'nces called Hauginge Langforde, in the countie of Wilts, & in the tenure & occupation of Henry Parkyns, gent., to have & to houlde to the saide Margarette, Thomas, & John Parkins successivelie for and duringe theire naturall lyves & the longest lyver of them. Item, I give & bequeathe to everie one of the daughters of the saide Margarette Parkyns fyve poundes. Item, I give Thomas Wilson & Alice Sandeowes, my servauntes, two entire markes, & to mother Joue, my servaunte, her fyndinge duringe her lieffe & yearlye in mouneye tenne shillinges. Item, I give to Richard Martyn, the sonne of Edward Martyn, Esq., the somme of twentie poundes. Item, I give to Brewer, my servaunte, his fyndinge so longe as he shall remayne in service with my cosen Francis Parkyns & yearlie in mouneye tenne

shillinges. Item, I give to Henry Bell, my servaunte, if he
surrender & give up his estate in Watermannes holde tenne
poundes. Item, I give to everye one of my servauntes, as well
manne servauntes as maide servauntes, that have lyved me
above five yeares, one whole yeares wages, & to them that
have served under fyve yeares one half yeares wage, & that
are not otherwise remembered in this my last will. Item, I
give & bequeathe to Edmonde Newtonne, my servaunte, tenne
poundes & the next copyhold that shall happen to comme voide
& be in to my saide cosigne Francis Parkins' handes for
terme of liefe of the saide Edmonde, so as he doe remayne &
contynewe in service with my said cosigne Francis Parkins.
Item, I give to my servaunte, Elizabeth Mathewe, tenne
poundes. Item, I will & my meaninge is that Thomas Beare
& Agnes his wieffe shall have, houlde, occupye, & enjoye for
tearme of theire lyves & the longest lyver of them the tenement
& copyhoulde landes the th' appurtenances theye doe nowe
houlde & occupye in Padworthye withowte payinge any yearlie
rente for the same, & I give them in monneye fortie shillinges.
yearlie, to be paide to them & the longest lyver of them during
their naturall lyves. Item, I will & my meaninge is that
Richard Astlett & Cislye, his wieffe, shall have & enjoye
the houlde theye dwell in Wihells withowte payinge any yearlie
rent for the same duringe their lyves & the longest lyver of
them. Item, I give to John Woddiche & Jone, his wieffe, twoe
Kyne & twoe Ewes & twoe Lambes. Item, I give & my
desyre is that my saide cosigne Francis Parkyns shall assure,
or cause to be assured, by coppye of courte rowlle unto my
servaunte, William Holwaye, for tearme of his lyfe rendeion
of the copyhoulde after the deceasse of Widdowe Kember lyinge
& beinge in Finchhampstead in the countie of Berk, nowe in
the tenure & occupation of the saide Widdowe Kember or her
assigns. Item, I give to John Galta, my servaunte, the monney
that he oweth me, beinge tenne poundes or thereabouts. Item,
I give to John Godfrye, my servaunte, one cowe, twoe ewes, &
twoe Lambes, & his fyndinge so longe as he shall remayne in
service with my cosigne, Francis Parkyns. Item, I give &
bequeathe to my cosigne, Richard Parkyns, sonne of my
cosigne, Henrie Parkyns, one annuitie, or yearlie rente of fyve

CHAP. V.

A.D. 1581.

WILL OF LADY MARVYN continued.

poundes, paiable to him quarterlie for & duringe the naturall liefe of the saide Richard. Item, I give & bequeathe to my cosigne, Richard Brewinge, fortie shillinges in monneye, & to his brother, Thomas Brewynge, fortie shillinges. * * * Here follow legacies to servants on the Wiltshire estate. *And the rest of all my gooddes & chattells not given & bequeathed I give & bequeath to my saide cosyne, Francis Parkyns, whome I order & make my sole & only executor of this my present latest will & testamente. And I doe ordaine Edmonde Plowden, Esq., & Edward Martyn, gentleman, to be overseers of this my last will, & doe give to the saide Edmonde Plowden, in token of good will, three poundes five shillinges eight pence. And to the saide Edward Martyn to buye a nagge withe all five poundes thirteen shillinges fower pence.*

In witness whereof I the saide Dame Elizabeth Marvyn to this my laste will & testamente have subscribed my name & put my seale in the presence of these whose names are subscribed the xxviii daie of Julye, in the yeare of our Lord God a thousande fyve hundrede fower score & one, in the xxiijth *yeare of the raigne of our soverayne Ladye Elizabethe, by the grace of God of Englande, France, & Ireland, Queene, defender of the faith, etc.*

Per Elizabethe Marvyne, Edwarde Martyn, George Tattursoll, Henry Parkyns, Robert Hollo, William Pulforde, Hughe Lynthighte.

Henry Parkyns, who is mentioned in the will as having reversionary rights, was nephew to her first husband, Richard Parkyns. He had married Margaret, the daughter of her youngest sister Anne, wife of William Wayte, of Wymering, in Hampshire. Henry Parkyns was the immediate ancestor of the Beenham branch of the family. See Appendix. The charitable benefaction which Lady Marvyn left as a charge on the property remains in force to this day, and bread, calico, and flannel are distributed to the poor parishioners, not only of Ufton and Padworth, but also of Steeple Langford and the other parishes in Wiltshire where Lady Marvyn's estates were situated, though her family have long ago ceased to hold any property there. The names of several of the servants to

Of Pole Manor.

whom she gives legacies, such as Beare, Wooddiche, Holwaye, and Astlett or Arlett, are still common at Ufton. Richard Brunynge was the cousin who had acted as Lady Marvyn's agent in the purchase of Pole Manor, and Edmond Plowden was the distinguished lawyer of the name whose daughter Francis Perkins, Lady Marvyn's great-nephew, had married.

The following is a table of Lady Marvyn's family, showing the relationship of the persons mentioned in the will:

Sir John Mompesson = Alice Leigh.

Elizabeth = 1st, Richard Parkyns, 2nd, Sir John Marvyn.	Susan, died unmarried.	Mary = Thomas Wells, of Bambridge.	Anne = William Wayte, of Wymeringe, co. Hants.

Gilbert Wells.	Anne = William Parkyns.	And others.

Francis Perkins.

Elinor.	Richard Brunynge.	Elizabeth Richard Norton.	Sir Susan Richard of Wollscott.	Wollaston,	Honor	William Wayte.	Mary	Richard Creswell.	Margaret	Henry Parkyns.

Richard.   Thomas.   John.   Anne.   Mary and others.

Panel from Orotry.

DESCENT OF THE FAMILY OF PERKINS OF UFTON FROM 1581 TO 1661.

(1st) Francis Perkins, = Anna, dau. of Edmond Plowden, of
died 1615.   Shiplake, co. Oxon.

(2nd) Fran- = Margaret,   Ed- = 1st, Jane   Kathe- = George   A dau. = Alyng.
cis Per-   dau. of   mond, Winch-   rine.   Tatter-
kins, died John Ey-   living comb.   sall.
1661.   ston, of   1660. 2nd, Eliza-
            Catmore.   beth James.

Francis Per- = Frances, dau.   John Perkins.   1. Mary.   4. Frances.
kins, died   of H. Winch-   died before   2. Elizabeth. 5. Elizabeth.
1660, before   comb, of   1660.   3. Anne.   6. Margaret.
his father.   Bucklebury.   7. Winifred.

(3rd) Francis Perkins.

Panel from Oratory.

Chapter vj.

Of the Recusants.

FRANCIS PERKINS was the first of the family whose name was sometimes, though not invariably, written in the modern style, as may have been noticed in Richard Parkyns' will. A.D. 1581.
Francis Perkins.

He was under age in 1566, for in that year, in accordance with a provision of the same will in case the living of Ufton Robert became vacant during his minority, Elizabeth the widow, made the presentation. Sarum Reg.

He not only inherited the estate of Ufton Robert from his Uncle Richard, but in 1581, he succeeded by the death of Lady Marvyn to Pole Manor in Ufton, and also to her manor of Great Bathampton and others of her Wiltshire estates, though not without dispute. Susan Mompesson the unmarried sister of the deceased, and various members of the Welles and Wayte families, as representatives of the two other sisters, maintained that a legacy, in their favour of the *stock of horses, ploughs, carts, sheep, and oxen*, had not been delivered to them by Francis, and that therefore his rights under the settlement made by Lady Marvyn were cancelled, and that they as her lawful heirs should succeed to her property. However, their claim was evidently disallowed, for Francis later on is found in possession. Chancery Proceedings
Eliz. P. 5. 54.

CHAP. vi.
A.D. 1581.

Anthony Wood, Athen. Oxon., vol. i., p. 506.

SERGEANT PLOWDEN.

Burke's History of Commoners.

He married Anna, the eldest daughter of Sergeant Plowden, of Shiplake, in Oxfordshire, who also owned *a fair estate in Burghfield*, namely, that of Wokefield, or Okefield, in the immediate neighbourhood of Ufton, which is, in fact, partly in the three parishes of Burghfield, Mortimer, and Sulhamstead. This estate was sold by Sergeant Plowden's son Francis in 1626 to Thomas Purcell.

Mr. Plowden was both distinguished as a lawyer, and much respected for the integrity of his character.

His connection with Francis Perkyns is alluded to in an account given by one Andrew Blundel of an incident in which his honourable and kindly nature is well shown.

He had received from the Queen the guardianship of young Francis Englefield, nephew of Sir Francis Englefield, of Englefield, but, instead of taking advantage of the office for his own profit, as was usually done in such cases, by bestowing his ward in marriage in exchange for a sum of money paid to himself, he formally made a gift of his authority to his ward. The scene is described as follows:

About the pointe of younge Englefielde's agge of XXI yeres Mrs. Englefield (the mother) Mr. Francis Fitten, her brother & young Englefield were at Shiplake. After dinner Mr. Plowden went into his newe parlor, called them unto him, called also Mr. Perkyns who then before had married his eldest daughter, ould Mr. Wollascott, younge Edmund Plowden, my cozen Humfry Sandford & myselfe & I know not whether any others. Then turned his talke to younge Mr. Englefield & said thus in effecte, Mr. Englefield you are my ward ... your expectation is greate and according to that I may now here receive for your wardship & marriage, & my ould Lord Montague hath offered for you, £2,000. Take it (says he) as a gift of £2,000 & in recompense I crave for no benefitte for myself or my own children.

The only request that the Sergeant made to Francis Englefield in return, was that he should continue to Humfrey Sandford, his son-in-law, the three lives' lease of lands at Englefield then held by Richard Sandford the father. A promise to this effect was readily made, but, sad to say, after the death of Edmund Plowden the Sergeant, as readily forgotten. Francis Englefield not only did not renew the lease, but turned the old man Richard Sandford out of his home. He exclaiming: *Wife, carry me to Plowden. He hath killed me! he hath killed me! with these words continually in his mouth, languished for about a month, & then for very sorrow & conceyte died.*

Elizabeth had wished to bestow the Lord Chancellorship on Sergeant Plowden, and wrote him a letter to that effect, making the condition that he should change his religion. His answer was as follows:

Hold me, dread Sovereign, excused. Your Majesty well knows, I find no reason to swerve from the Catholic Faith, in which you & I were brought up. I can never, therefore, countenance the persecution of its professors. I should not have in charge your Majesty's conscience one week, before I should incur your displeasure, if it be your Majesty's intent to continue the system of persecuting the retainers of the Catholic Faith.

It is much to Elizabeth's credit that this bold answer altered in nothing the esteem in which she continued to hold her faithful lawyer and servant to the end of his life. This was a time when many were subjected to temptations of the sort; and not a few who resisted, less fortunate than Sergeant Plowden, suffered loss and imprisonment, and even death, rather than sacrifice their religious convictions.

The life of Francis Perkins corresponded pretty nearly with the period of that great revolt against Papal authority in England which resulted in the Reformation. It is not here the place to enter into the causes that brought this change to a successful issue; the spark struck in Germany, no doubt found ready fuel in this country, where, from the earliest days of the Church's history, protests against ultramontanism, and struggles for ecclesiastical independence, had been going on with little intermission from one century to another. If the nation generally had not been looking for religious freedom, it can scarcely be imagined that the many arbitrary and cruel acts which accompanied the revolution, would have been submitted to and accepted as they were. For not a village, nor scarcely even a family, was unaffected by it. The suppression of the monasteries in 1539, put an end at one blow to a system which, as the members of the various confraternities were drawn from all ranks of life, from the highest to the lowest, must have been closely entwined with family and social life everywhere. In every country parsonage the priest was suddenly brought face to face with the question, whether he would cling to the past or follow the stream. The patrons of livings had to conform, as it was called, to the change from the supremacy of the pope to that of the king, or lose their right of presentation; and the perplexities and sufferings of this time of transition were no doubt, all the while, enormously aggravated by the interested and rapacious conduct of the king and his tools. If the minds of the many were convinced, so that they were ready to follow such leading, it must be allowed that it is to the credit of the few who were not so convinced, that they stood aloof, and ultimately suffered the loss of social and religious privileges, of fortune and even life itself, rather than give up their allegiance to the foreign prelate whom they believed to be the head of the Church. Among those few who did so refuse to conform were the family of Parkyns.

The first hint we have of ecclesiastical difficulties in the parish is connected with the presentations to the living. The patronage had always been in the gift of the lords of the manor. In 1566 Lady Marvyn, as has been said, presented, under the will of her late husband, Richard Parkyns, but from that date forward till the sale of the advowson to Oriel College this right of presentation was not again exercised by its proper owner. Recusants, as such persons were called in Queen Elizabeth's reign, who refused to take the oath of Royal supremacy, were, in fact, declared by law incapable of appointing to livings in their gift.

Other and severer laws were at the same time enacted against them. In 1563 the oath was imposed on all who should celebrate or hear mass, under the penalty of premunire for the first refusal, and death for treason for the second; and during succeeding years till the end of Elizabeth's reign, as well as during the reign of her successor, many and similar

Acts of Parliament were passed; one in 1571 made liable to the penalties of treason all who should put in use any bull or writing from the Bishop of Rome, or who should introduce or receive the things called Agnus Dei, or crosses, or pictures, or beads blessed by the Bishop of Rome; and ordering all persons who had left the realm without license to return under pain of forfeiting their goods and chattels; also, in 1581, that all who pretended to possess the power of absolution, or who should attempt to withdraw others from the established religion, should suffer for high treason; that the punishment for saying mass should be the payment of 200 marks and one year's imprisonment, and that for hearing mass 100 marks and imprisonment for the same time. That the fine for absence from the parish church should be £20 per month, and if the absence were prolonged to an entire year that the recusant should find securities for his good behaviour for £200 each. In 1584, that if any clergyman ordained by the authority of the Bishop of Rome were found within the realm after the expiration of 40 days that he should be adjudged guilty of high treason; that whosoever knew of his being in the kingdom and did not discover him within twelve days should be fined and imprisoned at the Queen's pleasure; that all students in Catholic seminaries abroad who did not return within six months should be punished as traitors. And in James I.'s reign, 1606, Catholic recusants were forbidden to appear at Court, to dwell within ten miles of the city of London, or to remain on any occasion more than five miles from their homes without special license. They were also declared incapable of practising surgery or physic, or in the Common or Civil Law, or of acting as judges, clerks, or officers in any court or corporation. But for all this most severe and repressive legislation, and for the cruel rigour with which, as must be added, it was put into execution, was there not a cause?

From the first moment of Elizabeth's accession she found arrayed against her and her friends all the adherents of her sister's policy, supported by the baulked ambition of Philip II. of Spain. It was a struggle for life and death which began between the two parties, and those who had lived through the persecutions of Mary's reign, and had felt hanging over their heads the threat of the introduction of the Holy Inquisition, might be pardoned if in their turn they wished to make sure that their opponents were left no power to harm. Nor was the danger only in the past. Dr. Jessopp in his excellent book on the Walpole family has shown that the first stringent Act passed by Parliament against all who should promulgate papal decrees was evoked by Pius V.'s Bull of Excommunication against Elizabeth depriving her of all her dominions, dignities, and privileges, forbidding her subjects to obey her, and absolving them entirely from their oath of allegiance. The succeeding Acts of 1581 and 1584 were expressly directed against the Jesuit missioners who swarmed into the country as they said to reconquer it for Rome, agents of Philip of Spain and eager promoters of any conspiracy that would serve to destroy the Queen. It was too true that the innocent suffered with the guilty, and that those whose only wish it was to follow the religion of their fathers in peace, and in all loyalty to the existing Government, were hunted, fined, and imprisoned, as well as the intriguing Jesuit priest from whom they had received the consolations of their faith. There is evidence that there was a very distinct difference of feeling among the recusants themselves. The old parish clergy and many others in the country resented the injudicious zeal so much mixed up with treason of the Jesuit missionaries who came from the Seminary at Douay, and later on from Valladolid. They resented the word missionary as an insult to the existing survival of loyal sons of the Roman Church in England; men who, as they said, would obey Cæsar and were most ready to spend their blood in the Queen's defence, though they would rather lose their lives than infringe what they considered to be the lawful authority of the Catholic Church. If the Jesuits had not interfered, they maintained, penal statutes would have been fewer and the odium in which recusants were held would have abated. Of this party was a certain priest, Father Bluet, whose protest against the mischief done by agitators is here quoted. He had come to England to bring alms to priests imprisoned for their faith, and, writing to Cardinals Borghese and Aragon in 1602, he says: *The Bishop of London, in whose power I*

Of the Recusants. 89

was by the Queen's command, showed me very many & divers
letters & books of Father Parsons, Father Holt, & other
English Jesuits, in which it plainly appeared that they invited
the King of Spain to invade the kingdom of England (as of
right due to him), & soliciting many private men that they
should kill the Queen either by poison or the sword.... He
asked me what I thought of these things, & whether the secular
priests were of the same mind. To which I replied that to my
certain knowledge neither the secular priests nor the principal
Catholics in England were ever conscious of such designs....
that we, the innocent priests, for many years were troubled,
tortured, & hanged, not on account of religion, or the Catholic
faith, or justice, but on account of treasons of this kind....
The Bishop of London communicated these my answers to the
Queen; & so, after various comparisons & conferences, the
Queen ordered the judges that they should abstain from the
blood of the priests unless any should be found guilty of such
designs; for the judges of the provinces, before they go to the
tribunals in the provinces, are wont to ask the Queen what
should be done as to the affairs of Catholics.

When this was done, a petition was offered to the Queen
that she would be inclined to clemency for some liberty of conscience on behalf of the Catholics, with this protestation, that
the priests & laity were faithful to her in all things which
belonged to her temporal affairs.... This supplication being
read, again & again she burst forth with these words: These
men, perceiving my lenity & clemency towards them, are not
content, but want to have all things at once. The King of
France (she said) in truth can, without any peril of honour,
life or kingdom, grant to the Huguenots liberty of religion, but
it is not so with me; for if I granted this liberty to the
Catholics, by that same deed, I lay myself, my honour, my life
& my crown, at their feet. For their highest pastor pronounced sentence against me whilst I was yet in my mother's
womb. (She referred to the sentence of Clement VII., touching
the marriage of Henry & her mother.) Moreover she said:
Pius V. has excommunicated me, & absolved my subjects from
the oath of fidelity; Gregory XIII., also, & Sextus V., at the
instance of the King of Spain (that he might extend his own

CHAP. vi. borders) *have renewed the same; & so it remains to our*
A.D. 1602. *peril.*

FATHER BLUET'S DECLARATION. Whether these were actually the words of Elizabeth herself, maintaining her own cause, or a representation by Father Bluet of what she might have been supposed to say, they are, surely, equally remarkable.

He goes on to say that there was a difference made *between the old priests, that is, those who were consecrated in the times of Henry & Mary, & the more recent priests whom they call seminaries. . . . The old priests having always lived peaceably & quietly. And when Queen Mary was dead, the old bishops & priests received this our Queen, & placed her on the throne of the Kingdom, & anointed her Queen; & though she removed them all from their Sees, on account of their ancient faith, & introduced others, nevertheless they, whether in prison or out of prison, always conducted themselves peaceably, nor have they attempted anything against the Crown. But those more recent Jesuits & Seminaries, far otherwise; for they have entered into the Kingdom secretly under the garb of religion & piety; nevertheless, they conspire for the death of the Prince & the ruin of their country, offering it as a booty to foreign Princes.*

Bluet, further on, quotes from a book written, in English, against the Queen at the time of the Spanish Armada, which declared the sentence of Sextus V. against her, saying: *That both Pius V. & other Popes, on account of the cowardice & weakness of Catholics, have permitted that they should legally & without sin, obey & serve Elizabeth as Queen de facto. Now Sextus revokes that liberty & order, commands & enjoins them, under pain of the greater excommunication, that in a collected multitude, they rush against Elizabeth, & throw her, like Jezebel, out of the window under the hoofs of Jehu's horses, or deliver her to the Catholic army to be punished. Then he reviles her with abuses & the worst names. Irritated by these things, she raged against priests & Catholics of both sexes, & without doubt, unless God had interfered by the death of the Earl of Leicester, she would have killed all the Catholics in the Kingdom. Many martyrs are crowned, & a great massacre declared.* And he adds: *Behold the fruit & result of the book, & of the King's fleet!*

Meanwhile, in the Spanish Seminaries, Father Parsons forced English youths and priests to subscribe to the Spanish Infanta as their lawful Queen. *Therefore,* says Bluet, *is it to be wondered at, if Elizabeth, irritated in this manner, raged against priests & people who are brought up & educated under such masters?*

It may well have been that the Parkyns family were of the number of those resigned and loyal folk who would have possessed their souls in patience if only they had been so allowed. Their names do not occur in the accounts of the various conspiracies of the time, nor do they seem to have been called upon to suffer death, or even imprisonment, as the price of constancy to their faith, and yet the persecution they endured was real enough. They, like the rest of the recusants on the proscribed lists ordered to be sent in by bishops and other officers throughout the country, were liable to be spied upon by their neighbours, and reported against if the least suspicion was entertained that they heard Mass in private or had sheltered a wandering priest. The informer was to receive half the fines, and one can readily imagine what a spur greed of gain became to the illwill or spite of some dishonest servant or petty tradesman living in the neighbourhood. Such an one was found in the person of Roger Plumpton, a tailor of the adjoining parish of Sulhamstead Abbot, who, on the evening of September 5, 1586, brought information to Reade Stafford, of Bradfield, and two of his brother magistrates, Thomas Parry, of Hampstead Marshall, and Humfry Foster, of Aldermaston, against *Frauncys Parkyns of Ufton,* described by them *as a gentleman of fayre living amongst us.*

In the report of the information which they sent to Sir Francis Walsingham, *Her Matie principall secretarye*, then living at his newly acquired property at Englefield, they state *that he* (Plumpton) *was able to disclose sundry matters practised, where he hath byne abydinge amongst Papists, hymselfe offereth to be an Instrument for the apprehension of a Seminary Priest.*

CHAP. vi.
A.D. 1586.

ACCUSATION
AGAINST
FRANCIS
PERKINS.

Whether the same Priest be in Mr. Parkyns house at this present, he is not well assured.

Roger Plumpton's accusations against Mr. Parkyns were as follows:

That one good wyffe Beare of Padworthe tolde hym that Mr. Frauncys Parkyns meeting with her demanded whether she stoode excomunicatt or noe, who answering Yea, he saide, Yt is noe mattre, If you knowe as mutch as I, you woulde soe remayne untill we see some other chaunge.

Item, he further Informeth that at sutch tyme as the Towne of Reading & other Parishes aboute us, made bonefyers & ringing in token of rejoycinge for her Ma^{ts} delivery owt of the daunger of theese late Trayters' rebellious practises, one Guy, s'vant to Frauncys Parkyns, cominge from Readinge, tolde his M^r thereof, who saide, Oh yt is a goodly piece of worke, be you sure yt is marvell that they threwe nott upp their cappes. Which words were spoken after a scornfull manner.

Further he sayth that their resorteth unto the dwelling house of the saide Frauncys Parkyns a certen unknowen person which is comenly lodged in a cocke lofte or some other secrett corner of the howse, & is not comenly seene abroade, but cominge abroade he weareth a blewe coate which person soe unknowen he vehemently suspecteth to be the same seminary Priest; for that on divers Wenesdayes, frydayes, & other festivall dayes, he hath seene most of the familye, one after another, slipping upp in a secrett manner to a highe Chaumber in the toppe of the howse, & theere continewe the space of an hower & a halfe or moore, & this Examinatt (Roger Plumpton) harkening as neere as he might to the place, hath often heard a litle bell rounge, which he Imagineth to be a sacring bell, wherby he conjectureth that they resorte to heare Masse.

Then he further saythe that Mr. ffrauncys Parkyns & his wieffe doe not repayre to the Church nor communicatt, neyther will thinke well of such their s'vants as be not of their religion; & further and lastly sayth that one George Tettersall, & divers other unknowen persons suspected to be papists resort to the house of the sayde ffrauncis Parkyns in secrett manner, sometymes by daye sometymes by night.

In consequence of this serious indictment, the same three Justices of the Peace, Thomas Parry, Humfrey Foster, and Reade Stafford were directed to repair to Mr. Parkyns' house at Ufton, to call him to account, which they accordingly did, on the following day; but not finding him at home, they forthwith made search in his studdy, clossette & all other seacreate places of the house, perusing all the books, Letres, & writinges in chests, cupboards, & boxes there remayninge, but founde nothinge contrary to the Lawes wherewith he might be charged, neither any straunger or unknown person. This search made, understanding by his wiff that himself with some of his servaunts weare at Illesley, tenne miles, of a hawking, we forthwith sent our letres requiring him in her Mat^{ts} name to make his personall appearaunce before us, which he did the same night, we, having before us all his servaunts, & one Beare, his tenant, did severally examine them; . . . we also examined one Mr. Hall, parson of Sulhamsted, & one Mr. Hobson, parson of Padworth, who, as we conjectured by Plympton's reporte, were able to Reveale further matter unto us concerning the resorte of seminarye Priests to Ufton, but they could not deliver us the certainty of any suche matter. . . . Three of the servaunts of the said Fraunces Parkins we have comitted to prison according to your honour's directions. We have likewise taken bond in fyve hundeth pound of the said Fraunces Parkins to make his personall apparaunce before your honour upon Saturday next, being the xvj.th day of the present September.

And there is added the following note on his appearance: *Perkins was before the like discharged concerninge the imputations, but is a recusant, & referred to Mr. Done to have conference with him who is to make report thereof.*

On the same occasion a humble neighbour of Mr. Parkyns', one Richard Higges, a labouring man, was also examined for recusancy. The incident is so characteristic of the times that no apology is made for transcribing the account of it. He was brought before these same magistrates for having had his child christened *by a priest at his own house in the latyn* service. The name of the priest he will not confesse, neyther what is become of hym. Being further examined, he answered that he mett the priest upon the downes near Wantidge, clad in a white fryse jurkyn, & a white paire of hoase, & imagined him to be a priest, for that he had a pen & ink horne at his gerdle & a booke in his bosome; but what his name is or where he dwelleth he will by no meanes confesse.

Poor Richard Higges was sent off to the *Maresshalsea* prison. It would be in accordance with what is known of the practice of the time to suppose that both he and Mr. Perkins' servants were kept that they might be worked upon by fear, or even torture, to betray what they knew of the name and whereabouts of the fugitive priest. Cruel as such means were, it is well-known that they were resorted to, at the time, by both sides alike, not only under Queen Elizabeth in England but even more freely in Spain and elsewhere on the Continent.

The popular rejoicings at Reading, about which Francis Perkins was said to have made scornful remarks, were on the occasion of the conviction of Babington and others, concerned in a conspiracy in favour of Mary Queen of Scots. They were executed on September 20th and 21st, in this same year 1586.

On another occasion, of which the date is not given, Roger Plumpton, again gave information concerning a priest, perhaps the same as above, who is called George Lingam; feigned names were, however, generally adopted by the priests during their wanderings.

He says, *The said Lingam willed one Roger Plumpton* (the treacherous informer himself) *to doe comendation to Mrs. Parkins, wyfe to Mr. ffra Parkins, esquier, & to tell her that one Lingam hath layen at Court of purpose to hearken for newes, sends her word of certayntie that the P. of Parma writ to the fr. Ambassador that the greatest piratt in England, Sir ffra. Drake, was taken, &., but newes came after, it was Sr R. Greenwill, also that vij of the Queen's best ships weare taken & sunk by K. Phillippe, that S^r ffra. Drake was fast cowped upp by that K., all which message was done to hir & to her husband.*

Plumpton's report goes on: *At the sayd Parkins' house was lodged at that tyme one Measea, a man ill affected. The sayd Lingam harbored & lodged sometymes at one Mr. Wilscots & at Englefield, who is at theise places called James Lingar, &, under collor of teaching on the virginalls, goeth from papist to papist, is thought also to bee a priest, so made in Queen Marie's tyme, & lyke to bee the man that was keapt in the topp of the sayd Parkins' house at a tyme when hir Ma*[tie] *was but ill served by hir officers in a search there made.*

The sayd Plumpton sayth it can not bee learned where a son of the sayd Parkins was christened, but thought to be done secretly by some seminarie. Sute made to this Plumpton by Parkins frends not to bring this matter into question.

James Anslye often useth to the sayd Parkins' house, & to one Alyng's howse, whoe married Parkins' sister & dwelleth in a wood near Englefild house.

This Anslye useth this speach to one Crosse that dwelleth in Deptford beyinge a M[r] *Carpenter in hir Ma*[ties] *ships; that the Queen of Scots is right heire apparent to the crowne of England, &c., & after was shifted away & could not since bee seene of anie that durst chardge him herewithall.*

A tenant of Englefild howse asked Plumpton on Whit sonday last what newes he heard of those beyond sea for relligion & sayd further that he heard a speach gyven owt that S[r] *ffra Englefild and the rest beyond sea for relligion would come home and keepe howse agayne shortly after midsomer.*

The sayd Plumpton afterwards asked Wytherton where he heard this speache, but he sayd he would not tell, & after was lyke to have spoyled the sayd Plumpton.

Fra. Parkins lodgeth sundry recusants whose names are under written:

M[rs] Tottersoll, mother to M[r] Parkins.	M[rs] Martha, a yong gentlewoman.
M[ris] Elizabeth, a waytyng gentlewoman to hir.	Friswyde, her chamber mayd.
	*One Corder hir cooke.
	* Marg.

M[r] Parkins, cousen to M[r] Fra. Parkins.
M[r] Richard Marvin.

CHAP. vi.
A.D. 1589.

SUBSCRIPTION AGAINST ARMADA.

Mrs Pollard.
Mr George Tottersoll & his wyfe.
Mr Edward Tottersoll.
Mr Mesca & his wyfe.
Mr Ric^d Parkins.
Mr Vachell.
Mr Pursell.
Mrs Marye Ployden.
One Aylen & his wyfe.
One Arselet's wyfe.
One Mr Hall.

There is also one Taylor, an alehowse-keeper in Englefild, that of longe tyme hathe beene a Carier of Letres between S^r ffra Englefild & other papists in Barkshire.

What a picture of the life of the times is here graphically brought before us in this mean man's disjointed jottings! The little society of recusants clinging together, passing the news of the day anxiously from one to another, often by treacherous messengers, the priest, by whose help alone they could enjoy any religious services, living amongst them in disguise, or hidden in secret chambers in a cocke loft ; not knowing whom among their servants or neighbours they could trust, or who might at any time deliver their friends to the scaffold, or themselves to imprisonment and penury. Truly it was not surprising if they were found sometimes disloyal in thought or word, as when Mrs. Parkins may have received with satisfaction the news of the sinking of the Queen's ships. From what can be ascertained, however, her friend was not very well informed; no such disaster as he describes befell either the British navy or Sir Richard Grenville at the time any more than that *greatest piratt* Sir Francis Drake. It seems rather at variance with the above reports that Francis Perkins' name should have been in the list of those who subscribed for the defence of the country against the Spanish Armada. But it appears that this so-called subscription was an enforced loan, in reality a tax. It was levied from 2,416 of the landowners in thirty-six different counties. Letters were written by the Queen to Walsingham in 1589, and by him sent to Lieu-

Spanish Armada, with Hist. Introduction, T. C. Noble, p. xxx.

tenants of the various counties, requiring the raising of the sum of £75,000 to meet the arrears of the expenses of the defence which the grants of Parliament had been insufficient to cover. The practice was to fix the sum of money which each individual was considered able to pay, and then to get it from him if possible. It was usually £25 or £50. The amount paid by *Francis Parkins* was £50, a proof that he must have been considered a wealthy man.

Of the persons whose names are given as inmates of Mr. Parkins' house, *Mrs. Tottersoll* was his mother. She had married, after the death of her first husband, William Parkyns, a Mr. George Tattersall, of Stapleford, in Wiltshire, and was now for the second time a widow. *Mr. Edward Tottersoll* was no doubt of the same family. Mr. Richard Marvyn was of the family of Lady Marvyn's second husband. *Mr. Measea,* or Thomas Meysey, had married Susan, the daughter of Henry Parkyns, of Illseley, and was therefore a cousin by marriage.

Mr. Parkyns' cousins, Francis and Richard, were sons of Francis Parkyns, of Padworth; they are named in Lady Marvyn's will.

Mr. John Vachell was of Burghfield, in Berkshire. In 1593, only a few years after the incidents related above, it was reported of him by the Lord Keeper Puckring, that *he had forborne to come to church these two years, but was reconciled in the Marshalsea.* Absenteeism from church was one of the punishable offences of the recusants, and the Marshalsea prison one of the corrective measures applied, in this case, as it seemed, with success.

Mr. Pursell, or Purcell, was subsequently the purchaser of Sergeant Plowden's estate of Wokefield.

Mistress Marye Ployden was the sister of Anna, wife of Francis Parkyns. She married afterwards Richard White, of Hutton in Sussex. The rest were probably servants of the household. Edward Lingen, a Jesuit, was taken prisoner with Henry Walpole in 1593. He may have been the same as the priest here called George Lingam, the constant practice of the priests being to travel under various names. In the list of recusants for the year 1592, Francis Perkins is styled *of Langford.* Probably he was then living at Great Bathampton, the property he had inherited from Lady Marvyn, in the parish of Steeple Langford, in Wiltshire.

The house at Ufton was let, and two-thirds of its annual rent and that of other lands and tenements, amounting to £20 13s. 4d., went as a fine for the owners' recusancy to the Crown. Francis Perkins also owed £80 in virtue of an Act of Parliament imposing fines of £20 a month for non-attendance at the parish church. Richard Perkins, his cousin, then living at Fieldhouse Farm, Ufton, and Margaret, widow of Henry Perkins, were each fined £260 for the same offence. When one remembers that the value of money at the time was at least four times as great as at present, one can realize better the weight of the burden thus laid on the backs of the poor papist recusants.

In 1599 Francis Perkins was still absent from Ufton, when another search for priests took place there. This time it was not Plumpton who gave the information, but a man named Gayler, whose brother had formerly been in Mr. Perkins' service.

The incident was described by various eye-witnesses, in answer to interrogations administered before the Court of Exchequer a few years later, in 1608, when certain legal proceedings took place connected with it, as will be related further on. The following narrative is gleaned from these answers, as nearly as possible in the original words, but put together in the order of events.

It appears, then, that this Gayler *came to a Mr. Henry Meere, a counsellor at the lawe, & told hym that he knewe of a great treasure that was hidd in a house of one Mr. Perkins, & yt was the mony of some ill effected persons, & to be ymployed to some ill purposes; & said that, of his good will to the said Mr. Meere, he acquainted him therewith, to thintent that he might take some course to benefitt them booth thereby; & to that end, he entreated Mr. Meere to move S*^{r}* Walter Rawley to begge yt of the Queenes Ma*^{tie}*. Whereupon the said Mr. Meere did accordingly move S*^{r}* Walter Rawley, but Mr. Walter did refuse to deale therein. Whereupon the saide Gayler, comminge after to Mr. Meere, to know S*^{r}* Walter Rawleys answer, & under-*

Of the Recusants. 99

standing Sr Walter's refusal, said, yt was no matter, for that now the Lo: Chamberlaine was made acquainted with the matter.

The Lord Chamberlain, Lord Hunsdon, thus informed, and susspectinge the trewth of that information, directed two letters or warrants to Sir Francis Knollys, knight, *the one of them being for the apprehending of one Jarrett a Jesuit escaped out of the Tower of London & one Garrett, twoe notorious Traytors supposed to be in the house of one Frauncis Parkins of Ufton, a place generally reputed to be a common receptacle for preistes, Jesuytes, Recusantes, and other such evill desposed persons; & the other letter declaring or expressinge an informacion made to the saide lorde Chamberlayne of some greate some of money that should be layde up there by Recusantes or other evill affected persons to the State, the which if he fownde to be true he should see the same in safe custodye untill such further order might be taken for the same, as by her Matie should be thought fyt.*

In pursuance of these orders, Sir Francis Knollys set out from his own house in Reading, on the night of July 17, 1599, with a party of men, including the informer Gayler, not knowing, as one of his attendants thought, *to what house he should goe untill he was a Myle or theiraboutes beyond the house, & being so furr gone, upon conference with some of the gentlemen in the company, called to his man Cray that then rode before & asked of him which was the way to Ufton, for that they had then rydd beyond the house as aforesaid. Whereupon they turnid towards Ufton & Sir Francis Knollys, when he knewe whither they should goe, declared his opinyon, that he thought yt better to forbeare enteringe the house untill Breake of day, than to adventure thereon in the dead of the night as then yt was.*

Arrived at the house at last, and after the party had *byne some while there, one of the company came to Sr Francis Knollys, being then in the Hall, & told him the Neste was found, then Sr Francis, having searched the rest of the House by virtue of the first letter, did furthwith repayer to the secrett place where the money was. The said secrett place was found by Gayler, that gave the first informacion to the Lorde Chamberlane. Sr Francis, before his entrie into any of the romes of the house for*

CHAP. vi.
———
A.D. 1599.
———
SEARCH OF
UFTON
COURT.

searche, did take into his Companie, the keeper of the house, whose name was Thomas Perkyns, & the keeper's wiffe, whoe both did accompanie the said Sr Francis thorowe all the romes that he went into. Everie rome, wherinto he came to searche, was eyther open before he came into yt, or els was openid by such of the house as did accompanie him, except a chamber which yt seymid had byne used for a Chappell, the dore of which Chappell Sr Francis, or some of the companie, did breake open with his foote, for that Thomas Perkyns said he had not the key therof. In that chamber or Chappell they found diverse relickes & popishe Trashe, as namely, holie water with a sprinkle therin and a crosse at the end of the sprinkle, besydes which, there was a little box with diverse smale white waffer cakes like Agneos Dei fitt for the sayinge or synynge of masse, & candles half burnt out such as usuallie masse is said withall, & diverse pictures & such other thinges wherby yt seemid unto them that some masse had byne said or song not longe before.

At his comyng to the secrett place Sr Francis did call Thomas Perkyns unto him & demanded of him whether he formerlie knew the said secrett place, who answered that he knew yt not; the secrett place had been opened before the comynge of Sr Francis, who had lightes wherby he myght well see into yt but went not into yt. And then Sr Francis caused the Chestes to be taken up & sett on the Flower in the next Chamber, & furthwith spoke to Thomas Perkyns to help him to some meanes to open the Chestes; Whereupon the said Perkyns went awaie to fetch a Smythe, & Sr Francis made some stay, expecting his return, who returned noe more durynge the tyme that Sr Francis contynewed in the house. The wiffe of Thomas Perkyns, however, was an Eye-wytnes & present at the openynge of the two chestes; in one wherof ther was a pokemantua locked, which was also opened & therin were found diverse bagges of gold, all which, as they were taken out, were laid into her lapp, & afterwardes caried into a closett in the said chamber, & the gold told out upon a Table ther by Sr Francis in her presence. And further, in the other cheste ther was diverse parcells of plate wherof a note was taken, also in her presence.

Then Sr Francis Knollys went from the house at Ufton together with the rest of the companie, excepting Gayler, with

Of the Recusants. 101

CHAP. VI.
A.D. 1599.
CHESTS CONVEYED TO ALDERMASTON.

the gold & plate, directlie to Sr Humfrey Foster's house, about a myle or two from ther, purposing to have left the said gold & plate with Sr Humfrey; but not fynding him at home, Sr Francis & the rest of the companie returned to Readinge, brynging the gold with them, leaving his servant at Sr Humfreys to bryng the plate after in a Carte.

CHAP. vi.
A.D. 1599.
LEGAL PROCEEDINGS AGAINST Sᴿ F. KNOLLYS.

Thus far the first part of the story; for the sequel it appears that the Perkyns family, in hopes of recovering some part of the loss, put up a man of straw, one Peter Beaconawes, who asserted that there had been, in the secret place, a bag containing £751 16s. 7d. in silver, which had been put there with the knowledge of Richard Parkins, brother to Thomas, who *let yt downe into the hole by a cord, pulling the boarde over the place againe as he found yt, & that Sʳ Francis Knollys, or some one of his company, had taken it, having no right thereto.*

In consequence Peter Beaconsawe brought an action of trespass against Sir Francis Knollys, and his servant Cray, in the Court of Common Pleas, which was *tryed by a Jury of twelve substanciall Freeholders of the County of South-hampton, who after full evidence gave a verdicte for Beaconsawe, & damages were assessed to £900 & costs £20.* But Sir Francis Knollys, meanwhile, had exhibited a bill of complaint against Beaconsawe in the Court of Exchequer. The witnesses called on Sir Francis Knollys' side are the narrators of the story related above. They were the two bearers of the letters from the Lord Chamberlain to Sir Francis, named Blande and Duffield, who were both present during the search of the house, John Vachell of Burghfield, and some others. Sir Francis Knollys and his servant Isaac Cray were also examined. The gist of their evidence went to prove that Sir Francis Knollys did not take the money; that Peter Beaconsawe was believed not to have been possessed of such a sum; that if the money had been put in the secret place, it was taken away before the arrival of the search party, probably by Richard Perkins; that Sir Francis had not known to whose house he was going, and therefore could have had no intention of finding Beaconsawe's money; and that the keeper of the house, with his wife and others, were with him in the house all the time, that they saw into the secret place, but had discovered nothing there except the chests of gold and plate which Sir Francis took safely to Aldermaston. Thereupon the Court of Exchequer issued an injunction to stay Beaconsawe's proceedings, and because he continued them in spite of it he was imprisoned for contempt of Court. Finally, on January 31, 1609, it was declared by the Right Honourable the Lord Chancellor, and the Barons of the Court of Exchequer, *that forasmuch as yt appeareth that if the defendant (Beaconsawe) had at any tyme the sum of money claimed in the house at Ufton, which was doubtful, it had been taken away by others before the complayncntes (Sr Francis Knollys & his servants) came there. Or that if it should have been taken by any that followed Sr Francis Knollys, without his knowledge, he was not responsible*, and that *this Court thinketh yt not reasonable nor agreeable to justice, nor to stand with the honor of the state & government, that Sr Francis Knollys being ymployed in the service by publique authority & warrant & doing his duty therin should be left subject to answer such warrant, & that therefore the defendant (Beaconsawe) shall not proceed in any manner of accion against the complayncntes touching the said summe of money & that they shall be discharged, freed, & acquitted forever.*

The two priests had escaped, apparently, but the loss of the money was not in any way made good. Thomas Perkins and his brother Richard here mentioned were cousins of Francis, being the sons of his father's younger brother, Francis Parkyns of Padworth (see pedigree in Appendix). Sir Francis Knollys was then, as is incidentally stated, living in Reading. He had received from Queen Elizabeth a grant of what remained of the old abbey buildings, and according to Coates he lived in the gatehouse, where divers old pictures of his family formerly hung in the upper room. He was a great favourite of the Queen's, being at one time a rival in her favour with Sir John Norreys. He was Treasurer of the Royal Household, Privy Councillor, and a Knight of the Garter. He and his family were buried in a transept of the Church of St. Lawrence, Reading, which he had built *for the peculiar use of himself and posteritie, as well for their seates there, as for their buriall-place underneath.* This transept was afterwards pulled down, and the street pavement outside the church now covers the graves.

It seems needless to comment upon this story, so graphically told by the actors themselves ; a glance at the plan of the upper floor of Ufton Court (chapter viii.) will show

<small>CHAP. VI.
A.D. 1615.</small>

<small>HIDING PLACE.</small>

a hiding-place, corresponding very accurately to the description given. Marked *a* in the plan is a hole in the floor, with an old oak board placed over it: that, and the adjoining room into which the chests were carried, and the little closet opening out of the room where the money was counted out on a table, are all still easily to be recognised. The place is unchanged, and bears its testimony to the accuracy of the above narrative.

<small>Ashmole, Antiq. of Berks, vol. III., p. 406.</small>

<small>I P.M., 13 James I., No. 181.</small>

In spite of the trouble which his adherence to the faith of his ancestors brought upon him, and the suspicion he incurred, Francis Perkins' name is nevertheless to be found on the list of the gentry in the Commission of the Peace of the year 1601. He died in 1615. In the Chancery Inquisition, taken afterwards, it is stated that he had held the estate of Ufton Robert of Peter Vanlore, Esq., as of his manor of Tidmarsh, in free socage and an annual rent of one pound of cummin, also sundry lands and tenements in Ufton Nervet and Sulhamstead, of Francis Lord Norris (see p. 20), and the manor of Ufton Pole of the heirs of Lady Marvyn. His tomb is in

Ufton parish church, and on it he is represented in ruff and trunk hose, breastplate, and tassets covering the thighs, with his wife lying by his side. Effigies of his two sons kneel below, the elder one in armour like his father, and on either side of them are two shields, bearing respectively the Parkyns and Plowden arms.

<small>F. Ashmole's MS. notes, Bodl. Lib.</small>

Above the monument were originally placed the Perkins shield and crest, but these have disappeared since the destruction of the old church. A brass plate is fixed on the wall at the back of the arch, bearing an inscription:

Of the Recusants.

which has been thus translated into English verse by the Rev. Canon Cornish:

> Trace his descent in his ancestral line,
>   The twelveth in order he, who sleeps beneath
> Earth hath its meed for merit, it was thine :
>   And Heaven hath greater, through its portal—death.
> He sleeps beneath the tomb which Anna made.
>   She by his side enjoys unbroken rest.
> 'Twas meet that they together should be laid
>   In that sweet union which their love had blest.

CHAP. VI.
A.D. 1615.
MONUMENT OF FRANCIS AND ANNA PERKINS.

The Latin inscription (see Appendix) was copied by Ashmole, and is published in his "Antiquities of Berks." Since his time another line was added, giving the dates of the deaths :

> Obit ille 1615 et illa 1635.

The bare statement here made, without explanation, that this Francis was twelfth in order of descent from his ancestors, is perplexing, as it does not correspond with the pedigree given in the Visitation of Arms, and signed on behalf of his son in 1623 (see Appendix). According to this account, he was the ninth in descent from the founder of the family, nor does it tally with the genealogical arrangement of the coats of arms on the monument of Richard Parkyns (see p. 57).

His wife Anna had the use of Ufton Court for her lifetime. She survived him twenty years. In her will she declares *I hold the Catholique, anntient, & Apostolique Roman faith, & I bequeath my body to the earth, to be buried without Pompe or vanity in the Parish Church of Ufton, neare unto my loving husband, where I have erected a Tombe.* She left all the goods, Chattells, Plate, stocke of Cattell or corne growing or in the barnes, &c., &c., to her second son Edmund Perkins and her nephew Francis Plowden the younger of Shiplake, as her executors, and appointed her brother Francis Plowden and her cousin John Perkins of Beenham overseers of her will. A memorandum is added to it, that *the said Anne Perkins did put the said Francis Plowden & Edmond*

Somerset House Pic. 73

Perkins into possession of the premisses by delivery of one silver spoone in presence of the said Francis Plowden.

The will was proved on June the 16th, 1636, by the oath of *Edward Perkins* her son and one of the executors named in it.

A mistake is made here, and also in some other documents, in giving the name as Edward instead of Edmund. Edmund Perkins, the second son of Francis and Anne, is represented on his father's monument in the dress of a civilian, while his elder brother is clad in armour. At the time of his father's death, 1615, he was probably about twenty-five, but he had already been married twice and was for the second time a widower. His first wife was Jane, one of the daughters of Francis Winchcomb of Bucklebury, of the family of *Jack of Newbury*. It was this lady in whose name the manor of Salham, *alias* Nunhide, had been purchased, in 1607, from William Foster of Aldermaston, with the various lands pertaining to it in the neighbouring parishes, including the plot of ground in Ufton, on which the disused parish church of Upton Nervet was then still standing. On her marriage with Edmund Perkins she received from her father as her portion £1,100, which was invested in the purchase of a manor and some lands in the parish of Hampreston in Dorsetshire, and was settled on Edmund Perkins and his children by Jane Winchcomb, and failing these on Francis Perkins his father. She died very soon afterwards, leaving one daughter; and Edmund married again, Elizabeth daughter of Sir Henry James, Knight, of London. She also was an heiress, having inherited from her grandfather, Martin James, a moiety of the estate of Serry's, or Seare's, Court, in the parish of Ivechurch in Kent.

She died, and was buried at Ufton on September the 13th, 1615. She left no children. In 1660 Edmund is mentioned in a settlement made by his brother Francis, as still living, and is described as of Brooke, in the parish of Bramshaw in Hampshire. It seems probable that he had in the interval married again, possibly the —— Kenyon, mentioned in the Visitation pedigree, and that he was the father of Edmund Perkins of Winckton (see Appendix).

The eldest son of Francis Perkins and Anna Plowden, also named Francis, was thirty years of age when he succeeded his father in 1615. He also was subjected to the many fines and penalties imposed on recusants. By an Act, dated 3rd year of James I., two-thirds of their property was sequestrated, and the rents so forfeited were leased out by the Crown at a low rate, generally to the informer, as a reward for his evidence. But sometimes an arrangement was found possible, by which the burden of this penalty was considerably lightened. A friend of a convicted recusant would apply for the lease of the sequestrated lands, and pay the rents in to their owner; and though the rent to the Crown had still to be deducted, yet as it did not amount to the full value of the land the recusant suffered less heavily.

Such an arrangement had been made by Francis Perkins in 1620, with Mr. Thomas Purcell of Okefield, who it may be remembered had been one of the guests in Mr. Perkins' house in 1587; but an informer was at hand to detect and put a stop to the subterfuge. By an appeal to the Court of Exchequer, it was shown *that whereas one Frauncis Parkins, late of Ufton Co. Berks, deceased, was in his lyfe tyme a Popishe Recusant, and whereas it was found by an Inquisicion taken at the Cittye of newe Salisburye that the said Frauncis Parkins was seysed (amongst other things) of one Capital Messuage in Ufton, & divers lands, &c., &c.; & whereas the kinge's Matie by his letters Pattente did grant unto one Thomas Pursell gent., two thirds of the said leases to have & to holde for twentye & one yeares. About sixe monethes paste the said Fraunces departed this life, & Francis Parkins, Esqr., beinge his eldeste sonne & next heyre is a Popisite Recusante, & is convicted for same Recusancy. Nowe so it is, that the said Thomas Pursell did suffer Frauncis Parkins deceased during his life time, & doth now suffer his sonne to receyve the Rentes, Issues & benefitt of the said premisses contrarye to the lawes of this Realme. May it therefore please your Lordshippes to awarde the Kinge's writte of subpena to be directed unto the said Thomas Pursell, commanding him to show cause if he can, why the same two partes should not be seysed unto his Maties handes.*

And the informer no doubt gained for himself the benefit of his information.

CHAP. VI.
A.D. 1637.
PETITION OF FR. PERKINS OF UFTON.
Recusant Rolls.

1625 saw Charles I. upon the throne, but the fines and sequestrations still continued. The Perkins of Ufton still refused to go to their parish church, for which special act of contumacy, besides their other burdens, a fine was levied on each separate member of £20 a month.

The law, also, which forbade recusants from leaving their homes without a special license was strictly enforced, as we conclude from a petition from this Francis Perkins. *To the Right Honble the Lords & others of His Maties Most Excll^t Privy Council,* dated 1637. It is as follows:

Domestic State Papers, R.O.

The Humble Petition of ffrancis Perkins of Ufton, in the County of Berks, Esqre, a recusant convict.

Sheweth—That whereas yor pet^r by means of his Recusancy is by the Statute confined not to passe without Lycense above 5 miles from the place of his dwelling or abode wherunto yor pet^r hath & doth in all humbleness submit & conform himself. Albeit by his Maties Ltres Patent under the Greate Seale of England granted about 10 or 11 y^{rs} since to his Matie 2 parts of yor pet^rs lands for his recusancie (wherupon his Matie hath ever since been duly answered to £50 p^r ann.); there is some clause or clauses that may seem to imply such a lycens, yet yor pet^r, not relying therupon & having urgent occasion to travell out of his said confynement, as well into the County of Wilts to receive his rents & otherwise to manage & dispose of some estate he hath there: as also to the Cities of London & Westminster, & other ways, about some suits & other necessary affairs, wherin his own personall agency be of great consequence unto him. Yo^r pet^r therefore humbly besecheth yor Lordshipps to grannt him yor honorable lycense to travell out of his said confynement for the space of six months next coming, in such manner as to yor Lo^{rs} wisedom shall seeme fitt & agreeable to the said Statute.

Patent Roll 3, ch. 1.

The letters patent he refers to had been issued in 1628, granting to William Eyston of Catmore, for the rent of £50, the two parts of the property of Francis Perkins of Ufton, which were sequestrated to the Crown *by reason of his recusancie*, and, that there should be no mistake as to the proportion forfeited, it is distinctly stated that the whole yearly rental of the manor of Ufton Robert was £24, and that the two parts amounted to £16. The proportion of the rents of Ufton Pole, Padworth, and the rest of the property are given at the same rate. This was another instance of a friendly arrangement. William Eyston was the brother-in-law of the young squire of Ufton, who had married his sister Margaret; and the Eyston family were faithful adherents of the Roman Church. How it happened that this family compact was allowed to hold good, as it did for many years, it is hard to say; perhaps the political disturbances, which were now looming in the distance, and which resulted in the death of the King and the establishment of the Commonwealth, distracted the attention of the Government.

During the course of the civil war Ufton was so fortunate as to be left in comparative quiet. The rival armies, as is well known, manœuvred backwards and forwards for some time along the valley of the Kennet, between Reading and Newbury, but the fighting came no nearer Ufton Court than Burghfield Bridge on one side and Padworth on the other. In this latter place, in the pretty shaded lane which leads along the brow of the hill towards Aldermaston, at about three-quarters of a mile from Ufton, according to Mr. Money's account in his interesting work on the battles of Newbury, there took place a sanguinary skirmish between some Roundhead troops under Lord Essex, who were making their way to Reading after the first battle of Newbury, and Prince Rupert's cavalry who there overtook them. The Parliamentarians succeeded eventually in beating off the attack and passed on, down the hill and across a ford of the river Kennet by Padworth, and so on to Theale, without coming by Ufton Court. Great must have been the anxiety and the subsequent relief felt there during that day.

But now the unfortunate lords of Ufton, after having so long suffered as traitors at the hands of the King, were severely taxed with the rest of their Royalist neighbours as malignants for their loyalty. The old fines were also continued, and at

CHAP. vi.
———
A.D. 1651.
———
PETITION
CONCERNING
L^Y MARVYN'S
CHARITY.

Roy. Comp.
Papers, 1st
series.

one time the parish had thereby nearly lost the benefaction which had till then continuously been administered according to Lady Marvyn's bequest. Whereupon the overseers of the parishes of Ufton and Padworth made their humble petition to the Parliamentary Commissioners, showing:

That whereas the estate of one Francis Perkins, a papist, is by good assurance in the lawe charged with the yearely payment of certen charitable gifts to the poore of the severall parishes aforesaid, which hath been duly paid yearely, untill such time as two parts of the said estate was disposed of by the commissioners for sequestration, which commissioners upon the setting of the two parts to one Ralp Harmswood, about six months since, have reserved a full yearely rent without making any allowance for the payment of the said charitable gifts. May it therefore please this Honble Committee to examine the matter, dated 15th May, 1651.

(Signed)   Richard Crawford,   William Mills,
           Tho. Aldridge,   Richard Webb.

Roy. Comp.
Papers, 2nd
series.

Unlike many petitions, this one had an effect. The commissioners ordered *that the said Charitable Gifts may be allowed & paid as formerly, that those poor families which, for many years past, have been therewith fedd & clothed, & to whom the same was charitably intended, may not starve & perish for want thereof.*

In 1642 Margaret, the wife of Francis Perkins, died before her husband. A most affectionate memorial was inscribed to her memory by him. It is on a small brass plate on the wall of the parish church, and has been translated as follows. (For original, see Appendix.)

Francis Perkins addresses his wife Margaret: Rest in Peace, my best beloved wife, & wait my coming for a while. I swear to you that if that coming be delayed, it is in obedience to the Divine command, & not from love of life. She died on the 1st March, 1641. Aged 55.

Katherine, the sister of this Francis Perkins of Ufton, and daughter of Francis and Anna (Plowden) had married

Of the Recusants.

a Mr. George Tattersall; and it was perhaps as her dower, that the manor of West Court Finchampstead, which had belonged to the Parkyns' family since about 1478, passed about this time into the possession of her husband's family. She is the ancestress of the present ducal family of Norfolk, as here shown:

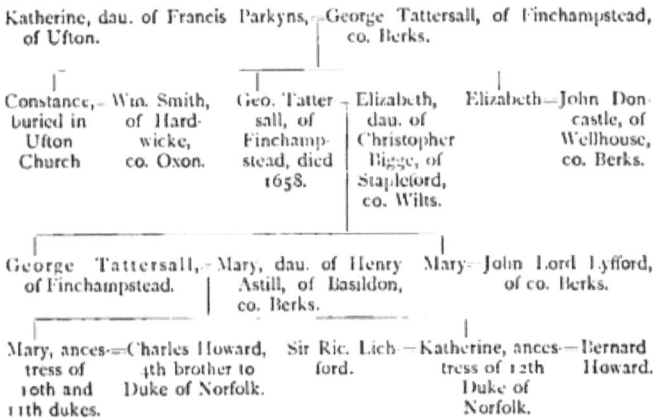

After the death of his wife, Francis Perkins executed a deed by which, *in consideration of the love & affection which he beareth unto Francis Perkins his sonne & heire apparent & other children of him the said Francis Perkins, & for setting of the manor lands & in the blood & name of him so long as it shall please Almighty God to continue the same,* he granted to Sir Richard Weston, Co. Surrey, & John Eyston of Lambourne, as trustees, all his manors & lands of Ufton Robert, Ufton Nervet, Ufton Pole & Padworth, & all his other estates, to the use of the said Francis Perkins his son & his heirs male; failing them, to the use of John Perkins his second son & his heirs male; then to his other sons lawfully to be begotten. Failing them, then to the use of Edmund Perkins his brother & his heirs male lawfully to be begotten, & in default of such, then to the use of John Perkins of Beenham & his heirs male.

CHAP. vi.
A.D. 1660.

And finally to the use of his own daughters & their heirs forever, provided they should not marry without his consent.

DEATH OF ELDEST SON.

One year before his own death, his eldest son died, leaving a widow and child, another Francis; and in consequence, the grandfather made a fresh deed, dated 1660, by which the property was entailed first on his grandson and his heirs male, and then on his brother, *Edmond Perkins of Brook, in the parish of Bramshaw, Co. Hants, & after his decease, then to the use of the sonnes of the said Edmond Perkins lawfully to be begotten.* In this deed there is no mention of his second son John (who may have died in the interval), nor of John Perkins of Beenham. The latter had meanwhile *conformed*, as it was said, to the Established Church, and taken office as churchwarden of his parish, which action on his part may account for his being cut out of all chance of inheriting the family property.

Five of the daughters of Francis Perkins are named in the Visitation pedigree as having married into the Hyde, Codrington, Mainwaring, Blunt and St. George families (see Appendix).

In the year 1661, the father himself followed his wife and son to the grave, in the seventy-ninth year of his age. In his will he made bequests to his unmarried daughters, and left all the rest of his property in trust for Francis Perkins, his grandson, according to the settlement already made. On his tombstone, a marble slab now placed under the altar, is an inscription, which is thus freely translated by Canon Cornish:

For original see Appendix.

*Here I, Francis Perkins am resting, son & heir
of Francis & Anna Perkins, who rest above me.
I married Margaret, daughter of John Eyston, of Catmore,
Esquire. She bore me six sons & ten daughters,
& under this marble we are both buried.
We lived in harmony, we sleep below,
In the same tomb our bodies are at rest.
God grant that we the same repose may know,
And with same salvation may be blest.*

Of the Recusants. 113

The epitaph to his eldest son, who had preceded him, is translated as follows:

FRANCIS, son of Francis & Margaret Perkins, who died in his father's lifetime, & was buried here in the year of our Lord 1660. His true age was 38.

Shield with Plowden Arms, 1615.

DESCENT OF THE FAMILY OF PERKINS OF UFTON FROM 1654 TO 1769.

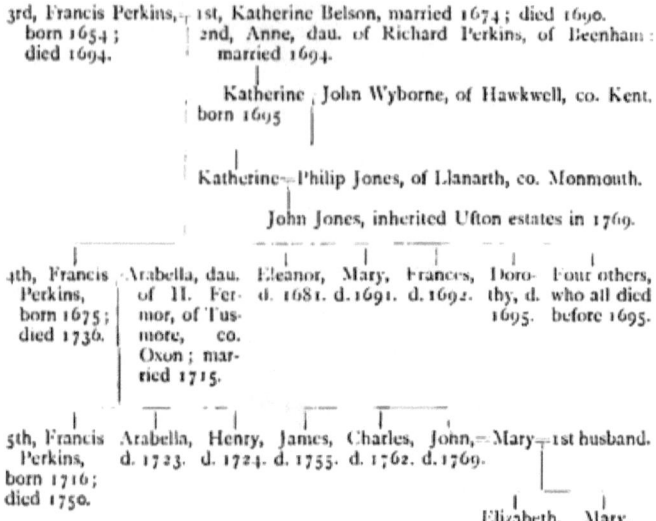

3rd, Francis Perkins, born 1654; died 1694.
— 1st, Katherine Belson, married 1674; died 1690.
— 2nd, Anne, dau. of Richard Perkins, of Beenham; married 1694.

Katherine, born 1695 — John Wyborne, of Hawkwell, co. Kent.

Katherine — Philip Jones, of Llanarth, co. Monmouth.

John Jones, inherited Ufton estates in 1769.

4th, Francis Perkins, born 1675; died 1736. — Arabella, dau. of H. Fermor, of Tusmore, co. Oxon; married 1715.

Eleanor, d. 1681. | Mary, d. 1691. | Frances, d. 1692. | Dorothy, d. 1695. | Four others, who all died before 1695.

5th, Francis Perkins, born 1716; died 1750. | Arabella, d. 1723. | Henry, d. 1724. | James, d. 1755. | Charles, d. 1762. | John, d. 1769. — Mary — 1st husband.

Elizabeth. Mary.

Distant View of Ufton Court.

Chapter vij.

Of Later Times.

HE young Francis Perkins, at the time of his grandfather's death, was only seven years old. His mother was Frances, the daughter of Henry Winchcomb, of Bucklebury, a descendant of the well-known Jack of Newbury, who is described by Fuller as *the most considerable clothier, without fancy or fiction, England ever beheld.* He kept a hundred looms at work in his own house, and in the expedition against James IV. of Scotland, he equipped a contingent of a hundred men for the service of Henry VIII., *as well armed & better clothed than any.* Tradition relates that he feasted Henry VIII. and Queen Catherine of Aragon at his own house at Newbury. This house is still standing, though cut up into different tenements.

After the early death of her first husband Frances married again, a Mr. James Hyde. She lived at Ufton Court with her son, and died in 1686. She is buried in Ufton Church, and on her tombstone is an inscription, translated as follows:

Sacred to the memory of Frances, daughter of Henry Winchcomb, of Bucklebury, Esqr., relict of Francis Perkins, who rests beneath, to whom she bore one son. After this she

> married James Hyde, Gentleman, whom she left on the 21st of March, 1686, to rest in the tomb of her first husband. Aged 63.
>
> *Frances again is with me as of yore,*
> *Ashes to ashes love unites once more.*

CHAP. vii.
A.D. 1674.

KATHERINE BELSON (1st WIFE).

Marriage Settlement.

Francis her son married, in 1674, when he was only twenty, Katherine, the daughter of Augustine Belson, of Dorking, in the county of Surrey. He settled upon her all his *manors & lands in Ufton Robert, Ufton Nervet, Ufton Poole & Padworth; & in Borwardescote or Buscot Snowswick, Pinockswick, Lougham & Littleham; also the Manor House of Ufton & the demesne lands late in the occupation of Mr. James Hyde & all those parts of the Park called Settmore mead & Calves mead, which lie next Ufton farm, & are divided from the other parts of Ufton by the running ditch or gutter called Shooters brook.*

From this recapitulation of the property it appears that, in spite of fines and sequestrations, it had still been retained pretty nearly entire.

Katherine Belson died in 1690. Her husband writes on her tombstone:

> *I, Francis Perkins, in my sorrow have placed this in memory of Catherine, who is at rest beneath this marble, daughter of Augustine Belson, Esq., & my deeply loved wife, who, united to me by the bond of love & religion, completed eighteen years of married life, & was the mother of nine children. Happy in her faith in Christ, still happier in hope, she bore this life as she had strength to bear it, in hope of a better, to which hope, after a long and severe sickness, she attained, to the sorrow of earth, to the joy of heaven on the 1st of June,* A.D. *1690, aged 37. Pray for her.*

His eldest daughter died in the following year; on the same stone he records:

> *My first born & most beloved Maria Perkins was taken from her father to shine in glory with her mother, heiress of her virtues, sharer of her grace.*
>
> *Mother & child repose beneath this stone.*
> *Two were their bodies, but their hearts were one.*

*In her fair maidenhood she graced the Heavens
on the 12th of March, A.D. 1691.*

Another daughter, Eleanor, had died in 1681; and within two years after the mother's death, two more, Frances and Dorothy were laid beside her in the grave.

Four years after the death of his first wife, Francis Perkins married again a distant cousin of his own, Anne Perkins, the daughter, and eventually one of the coheirs of Richard Perkins of Beenham (see Appendix). On her, her husband settled Old Farm in Padworth and Fieldhouse Farm on the north side of the river Kennet. He began, about the same time, considerable alterations and improvements to his house of Great Bathampton at Steeple Longford in Wiltshire. Ufton Court was let for seven years to a Mr. William Wareham, or, as it is said in the agreement, *part of Ufton Court*, the probable explanation being that then, as afterwards, the south wing of the house was given up for the chapel and the use of a resident priest. The days had gone by when much notice was taken of priests or Mass-saying; the Government was satisfied with the payment of the heavy fines which were still continued, and the double land-tax levied on all Roman Catholic estates. Recusants had ceased to be an element of danger to the State, and were now left in comparative peace.

This Francis died only a year after his second marriage. The epitaph on his tombstone is as follows (translated):

*Beneath this marble slab there rest in peace
the ashes of Francis Perkins, Esqr,
Lord of this manor, who when five years had not yet passed,
came to the tomb of his first wife, Catherine,
who rests beneath. One only son survived him,
heir of his virtues as well as his estate.
He was a man of ripe understanding, fertile mother-wit
richly adorned with every grace of mind and body.
He left a widow Anna, daughter of Richard Perkins, Esqr,
of Beenham, and one posthumous daughter,
of very great beauty and promise survived.
He was just, pious, and honourable*

CHAP. VII.

A.D. 1694.

ANNE PERKINS (2nd WIFE).

CHAP. VII.
———
A.D. 1694.

FRANCIS
PERKINS
(4th).

> His every debt he faithfully rendered,
> To God, Cæsar, and his neighbour, and his soul to heaven
> the 21st day of February in the year 1694.
> Pray for him.

It is not a little remarkable that out of his large family one only son should have survived him, and that from the failure of heirs male altogether in the next generation the estates should have eventually passed to the grandson of his youngest and posthumous daughter.

The young heir could not have been more than twenty when he came into the family estates; he found them in the charge of a bailiff, one John Berrington, who had been in his father's service for some time, and who continued in that of the son till his own death in 1743. A good many accounts connected with various matters which are still preserved are signed by him. There is the record of the expenses of the workmen employed about the buildings at Great Bathampton, and also sundry small items which are interesting as showing the current prices of the day. Here are some examples:

	£	s.	d.
ffor a bottle of white wine	00	01	10
ffor a bottle of sack	00	02	00
ffor a pint of Muskin dine (Muscadine wine)	00	01	00
ffor a pound of lofe shuger (loaf sugar)	00	01	00
ffor a ¼ of a pound of tee sent into Essex	00	04	00
ffor 5 lottery tickets	00	05	00

Among his private accounts he pays for his daughter's board while she was away from home:

	£	s.	d.
ffor one yeares bord doe at Chrismass	10	00	00
ffor making the boddey of heir old cote into a pare of stayes & for making heir a gound	00	03	00
ffor a yard of mussullin	00	05	00
Paid for heir pole	00	04	04

That last mysterious subject of expense is not further explained. But the most important deeds with which he had to do in his capacity of bailiff or agent are those connected with the purchase of the Manor of Ufton Nervet and other lands, at that time in the possession of Montague Earl of Abingdon.

It will be remembered that the present parish of Ufton had been, from the earliest times of which we have any record, held as two separate estates or manors (see p. 5), of which the one named after Richard Nervut, in the thirteenth century had belonged to the Abbey of Reading, and at the dissolution of the monastery had been granted to Sir John Williams, and from him it had passed to his descendants, the Norreys family, and through them to Lord Abingdon (see p. 20).

In 1709 the manor and its appurtenances was purchased on behalf of Francis Perkins of Ufton Robert by Lord Stawell, the then owner of Aldermaston and Leonard Belson, as his trustees.

And at the same time a plot of land, comprising the meadows of Rockmore and Crondalles, and Crondalles Grove, in all about thirty-five acres, which had likewise been part of the confiscated abbey property bestowed upon Sir John Williams, was also purchased for Francis Perkins by his bailiff John Berrington.

This small property, last mentioned, was at the time in the possession of James Bertie, also a descendant of Sir John Williams. Further particulars relating to it have been given at page 28.

Now therefore, at last, the whole of the land comprised within the two united parishes of Ufton Robert and Ufton Nervet was, with the exception of some very small holdings, consolidated into one estate, and has ever since so remained.

Francis Perkins, who was so fortunate as to be able thus to extend the family property, was also fortunate in his marriage. In 1715 he won the hand of the reigning belle of London, Mistress Arabella Fermor.

This lady was the daughter of Henry Fermor of Tusmore, in Oxfordshire. The fame of her beauty and her charms, as celebrated both by poets and painters, has come down to posterity. There are three portraits of her in existence,

CHAP. VII.
A.D. 1715.

ARABELLA
FERMOR.

which by the kind permission of their owners are here reproduced. The earliest represents her as a very young girl, and is in the possession of Mr. W. W. Cowslade of Earley, near Reading. Miss Mitford thus describes it.

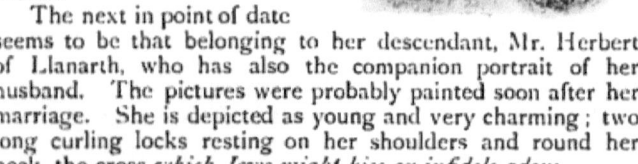

Mrs. Lenoir's nieces possess a portrait of the lovely Arabella Fermor, when she was twelve or thirteen years of age . . . a high broad forehead, dark eyes richly fringed and deeply set, a straight nose, pouting lips, and a short chin finely moulded. The dress is dark and graceful, with a little white turned back about the neck and loose sleeves.

The next in point of date seems to be that belonging to her descendant, Mr. Herbert of Llanarth, who has also the companion portrait of her husband. The pictures were probably painted soon after her marriage. She is depicted as young and very charming; two long curling locks resting on her shoulders and round her neck, the cross *which Jews might kiss or infidels adore.*

The portrait of Mr. Perkins, her husband, represents a handsome man of about five-and-twenty, though it detracts considerably from his good looks that he is wearing the hideous and cumbersome wig of the period. Their names are, in the originals, printed on the background of each painting; probably, however, these were added at a later period. The two pictures hung once in Ufton Court, till they were taken away and carried to Llanarth, where they are now preserved, after the death of the last Mr. Perkins of Ufton and the dispersion of the family possessions. It is to be lamented that these are the only two family portraits which have been traced as coming from the Court, though doubtless many others existed, which are now perhaps scattered among

different collections of such works of art, or with new names adopted into other families.

The third portrait belongs to Mrs. Welby-Parry, having

CHAP. VII.
A.D. 1715.
ARABELLA FERMOR.

formed part of the collection of the late Mr. Hartley of Bucklebury. It is said to be by Sir Godfrey Kneller, and its artistic merit quite bears out the supposition. It is of a woman in the prime of her beauty and grace; the pose is very elegant, and the colouring charming; in it she still wears the fashionable love-lock of the day. All three have much individuality and many points of resemblance. Hair of a warm golden shade, a slender neck and sloping shoulders, almond-shaped eyes with well-formed level eyebrows, are characteristics of them all. In fact, what is so often not the case, the representations of beauty which artists have handed down to us fully bear out in this case the praises of contemporary

16--2

CHAP. vii.
A.D. 1715.
THE RAPE OF THE LOCK.

writers. Among these, the now not much read poet Parnell sings of the dismay of the "jeunesse dorée" of the time when this fascinating lady left London for the country in the summer:

> *From town fair Arabella flies:*
> *The beaux, unpowdered, grieve;*
> *The rivers play before her eyes,*
> *The breezes softly breathing rise,*
> *The spring begins to live.*
>
> * * * *
>
> *Her lovers swore they must expire,*
> *Yet quickly find their ease.*
> *For as she goes, their flames retire:*
> *Love thrives before a nearer fire;*
> *Esteem, by distant rays.*
>
> *Yet soon the Fair one will return*
> *When summer quits the plain:*
> *Ye rivers, pour the weeping urn,*
> *Ye breezes, sadly sighing, mourn,*
> *Ye lovers burn again;*

and so on through several stanzas.

But in spite of the admiration of the world of fashion, which she no doubt enjoyed in her lifetime, and in spite even of Parnell's verses, it is possible that the thought of her beauty would by this time have passed away into the land where all things are forgotten, had it not been that she was the inspiring theme of perhaps the most successful of all Pope's poetical works, *The Rape of the Lock*, in which the absurdities of the mock-heroic and the graceful imagery of poetic fancy are blended with the unrivalled skill of genius. The incident which suggested its composition was an indiscretion of which Lord Petre, a young man of twenty, had been guilty, when on a certain occasion he, unbeknown to the fair lady, cut off and stole a lock of her hair. She was very angry, and a serious quarrel took place between the two families. Whereupon Pope's friend, John Caryll of Lady Holt, in Sussex, proposed to him that he should write something slight and amusing on the subject, in hopes that good-natured raillery might appease the ill-feeling that had been excited. The poem was in every way suited for its purpose; unfortunately, however, Pope, as it appears, was not personally acquainted with Mistress Arabella; he published it without asking her leave, and, moreover, appended to it a motto, which was taken by her friends to imply that she had asked him to compose the poem. Instead of mending matters, therefore, he only by his want of tact drew another quarrel upon himself. *I hear*, he writes to Caryll, some little time after the publication, *the celebrated lady herself is offended, &, which is stranger, not at herself, but me. Is not this enough to make a writer never be tender of another's character or fame?* In consequence, he brought out another edition, suppressed the objectionable motto, and prefixed a propitiatory letter of dedication to Arabella. In this he assures her that the incidents of the poem are all *as fabulous as the vision at the beginning, except the loss of your hair, which I always mention with reverence; . . . the character of Belinda as it is now managed resembles you in nothing but beauty,* he goes on. *It will be vain to deny that I have some regard for this piece since I dedicate it to you. . . . If it had as many graces as there are in your Person or in your Mind; yet I could never hope it should pass through the world half so uncensured as you have done. But let its fortune be what it may, mine is happy enough to have given me this occasion of assuring you that I am, &. &.*

The lady seems to have been pacified, and perhaps even accorded Pope her friendship, for on the occasion of her marriage he wrote her an almost affectionate letter. He says, *It may be expected, perhaps, that one who has the title of poet should say something more polite on this occasion, but I am, really, more a well-wisher to your felicity than a celebrator of your beauty. Besides, you are now a married woman, & in a way to be a great many better things than a fine lady, such as an excellent wife, a faithful friend, a tender parent, & at last, as the consequence of them all, a saint in heaven.*

Pope was at one time a great deal at Mapledurham, which is not more than seven or eight miles from Ufton Court. It is possible, therefore, that he may have come to visit the lady he so much admired, in her married home; there is, however, no actual record of his having done so.

Comparing Pope's account of Arabella's beauty with the existing portraits, it is strange that, as she is represented in all three pictures with fair auburn hair, he should have expressly described it as black.

> *These two in sable ringlets taught to break*
> *Once gave new beauties to the snowy neck;*
> *The sister lock now sits uncouth, alone,*
> *And in its fellow's fate foresees its own.*

That he should have made such a mistake seems to confirm Mr. Courthope's opinion, expressed in his recent edition of Pope's works, that the poet was not acquainted with the lady when he first sang the praises of her beauty.

At her marriage, in 1715, her husband settled on her the *messuage commonly called Ufton Court, now in his own occupation, & all that farm of Ufton known as Poole lands & church grounds. Also the farm called Ashpoles, then in the occupation of John Berrington, the bailiff* (there is a plot still so called not far from the church). *Also the farms called Snowsewick & Penniswick, & other lands in Buscot, & the messuage & farm called Great Bathampton, in the parish of Steeple Langford, co. Wilts. Also Perkins' farm in Hanging Langford — in all of the value of £600 yearly.*

There is a tradition that it was for Arabella Fermor that Ufton Court was very much refashioned and enlarged. Certainly one half of the frontage (as shown in the illustration, chap. viii.) was, prior to further alterations made in 1838, of the style prevalent at the time of her marriage. Parts of the interior, also, were modernized; the hall and dining-room, while retaining their Elizabethan ceilings, were entirely re-panelled, and the style would fix this alteration also to early in the eighteenth century.

Arabella bore to her husband one daughter, named also Arabella, who died in childhood in the year 1723, and five sons.

Her second son, Henry, died in 1724, also young. Her

husband died in 1736, leaving his wife for her present support
£52 10s. His landed property he left to Sir Henry Englefield of White Knights, William Wollascott of Woolhampton,
John Hyde of Hyde End, and Mr. John Berrington the
bailiff, in trust for his eldest son, and to his younger sons
he left £100 apiece, *to place them forth apprentices to some
trade, profession, or employment.*

Arabella only survived her husband one year.

Another Francis was Squire of Ufton, but the race was
now coming to an end; he died at the age of thirty-four,
unmarried. The year before his death, 1749, Ufton Court
was let for a term of three years, at a rent of £89 4s. 6d., to
Lord Kingston, *with furniture now remaining except china,
linen & plate.* This Lord Kingston's name is to be found
about the same time in a list, still preserved, of the members
of a club which met every fortnight during the summer
months, between the years 1727 and 1815, at the Hind's
Head Inn at Aldermaston, for playing at bowls and dinner.
It included nearly all the gentry and a good many of the
clergy in the district. Francis Perkins, the son of Arabella,
belonged to it, as did also his younger brothers. It seems to
have been a most friendly and pleasant institution, and that
the Ufton family attended it is a proof that by this time
religious animosity no longer caused estrangement among
neighbours.

James and Charles, brothers of Francis, succeeded one
after the other to the property. It was in their lifetime that
the family fortune suffered serious diminution. James Perkins
sold the Buscot estate, and later on the Wiltshire property.
Great Balhampton, Langford, and Wylie were by Charles
Perkins' desire sold after his death to pay his debts. As no
explanation is given, one may suppose that either money had
been swallowed up in the speculations that were rife at the time,
or that these quiet country squires had too rashly followed
the extravagant fashions of the day of their richer neighbours.
Charles bequeathed his property to his youngest brother,
John, and to his children; failing them, it was to go to his
cousin Jones, daughter of his late Aunt Wyborne, and in
default to Sir Henry Englefield, of White Knights, and

CHAP. VII.
A.D. 1769.
JOHN PERKINS.

then in default to *my neighbour, Christopher Griffith, of Padworth.*

A reference to the table of descent, p. 114, will explain how it was that the daughter of his aunt Wyborne was next in descent to his own brothers and their children. John Perkins, the youngest brother, succeeded to the property in 1760. He married, but had no children, and was the last of his name of Ufton. He died in 1769. In his will he said: *Having survived Mary, my late wife, I make provision for her two daughters.* He described them as *Elizabeth, now residing in the house with me, & Mary, now being at a boarding school at Newbury,* and he left them, *when they shall respectively attain the age of* 21, £1,000 *apiece.* To his housekeeper, Mary Wilson, he left £20, and the rest of his personal estate he left to Henry Deane, of Reading, who had been his man of business, and to Francis Prior, of Padworth. He concluded: *I desire to be interred with as little ceremony & expense as decency will permit, regard being had to what I caused to be done on the decease of my late dear wife, but with* 18 *instead of* 12 *poor men & women to attend on that occasion.*

Henry Deane, the legatee, was the successor of John Berrington in the office of agent to the property. Francis Prior was a Roman Catholic gentleman, a neighbour and very intimate friend of the family. He held a lease for life from the squires of Ufton of the house belonging to the Perkins estate in Padworth called Pam Hall — *an exceeding good dwelling house, brick & tiled, with yard & garden,* as it is described in a note on the rents of the Ufton estate dated 1784. It is now pulled down. This Francis Prior died in 1788, and was buried at Ufton. There is a remarkable testimony to the esteem in which he was held in an entry in the Padworth Register, which is as follows:

*On Thursday, Dec*ʳ 4, 1788, *about* 4 *o'clock in the morning, Mr. F. Prior of Padworth departed this life. He was a man universally beloved by all that knew him; & this esteem was raised in them from the goodness of his heart & his steady adherence to his religious principles, which he shewed by an upright conduct of life & conversation. This small tribute to*

his memory is left upon record to show how much he was esteemed by the rector of this parish & his family.
Memento mori.

<small>CHAP. VII.
A.D. 1769.</small>

This from a near neighbour who must have known him well, and who could not have altogether agreed with the religious principles he alludes to, is a touching testimony to the real worth of the man.

<small>F. Prior of Padworth.</small>

His name is mentioned again in connection with that of his friend and landlord, John Perkins. It is at the death-bed of the latter, during a conversation related by Father Madew, the then resident priest at Ufton Court. He, Madew, was evidently aware that at his patron's death the house and property were to pass away to comparative strangers, and, anxious for the interests of the little congregation of the faithful to which he ministered, he writes down what occurred:

<small>Cath. Reg. of Ufton Court and Woolhampton, ed. by F. A. Crisp.</small>

I, Edward Madew, then being in the room with John Perkins, Esqr., asked ye said John Perkins if he had made a disposition of his church stuff; that, in case he had not, I hoped he would leave it for ye benefit of the congregation & in trust to M^r. Prior or to M^r. Edward Madew. To which he answered, I think it ye best way, I do give it for that purpose, & repeated over again, I think it ye best way. M^{rs}. Mary Wilson being then present, I told her to bear witness of what M^r. Perkins said. And thereupon follows the declaration of Mrs. Wilson, the housekeeper: *The contents above I declare to be literally true, as witness my name, Mary Wilson.*

It has been seen that the prohibitory laws against Roman Catholics had in practice been gradually relaxed. Yet as late as Pope's time they were still debarred from entering the army or navy; they could not be barristers, or magistrates, or sheriffs, or members of Parliament. *Truly*, as he exclaims, *ambition is a vice that is timely mortified in us poor Papists!*

<small>Pope's Letter, Courthope's edition.</small>

In his case the usual fines still levied from them had been excused, an exemption being made in his favour on account of his literary merits. In a letter in which he thanks the Earl of Halifax for this mark of favour, he says: *It is indeed a high strain of generosity in you to think of making me easy all my life, only because I have been so happy as to divert you* some hours; but if I may have leave to add, it is because you think me no enemy to my native country, there will appear a better reason.

In 1746, according to the Annual Register, orders had been given to the clerks of the peace throughout the country to send in a list of the Roman Catholics in their districts and the landed property they were possessed of, and a like direction was given in 1767 by the bishops to their clergy, in consequence of an order from the House of Lords, that it might be seen whether they increase in prosperity or no. *It was not till February, 1794*—only two years before the death of the last Mr. Perkins of Ufton Court—*that the rule by which Roman Catholics were charged a double rate to the land tax was cancelled, to the great satisfaction of the liberal minded of all persuasions.* No doubt the infliction of such penalties for the sake of religion seems nowadays most unreasonable bigotry and tyranny; yet it must be understood that such repressive legislation was far more political than religious. Men were still living in 1750 who could remember the sacrifice made by the nation in freeing themselves from the Romanising rule of James II.; and since then no long time had ever passed without some rising in Scotland or some conspiracy at home in favour of the return of the Stuarts. One William Perkins, a Roman Catholic gentleman of Warwickshire—not, however, immediately related to the Ufton family—suffered death in the reign of William and Mary for having secretly collected arms and followers to join and assist an invasion from abroad, and died declaring that he thought it no sin to fight for his lawful Sovereign. If we admire his heroism and loyalty, we must allow that no Government can continue to exist unless it takes means to suppress such as conspire for its overthrow. As late as 1745, when the Scotch army under the young Pretender pushed on as far south as Derby, inviting all who wished for the return of the old faith to join his standard, the Roman Catholics scattered about the country were naturally looked upon with suspicion, as a source of danger to the State.

After that, on three separate occasions, it is believed that Prince Charles Edward paid visits to England, and went among his friends and adherents with a view of discovering whether a rising could be arranged with any chance of success. On the first occasion (1750) he spent a week in London, and it was then that, according to his own journal, he was formally received into the English Reformed Church, in hopes of thereby propitiating the nation at large. The second occasion was in 1752, when an attempt was actually planned to place him on the throne. Alexander Murray, a brother of Lord Elibank, was to march on St. James's Palace, and Charles was to proclaim himself. On his third visit during the following year (1754) he travelled about the country, and was at Nottingham when word was brought him that there was danger of his being discovered, and he accordingly returned to the Continent. It must have been then, if tradition says truly, that he visited Ufton Court. According to a letter, already referred to, written by Mr. Congreve, of Aldermaston, in 1838, a Mr. Byles, a very old apothecary who had died at Aldermaston thirty-three years before, told him (Mr. Congreve) that the Pretender Prince Charles Edward had once been at Ufton Court, not, as he explained, in '45, but a few years afterwards. This fact was also affirmed by the late Sir Paul Hunter, of Mortimer, who had heard it from his grandfather. I give the story for what it is worth, with the authorities from which I have obtained it. There is nothing improbable in it, though no recollection of the incident has survived in the neighbourhood. The Prince while travelling about the country would naturally stay at the houses of such Roman Catholic gentlemen as he thought might be favourable to his cause, and that Ufton Court contained hiding places and secret ways of escape in case of surprise might also be in its favour as a temporary halting-place.

It is said on the authority of Hume the historian that the Prince was once more in England on the occasion of George III.'s coronation; but long before that time the cause of the Stuarts had been felt to be hopeless, and Englishmen at last settled down as one nation under one Government, and persecution and repressive legislation gradually ceased.

Mention has been made of a resident priest at Ufton. The first who is known of in that capacity is a Father Price, who was at Ufton about the year 1758. Probably before that time Roman Catholics only enjoyed the services of travelling priests, or missionaries, as they called themselves, who never stayed long in any one place, but passed from house to house.

Father Madew, the next priest whose name has been found, says of himself that he *came to Ufton Court*, though not apparently for the first time, *September y^e* 18, 1761, and that he *spent on ye road & ye carriage of my goods* £1 7s. 6d.

He was in the habit of keeping notes, which were at the same time a diary, account book, and church register, of which some loose leaves are preserved at Woolhampton College. Dr. Conway, the principal, has kindly allowed me to copy from them.

About his personal affairs he records that in May, 1762, he made a journey to Bath, evidently to attend some funeral, that his journey cost £2 11s., that he *gave ye three gentlemen who assisted at ye dirge* £3 3s. For which amount and a further sum of £5 5s. he notes having given a receipt to Mr. Perkins of Ufton Court.

In chapter viij. will be found quoted his memorandum about the money he left in the cupboard in his room at Ufton Court. On another occasion he says: *I leave in two purses in ye table drawer & ye other in ye desk, fifty two pounds ten shillings.*

Signed, Ed. Madew.

The expenses are multifarious—some for the little chapel, no doubt, and some for himself—all mixed up together. Here is a specimen:

	£	s.	d.
Feb. 4, 1762.—*Paid to M^r. Ingram for candles & breads*	1	0	7
Jan. 27, 1763.—*Paid to M^r. Ingram for candles & books*	1	14	0
Mar. 24.—*Paid to M^r. Ingram for books & snuff*	1	0	6
June 11.—*Paid to M^r. Ingram for clothes & snuff*	10	7	6
Jan 22, 1764.—*Candles, &., to M^r. Ingram*	3	1	10

Mr. Ingram must have been the predecessor of the miscellaneous village shopkeeper of the present day. But besides such things he records in a regular register the deaths of seven of the Perkins family, beginning with *Francis Perkins'* grandfather died Feb y 7th, 1694, mentioning the death of Arabella and her husband, and of their four sons. Curiously, he takes no notice of the two children who died in 1723 and 1724. He notes only the deaths of the heads of the family.

Then he records the baptisms, some of them children of Ufton parents, but many from the neighbouring villages. He gives a whole list of the congregation at Ufton in the year 1749, to the number of 98, including Mrs. Prior and her son, Mrs. Berrington and maid, and many names still familiar in Ufton, and finally mentions that confirmations were held at one time at Mr. Doughty's, at Beenham, and on two other occasions at Ufton Court, by Bishop Chaloner. This ecclesiastic, whose title was Bishop of Debra, was Vicar Apostolic of the London district. He was the author of a book of memoirs of the missionary priests. He is buried in the parish churchyard of Milton, in Berkshire.

A last entry concerning Madew is written by his successor:

On Sunday, May 13th, 1782, died, age 79, the Rev. F. Edward Madew, O.S.F., a jubiliarian, many years missionary at Ufton Court, where he died. He had likewise been missionary in Warwickshire, at Mapledurham, Oxon, & at Beenham & Ufton, Berks.

Signed, G. A. Baynham, P.S.F.

The term "jubiliarian" has been explained to signify that he had been fifty years a priest. The F. prefixed to his name no doubt stands for Father and O.S.F. for Order of St. Francis.

It will be noticed that he survived the last of his patrons at Ufton for many years. Not only was the church stuff left for the use of the congregation, but also a priest was maintained in the house even after the property was sold. G. A. Baynham, who signed the above, lived on alone in the deserted Court till his death on March 29, 1803.

An old woman, only lately dead, used to relate how she well remembered running up from the village as a child one cold, bleak spring morning to see his funeral procession pass along the avenue, on the way to the churchyard which receives

CHAP. VII.
A.D. 1802.

SALE OF MANOR OF UFTON.

all who agree or disagree in this life when at last they rest from their labours and are at peace.

Ufton Court and the estate immediately surrounding it passed to the grandson of Katherine Wyborne, Mr. John Jones, of Llanarth; but it was then a desolate, neglected, and ruinous place, and was never lived in by its new owners. At last, in 1802, it was sold to Mr. Congreve, the owner of Aldermaston, and while in his possession the Court fell more and more into ruin. A great part of the oak panelling was stripped from the walls, some of it having been used in Aldermaston Church, and a great deal of timber was cut down on the estate, and when it was again resold in 1837 the house was described in the agent's advertisement as unfit for a gentleman's residence.

Fortunately it fell into kind hands. Mr. Benyon de Beauvoir, of Englefield, who was the purchaser, in order to make use of it as tenements for his labourers, put it into a thorough state of repair, and under the care of Mr. Benyon, his successor, the present owner, it bids fair to last yet for many long years to come—a specimen, not of a nobleman's castle or a rich man's palace, but of the home of an English country gentleman of the olden time.

1709

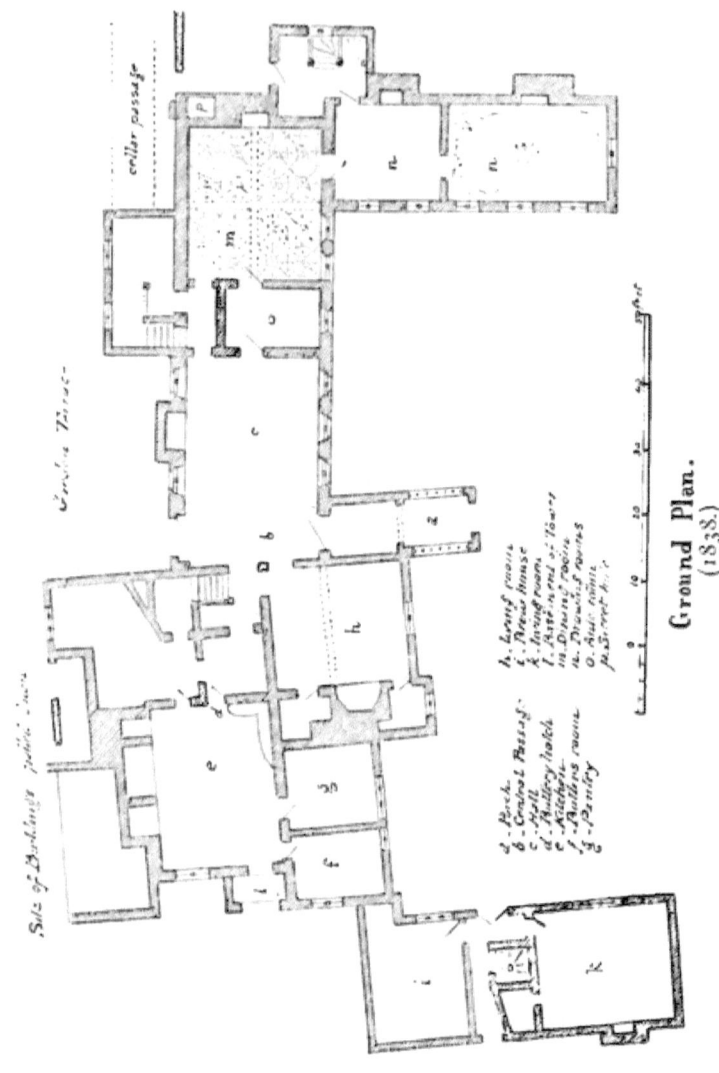

Ground Plan. (1838.)

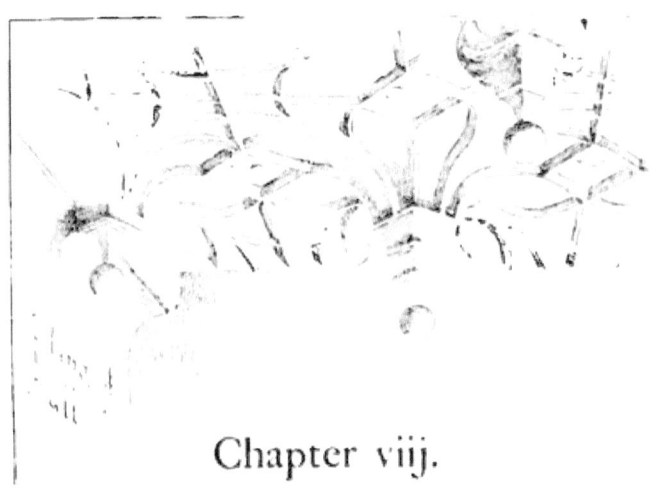

Chapter viij.

Of the Court.

FTON COURT stands almost on the edge of Sulhams, a long stretch of high land which runs parallel to the course of the river Kennet on its southern side. The line of hill is interrupted here and there at intervals by deep gullies, down which small tributary streamlets make their way to the valley below, and it is on the slope of one of these gullies, thickly clothed with wood, that the old manor-house is built.

Thus it enjoys all the advantages of an elevated situation on a dry gravel plateau here stretching southward into Hampshire and, at the same time, it is hidden away in the folds of wood and hill so as scarcely to be discoverable at any distance. A pedestrian, making his way up from the valley along lanes bordered with oaks and holly-trees of unusually fine growth, may come almost upon it before he is aware of its existence.

And if to us, nowadays, the first of these advantages, namely, that of a high and dry soil, seems the more important,

CHAP. VIII.
APPROACH.

there were no doubt times when, to our ancestors, that other advantage of being concealed from the observation of parties travelling along the roads was also of value; indeed, from many instances that exist, it would seem to have far outbalanced any pleasure to be sought from an extensive view from the windows.

There are examples in the immediate neighbourhood. The manor-house of Woolhampton, though standing on very high ground, is withdrawn only a hundred yards behind the brow of a hill from whence a splendid view could have been enjoyed, but where the house itself would have been a conspicuous object from the highway which passes below. Also, the old country residence of the abbots of Reading, now known as Bere Court, which is even more carefully concealed than Ufton Court, lying as it does in a deep hollow among the downs which border upon the valley of the Thames.

The approach to Ufton Court from the east is between a double avenue of oaks. The actual trees are comparatively young, and must have been planted about eighty years ago to replace the older avenue represented in Roque's Topographical Survey, dated 1761. From his map it appears that there were then several avenues of trees leading up to the same point in front of the house from different sides, after the fashion of the time of Louis XIV. All traces of these have, however, disappeared.

Close to the court, and flanking the road on the left, is a huge barn, part of the buildings of the home farm. It has a fine, though rude, timber roof, which, together with the cusped ornaments of the slit lights, speak of its great antiquity. Opposite to it once stood

the stables, a pile of red brick buildings in the Queen Anne style. From the exact similarity of the principal doorway to that of the old stables of Aldermaston House, still standing, it appears that the two buildings must have been erected at the same time, and perhaps by the same architect. The road to the house was between the stables and the barn, according to an arrangement not unusual in the neighbourhood. An instance is the Mansion of Strathfieldsaye.

The long low façade of the Court as seen from this side is strikingly picturesque. With the two wings and central porch, there are no less than nineteen gables to this front alone; the storeys project and overhang one beyond the other; the lattice casements jut out still further on brackets from the walls; irregular corners and recesses everywhere present themselves, and the whole is crowned with clusters of well-proportioned chimneys, not twisted, but set in angles so as to produce a very artistic effect.

On a nearer approach triangular leaden shields may be seen, placed at the junction between each pair of gables. These hold long leaden water-spouts projecting over the gravel drive below. They are now relieved of their functions, and only serve to heighten the picturesque effect of the roof that they were intended to drain. On the shields are inscribed the initials "F. P.," for Francis Perkins, with the date 1664, which, however, refers only to the addition of the pipes themselves, not to the building of the house—in part, at least, much more ancient.

This side of the Court is constructed of a framework of oaken posts and beams, filled in with brick or rubble of the style known as *post and pan*; the walls are not therefore thicker than the width of the timbers. The combined strength and elasticity of the materials has proved, however, more enduring than many a broad stone wall. The outer surface has been in comparatively recent times partially covered with rough cast plaster, no doubt as a protection from the damp and cold. Carved wooden shields once ornamented the chief gables. A fragment of one of these only remains, that over the porch having been recently put up.

The principal frontage is to the east, according to a very usual practice. Mr. Denton, in his work on England in the sixteenth century, says that manor-houses were often so built

CHAP. VIII.
FAÇADE.

Tempest, Act I.

"sheltered from the blustering, sickly south winds and from the boisterous west." He quotes Shakespeare to prove the prevailing opinion in his day as to the character of these winds. Caliban says, *A south wind blow on ye & blister you all over;* the east wind was thought to bring serene weather, and the north to be a preservative from corruption.

The building is in the form of the letter E, a well-known fashion of the time of Queen Elizabeth, and generally supposed to have reference to her name, though in this case, as the lords of Ufton were fervent adherents of the old faith, so severely repressed during her reign, the supposition does not seem very likely.

There are at least three distinct styles of architecture to be noticed in the house, denoting that it was either added to or altered on several occasions. The oldest or Gothic portions form the nucleus of the whole, and comprise the kitchen and buttery. In front of this is the Elizabethan façade, the porch, the hall and dining-room, the staircase, the library, and the whole of the south wing. To a later period, which may roughly be called the time of Queen Anne, belong the north wing and a block of building which projects on to the terrace behind (see ground plan).

It must be understood that the above is only an approximate division of the styles of the various parts of the house, as in many instances traces of all three styles are to be found mixed together.

It may be interesting, before describing the interior of the house, to note what was the usual arrangement of the dwelling rooms in manor-houses in the fifteenth century; that is, when what must be considered as the oldest part of Ufton Court was built.

Whitaker, 15th century.

Mr. Whitaker describes the manor-houses of that period as divided in half, from front to back, by a passage leading from the central porch, which passage went through the lower end of the hall, and was divided from it on the right only by a wooden screen. Above the passage, and open to the hall, was a gallery used for musicians on festive occasions, and on that account called the minstrels' or singers' gallery. Beyond the hall, and still on the right-hand side of the entrance, were

the ladies' withdrawing-rooms, and, in later times, a private
dining-room for the master of the house and his family. On
the other or left side of the central passage were the kitchen
and offices, with bedrooms above: this arrangement may very
clearly be traced at Ufton Court.

The central passage opens from the porch by a heavily-
nailed door, and traverses the house from east to west, leading
on to the garden and terrace behind. To the left of the
passage and at the foot of the principal staircase a gothic
doorway, with an oak door and a rude old wooden bolt, leads
through the buttery to the kitchen, which still at present
serves for the same use as it did 300 years ago.

The Kitchen.

It is of very massive construction. Huge oaken posts,
with bases, support a lofty roof, which is divided lengthways
into three compartments
by two wide arches, the
intervening bays being
also spanned by arches.
The chimney is the size
of a small room, and
inside the hearth two
wooden settles were to
be seen, till the exi-
gencies of modern civi-
lization required the
insertion of a kitchener,
which now conceals
them. At the upper
end is a buttery hatch;
this and the door near
it are framed with
pointed arches of the

same date as the roof. While the house was left untenanted,
after 1769, it is said that this part of it fell so completely into
ruins that a cart and horses could have been driven through
a breach in the outer wall. When it was rebuilt a battle-

CHAP. VIII.
BUILDINGS NOW DESTROYED.

mented tower, which originally stood at the outside entrance, was taken away. Its appearance can be seen in the interesting sketch supplied me by the kindness of Mr. C. A. Buckler, the original drawing having been made by his father before the alteration in 1837. Its fortified appearance must have formed a strong contrast to the later domestic architecture of the rest of the house.

The date of this kitchen is very difficult to determine, its features being simple and rude and with but few determining peculiarities. It has been thought, however, to belong to the early part of the fifteenth century—that is, before the reign

of Henry VII.—in which case the tower and oak-built hall are probably survivals of the manor-house of Pole Manor as it was in the days of the Lovels, whose tenure ended in 1487. In much later times the kitchen has been divided into two storeys, two bedrooms being in the upper floor; an inner one, called Hide Hall, in the inventory of the house at the time of the sale in 1770, and an outer one, there named the Priest's-room.

In Mr. Buckler's drawing may be seen a large block of buildings, which formerly extended from the corner of the kitchen across the road now leading round the house. It contained the steward's house, brew-house, and other offices. When it was pulled down, soon after the date of the drawing, a considerable sum of money was found in a cavity behind a chimney.

The Central Porch

belongs to the second or Elizabethan period. It is very handsomely ornamented with carving, and is lighted by two side openings fitted with balustrades. It is easy to see,

where a frame of rougher timber work divides the porch lengthways, that a later projection was added on to the original entrance. The same addition can be detected in the room immediately to the left of the porch, which must have been at first only half its present size. Over the porch in an upper storey is a charming little square room, lighted by windows on its three outer sides, and forming the very ideal of a lady's bower, and from it there is a very pretty view down the avenue. Continuing from the porch on the ground-floor is the central passage, now divided by a solid wall on the right from

The Hall.

As we enter, the most striking feature attracting the attention is the lofty coved ceiling of stucco work, ornamented with elaborately intersecting tracery, heavy pendants, and a graceful frieze. On the wall at the opposite end and close below the ceiling is a device worthy of notice, as giving a possible clue to the date of the decorations of the hall, and perhaps also to much of the building of the house itself. It consists of three diamond-shaped lozenges interwoven. The centre one contains a shield, bare of any device; those on either side hold the initials R. P. E. and I. M. E. The only persons to whom they can refer are Richard and Elizabeth Parkyns and John and Elizabeth Marvyn. Now, the Elizabeth who married, first Richard Parkyns, and secondly Sir John Marvyn, was the Lady Marvyn who died in 1581. It seems a fair presumption that it was she herself who caused the initials of both her husbands to be put up thus side by side entwined with her own; and if so, it is probable that it was during her second widowhood that this ceiling and the rest of the Elizabethan additions to Ufton Court were made. Sir John Marvyn died in 1566. Thus the date of the erection is fixed to between that year and 1581, when Lady Marvyn herself died. The initials are repeated on the central pendant.

If reference is now made to the illustration on the opposite page, taken from a drawing made by Mr. Buckler in 1838, it will be noticed that the division between the hall and the passage is simply indicated by a dotted line, and that the further or back wall of the passage is open to view; the same will be also seen in the architect's ground-plan of the same

The Hall Upton Court
J.C. Buckler

date. Dotted lines in architectural drawings denote that there is a structural division above where there is no corresponding wall or division below. Thus it is clear that at the time these drawings were made there was no wall, as now, dividing the hall from the central passage, nor even apparently the screen which must originally have stood there, but that there still remained the overhanging gallery forming an upper story over the passage, which was, as shown in Mr. Buckler's drawing, concealed behind a partition of panelled woodwork. The panelling is still to be discovered under a coat of plaster and whitewash; it is only of thin oak boards, palpably out of place, and stuck up there merely to shut off the originally open gallery as a separate room. In this small room may be seen one remaining bay of the rude, simple roof of the original hall as it was before the handsome stucco ceiling was added. The older roof here seen is of slightly arched oak beams, supported by stanchions, which are continued down the walls. On one of them is a carved shield bearing an enigmatical monogram or device, as shown in the sketch.

The hall has been much tampered with at different times. The pavement is of the same date as the stucco ceiling, but the walls have been, at some subsequent time, probably early in the eighteenth century, lined with a high wainscot of deal with long panels, and a chimney-piece and tall windows were inserted to match. Two of the tall windows remain, those looking out on the back or garden side of the house; but those opposite, which were still there when Mr. Buckler made his sketch in 1838, were replaced by small low casements when Mr. Benyon De Beauvoir adapted the Court as cottages for his labourers. The appearance of the eastern exterior of the hall before this last alteration was made can be seen from the drawing which Major Thoyts has kindly allowed me to reproduce from the original sketch in his possession.

As to what was the character of the external architecture in Elizabethan and earlier times, we are left almost wholly to conjecture. Early halls of the style are usually lit by tall

mullioned windows reaching nearly to the ceiling. It may
have been so in this case, but no indications are left from
which to judge.

From this hall the charitable bequests of Lady Marvyn—

bread and good flannel and calico (see p. 75)—are still distributed to the poor of Ufton and Padworth every Mid-Lent by their respective rectors and churchwardens; and, according to an old and carefully observed custom, the Ufton folk receive their portions out of one window, while their neighbours of Padworth are served through another.

Two doors at the upper end of the hall lead, one through an ante-room, and the other by a short passage into

The Dining-Room.

It is a good-sized square room, though very low. The ceiling, divided into four compartments by carved cross-beams, is of stucco, of a very good design, and is of the same date as that of the hall. Here also panelling of the style of Queen Anne has replaced the older wall-coverings.

CHAP. VIII.

THE STAIRCASE.

Early Dom. Arch., J. H. Parker, 1853.

The Staircase.

Mr. Parker, in describing the usual arrangement of ancient halls, says that "in the end wall behind the screen were, in smaller houses, two doors, one opening into the buttery, and the other into a pantry or other servants' apartment." Such is exactly the case at Ufton Court (see Mr. Buckler's drawing of the hall). The two doorways here are curious examples of an imitation Gothic style, which, according to the same authority above quoted, is frequently to be found in houses of the time of Elizabeth and James I.; easily to be detected in this case by the clumsiness of the mouldings and the plain, cuspless circular ornaments.

A good wide square staircase, with handsome balustrades and finials, leads to the upper story. In a room on the first landing there is a stone, low-arched fireplace, on which is scrawled a now much obliterated inscription. A sketch made of it by Mr. Buckler in 1819 is here reproduced. It probably refers to William Parkyns who died in 1558 (see p. 61), but it has been unfortunately much defaced in modern times, and without this record would be now unintelligible.

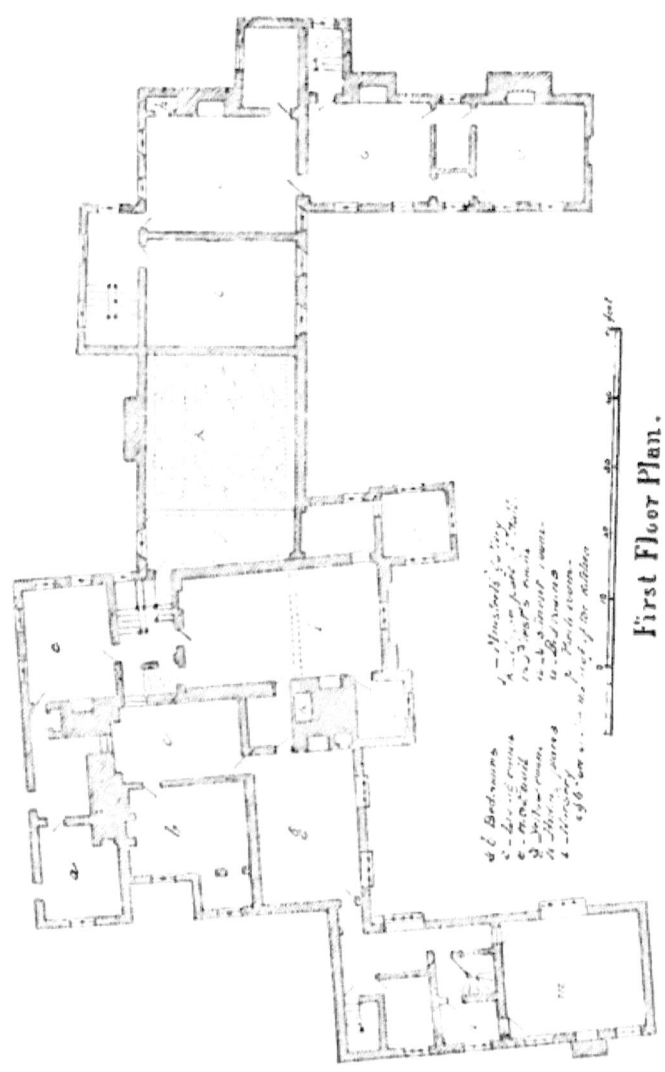

First Floor Plan.

CHAP. VIII.

THE STAIRCASE.

The Library

is a charming long, low room, still retaining its sixteenth century panelling and a highly decorated mantelpiece of oak, with inlaid patterns in some lighter wood. A crescent, also inlaid, fills a centre compartment. Near this device, and just above a centre pilaster, is a roughly-cut inscription, as shown in the illustration. The initials belong to Francis Perkins,

the nephew and heir of Richard Parkyns and Lady Marvyn, and the date is two years after the death of the latter. This carving is too roughly done to have been the workmanship of the artisan who made the mantelpiece; it was more probably cut by some amateur, perhaps Francis Perkins himself, when he had come into possession of his aunt's inheritance after her death in 1581. It is interesting to compare the style of this mantelpiece with some very similar woodwork in the dining-hall of Charterhouse, of about the date of 1554 — a date which very much confirms the conjectures that have been made as to the time when this part of Ufton Court was built. The two coats-of-arms that have been painted on either side are modern. The lattice-work of the windows in this room and many other parts of the house is remarkably pretty.

In this library there is said to have been formerly a folio copy of Shakespeare, date 1632 (second folio), which came into the possession of Mr. R. P. Collier, the well-known Shakespearian commentator. He claimed to have discovered in it some very early MS. notes, written possibly, as it was thought, by a contemporary critic. On examination by experts, however, it was concluded that these were not authentic. A fierce dispute raged about them among the learned for some time, and a whole library of books and pamphlets was written on the subject. The folio, which is called the *Perkins Shakespeare*, is now in the possession of the Duke of Devonshire.

Other valuable curiosities in the way of books, which have been picked up lately in the district, are supposed by a writer in the *Athenæum*, 1857, to have come from this collection. Among them, another copy of Shakespeare, first folio date 1623, which was bought out of a carpenter's shop near Maidenhead; a copy of Spenser's works, folio 1613; a second edition of Philip Stubbs' *Anatomy of Abuses*, and three tracts by the celebrated Robert Green, published between 1589 and 1617, called *The Groat's-worth of Witham*, in which Shakespeare is described as the only *Shake-scene in the country*.

The Oratory or Vestment Room.

It has been already said that the owners of Ufton Court were Roman Catholics. They never wavered in their allegiance to their faith, and in spite of much persecution they appear, latterly, at any rate, to have succeeded in retaining a private chaplain in their family and in enjoying the rites of their religion. A small square room, hardly larger than a closet, was devoted to the purposes of a confessional, or oratory, in which there are considerable remains of decoration. The walls are lined with oak and are painted in squares, containing alternately the monograms I. H. S. and M. R., the latter for *Maria Regina*. These are interwoven with many loops and gem-like ornaments, which, if not very well executed nor in purest taste, yet are interesting as being strictly in the Renaissance or Jacobean style.

In the narrow panels, which form a sort of frieze near the ceiling, are still just discernible the initials A. P., which may refer to the Anna Perkins whose effigy is in the church, and who died in 1635.

It has been thought that the careful decoration of this room is not to be accounted for merely on the ground of its being a confessional for penitents, but that it was probably also used for the reservation of the Blessed Sacrament, and this idea gains probability from a description of just such a small chamber in an old romance called *The Storye of the Knyghte*

CHAP. VIII.

THE ORATORY.

Storye of the Knyghte Parys and the fayr Vyenne, printed by Caxton, 1485, Sign. B, ii b.

Parys & the fayr Vyenne, printed by Caxton in 1485. The *fayr Vyenne* is being shown by the mother of Parys over his castle, and they *com on a syde of the Chamber where they foude a lytel dore, of whyche henge a lytel key by a thonge, & anon they opened the dore & entrd therein. And there was an oratorye wherein was the Majeste of our Lord Jhesu Cryst upon a lytel auter, & at eche corner was a candelstyke of sylver & thyder cam Parys for to make hys sacrifyce when he aroos & whan he wente to hys bedde.*

The painting on the ceiling and the stained glass are both modern additions.

It is probable that this small chamber did not open on to the passage, but that its only entrance was originally through the door by which it still communicates with the adjoining room, which, in the plan of the house, is called

The Priest's Living Room.

Among some papers preserved at Woolhampton College have lately been found a few loose sheets, on which are written the notes, at once diaries and registers, kept by the two last priests resident at Ufton. One entry runs as follows:

August ye first, 1762.

I leave in ye little cubbard by ye Fireside in my room at Ufton Court twelve Pounds one shilling.

E^d. *Madew, O.S.F.*

A little recess in the wall by the fireside in this room still exists to answer to the description of *ye little cubbard*. Its door has gone, but a great deal of oak panelling is known to have been taken away from Ufton Court by Mr. Congreve, of Aldermaston, during the time of his ownership; and there are signs that show that this room, among others, was formerly panelled. If so, the cupboard door which the priest locked on the sum of money that he left in store was perhaps a secret one forming part of the panelling itself. A modern door has been recently affixed.

The Chapel

is above, and occupies the whole of the upper story of the south wing. No decoration, if any such once existed, has been preserved, nor any sign of its former use, except some marks in the floor where the altar-rails were once fixed, unless the slightly arched doorway may also be so considered. It is improbable that it was ever consecrated. In times of persecution such was

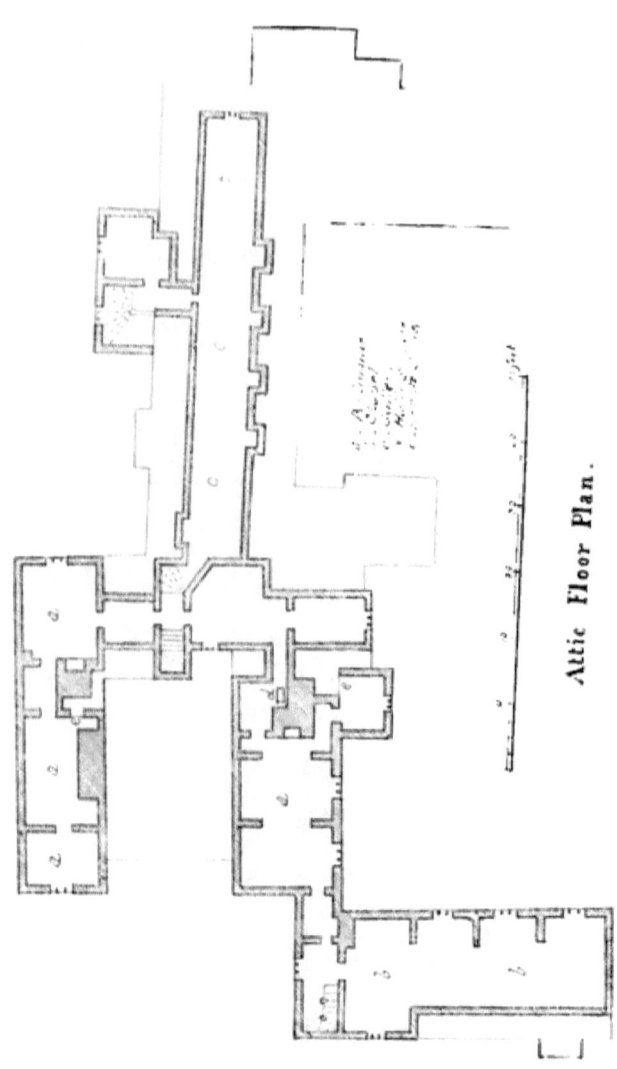

Attic Floor Plan.

rarely the case. A small portable and consecrated altar was generally used, which was simply a slab of marble about the size of a folio volume, which could be easily taken away and concealed. Those who had the privilege of the acquaintance of the late Dr. Rock will remember a beautiful specimen of such an altar in his possession, engraved with a great variety of mystical emblems, including those of the four elements, and will recall the interesting explanation of it that he was wont to give.

The south wing containing these rooms for religious purposes and for the use of the priest, has also a separate staircase, and on the ground floor a door opening to the front of the house. It formed, in fact, a separate dwelling for the family chaplain, communicating only with the rest of the house through the library; and as he probably combined in his own person the duties of priest and tutor to the younger members of the household, it is easy to understand the convenience of such an arrangement. Something similar is often to be seen in country houses in Italy to this day, where the chapel and the chaplain's house are all under the same roof with the *Casa di Padrone*, each having its separate entrance, and the whole together forming one large rambling semi-connected, but wholly picturesque, range of buildings.

Unmistakable proofs of the trials and persecutions which harassed the daily life of our Roman Catholic fellow-countrymen three hundred years ago are to be seen in the

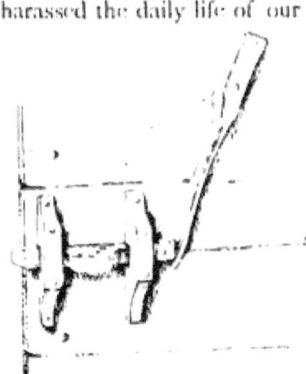

Hiding Places,

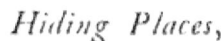

of which several exist in this house. Some are openings under the rafters in the sloping roof; others are trapdoors in the floor leading to small, dark chambers generally constructed against or behind the massive chimneys. They are mostly fitted with wooden spring locks.

One is a hole about 9 feet deep, 3 feet 10 inches long, and 2 feet 5 inches wide, a broad oak plank forming the covering. These are the present dimensions; but in the plan of the house, dated 1838, to which reference has before been made, they are shown to be considerably larger. In this hole the ladder still stands, down which perhaps some poor fugitive priest stumbled to lie hidden while the house was being searched by pursuivants, with warrants for his arrest, and while the trembling squire diverted their attention as best he might, knowing that the lives of both of them would have answered for it if an emissary of the Pope of Rome had been found within the walls. That such incidents were fact, not fiction, has been proved by the story given in the chapter on the Perkins family, where the official reports of two such house-searchings have been quoted from the original documents in the Record Office.

In the last described place of concealment are said to have been found at the beginning of this century a small ivory figure and two old guns. These are now in the possession of the lord of the manor, Mr. Benyon, at Englefield House.

Another hiding-place is at the extreme north-west corner of the house. It is a deep, well-like hole in the floor of a cupboard upstairs. It measures 4 feet 6 inches by 2 feet 3 inches, and when explored was found to consist of two chambers, the upper one 4 feet deep, with a wooden floor, the lower going down below the level of the basement. It is now blocked with rubble, but it probably once communicated with the cellars under that part of the house which abut at their farther end on to the wall of the vaulted passage below the terrace at the back. An opening between the two would make an easy way of escape from the house out into the meadow beyond, and so into the woods.

As is well known, these contrivances are by no means unusual. In Compton Winyates the beautiful Elizabethan house belonging to Lord Northampton in South Warwickshire, there is a whole network of passages, starting from a small chapel which is carefully hidden under the roof. Walter Scott's description of Woodstock will occur to everyone; and still more to the point are the accounts collected together in Foley's "Records of the Jesuits in England"—accounts of dangers, concealments, hairbreadth escapes, and catastrophes in scenes just such as have been above described, written by the hunted sufferers themselves in their letters and diaries. Reading these, the use of the hiding places at Ufton Court is easily understood.

It is from these records that we learn that there lived at that time a lay-brother of the Jesuit order, whose name was Nicholas or John Owen, often called *Little John*, as he was remarkably small of stature. It is not unlikely that he was a builder by trade; but at any rate he *was a man of talent & admirable prudence, & by his skill in contriving hiding places for the priests, hunted to death by searchers & pursuivants, he saved the lives of many.*

He is known to have supplied the plans for the building of Hinlip Hall, then belonging to Mr. Thomas Abington, which was arranged throughout as a place of refuge for priests. "Almost every room had a recess, a passage, a trapdoor, and a secret stair; the walls were hollow, the ceilings false, and the chimneys had double flues, one as a passage for the smoke and a second for the priest." He often, in other cases, was *both architect & builder, working with inexhaustible industry & labour; for generally the thickest walls had to be broken into & large stones extracted, requiring stronger arms than were attached to a body so small as to give him the nickname of Little John.* His custom was to regard these labours as religious works, and to receive the Holy Eucharist before beginning. He is spoken of as a *great servant of God in a diminutive body.*

For eighteen years Owen was a faithful attendant—first of Father Henry Garnett, Superior of the Jesuits, and afterwards of Father John Gerard. He was taken prisoner in company with Garnett at Little Malvern Court, then in possession of the Berington family, where he and a party of fugitives were starved out of their places of concealment by

CHAP. viii.
BROTHER OWEN.

the searchers. Eventually he died under torture in the Tower, refusing to give any information that could lead to the discovery of his friends.

Though no direct evidence exists that *Little John* was the designer of the hiding-places at Ufton, yet, as he is known to have gone much about to the houses of various recusants in order to contrive these arrangements, it seems possible that such was the case. The two Jesuit priests who were said to have been concealed here at the time of the search in 1599 (see p. 99) are named as Garrett and Jarrett. No such names are to be found among Jesuit records; one must therefore suppose either that they were assumed names—a practice very commonly followed—or else that perhaps they are mistakes of writing, and were intended for Garnet and Gerard. In this case the probability that Brother Owen had to do with Ufton Court is much increased.

The Upper Story.

Of the sleeping-rooms it may be remarked that in almost every case they have at least one small closet attached. In Croker's notes to the Life of Pope, published by Courthorpe, there is a comment on a passage in the "Rape of the Lock" (Canto I.) which throws a light on this arrangement:

Belinda rung a hand-bell, which, not being answered, she knocked with her slipper. Bell hanging was not introduced into our domestic apartments till long after the date of the "Rape of the Lock." I myself, he goes on to say, *about the year* 1790, *remember that it was still the practice for ladies to summon their attendants to their bed-chambers by knocking with a high-heeled shoe. Servants, too, were accustomed to wait in ante-rooms, whence they were summoned by hand-bells; & this explains the extraordinary number of such rooms in the houses of the last century.*

Over and above the dwelling-rooms there is a confusing

labyrinth of winding passages and objectless corners; there are several unaccounted-for spaces, and a long gallery which ends in nothing. One is here irresistibly reminded of Dickens's description of Bleak House: *Where you go up & down steps, where you come upon more rooms when you think you have seen all there are, where there is a bountiful provision of little holes & passages, & where you find still older cottage rooms in unexpected places, with lattice windows & green growth pressing through them.* It is the very place for ghosts, if they at all observed suitabilities. Longfellow has said that

> *All houses wherein men have lived & died*
> *Are haunted houses;*

but, except in that sense, a strict adherence to truth compels me to confess that of ghosts at Ufton Court there are none, nor has one ever been seen or heard within the knowledge of living man or woman.

Yet it must be admitted that there are occasions when it is hard to believe that supernatural occupants are not in possession of the place. If the Court should be seen in the dusk of the evening by some one driving up in a lighted carriage, he will be surprised as he approaches to see it lit up from top to bottom. A grand entertainment appears to be going on in the hall, and the whole house seems full of guests and servants hurrying along the passages and carrying lights from room to room. Not a sound is heard, but to the eye the scene is one of revelry and wild excitement. Coming nearer, and before he recovers from his astonishment, in a moment the whole is changed, and darkness falls upon the night, except perhaps where a quiet glow from some window shows signs of a warm fire and a welcome within. The reader is assured that a strictly natural cause can be found for this effect; what that is is left to his intelligence to discover. One thing only may be averred, that it is not the effect of imagination or even of over-conviviality.

Returning to the ground-floor, a door at the further end of the Hall leads into a small panelled anteroom from which, by a door now blocked up, access was formerly had, through the dining-room, to the rooms in the North wing.

The Drawing-rooms

are of the time of Queen Anne, and, with the bedrooms over them, occupy the north wing. The staircase, however, leading to the upper story appears to be Elizabethan, by which we understand that this wing must have formed part of the original sixteenth-century building.

The appearance of this part of the house was very much altered after 1838, when Mr. Benyon De Beauvoir converted it into dwellings for his labourers; before that date the external walls were of brick, and tall windows on both floors admitted plenty of light (see illustration, p. 147). Inside some of the tall window-frames still remain, but they have been in most instances blocked up, and small low windows inserted, made exactly to imitate those in the south wing. It must be allowed that this last alteration has been much in favour of the harmonious architectural effect of the façade. The two drawing-rooms are narrow; they are panelled, and have handsome wooden cornices and doorways, and the larger of the two has a gracefully ornamented stucco ceiling. The ornamental panel over the fireplace is original, but the mantelpiece itself is modern; as are also all the carved mantelpieces in the house, except that in the library. The only entrance to these rooms in former times was through the dining-room, an arrangement which would be hardly thought convenient now.

To guide us in forming some idea as to how the ladies and their husbands lived who inhabited these rooms, we can refer to a catalogue of the household goods of *the Manor-house called Ufton Court*, which were sold by auction on October 23, 1770, the year following the death of John, the last Squire Perkins of Ufton. But either all the better articles had been taken away before, or they were reserved, for neither family portraits nor books appear in the list. It is noticeable that the furniture neither of the chapel nor of the priest's room is mentioned. The priest stayed on at Ufton, and the chapel was in use as late as 1802.

The various rooms enumerated are mostly described by

the materials of their furniture, such as *the check bedchamber*, the *cotton bedchamber*, and so on. The long gallery is mentioned, in which it is said there were 16 old chairs and 66 old maps and prints. There was the bedchamber over the porch and the room adjoining; there was the nursery, also mentioned in the plan, and the old nursery. One room was called *Hide Hall*, and contained a four-post bed and needlework furniture. Perhaps it was so called in remembrance of the mother of one of the Perkins squires, who married again a Mr. James Hide. She lived at Ufton during her son's minority, and died and was buried here in 1686.

Char. viii. Catalogue of Furniture.

The drawing-room contained an *oval pier glass in a neat carved frame* and *eight India pictures*. There were in the study a harpsichord, a back-gammon table, and an ombre-table, a favourite game in Queen Anne's reign.

> *Belinda now, whom thirst of fame invites,*
> *Burns to encounter two adventurous knights,*
> *At ombre singly to decide their doom.*

Rape of the Lock, Pope.

In the *little parlour* there was a dining-table and a cherry-tree ditto; in the *eating parlour* a chamber organ and a large Turkey carpet; in the *servants' hall* a wig-block, and in the *great hall* a large linen chest, a bookcase with sash front, and a pillion with a camlet case.

Behind the house the old walled garden still exists, reached by a very pretty flight of stone steps which descend

The Garden.

from the terrace. It requires but little imagination to people again garden and terrace with belles in hoops and brocade,

CHAP. viii.
THE GARDEN.

and beaux snuff-box and clouded cane in hand; Belinda and her gay London friends, with Pope and Swift, perhaps, among them; or, as in Mr. Burnside's charming song, one may dream of

That old garden with its lilies fair & tall,
And the maid who walked within it . . .
In her petticoat of satin & her gaily-flowered gown,
And the perfume & the powder in her hair of sunny brown.

See page 166.

But even in neglect and decay this spot has a beauty and a special charm of its own. The grassy paths are bordered with lilies and roses and a crowd of other old English flowers, and the whole is set in the frame of the old ivy-mantled brick wall, glowing with tones which time alone can give. At the lower end is an old gateway opening to the meadow beyond, and flanked on the outside by two venerable yew-trees. Unhappily, a very heavy snowstorm during the winter of 1886 did more severe injury to these trees than they had suffered during all the previous centuries of their existence. The ground here descends rapidly to the little stream called Shooter's Brook, which forms the boundary of the parish. Nine fishponds connected by sluices follow the slope of the hill, in which were stored and fatted the carp and perch that were wanted for the squire's table on the fast days of the Church. That these formed no unimportant part of the manorial *menu* seems proved by the excellence of the materials with which they were dished up.

Given in the Appendix.

In the chaplain's note-book, among other useful recipes—such as *syrup for consumption,* by which *many have been cured when taken in time,* and *a cure for ye bite of a mad dog,* and *an infallible cure for ague*—is the following for fish sauce: *Take half a pint of Port wine for carp, for other fish white wine or Rasen wine, y^t is not sweet, 2 anchovies, a little scrap^t horse radish, a little pounded pepper, half a dozen shalotz or a middling onion, a little mushroom powder or ketchup, gently simmer these ingredients together till the liquor is near 3 parts wasted, then thicken it up with half a lb. of butter, sharpen it with a lemon or pickle, according to taste—oysters are a good*

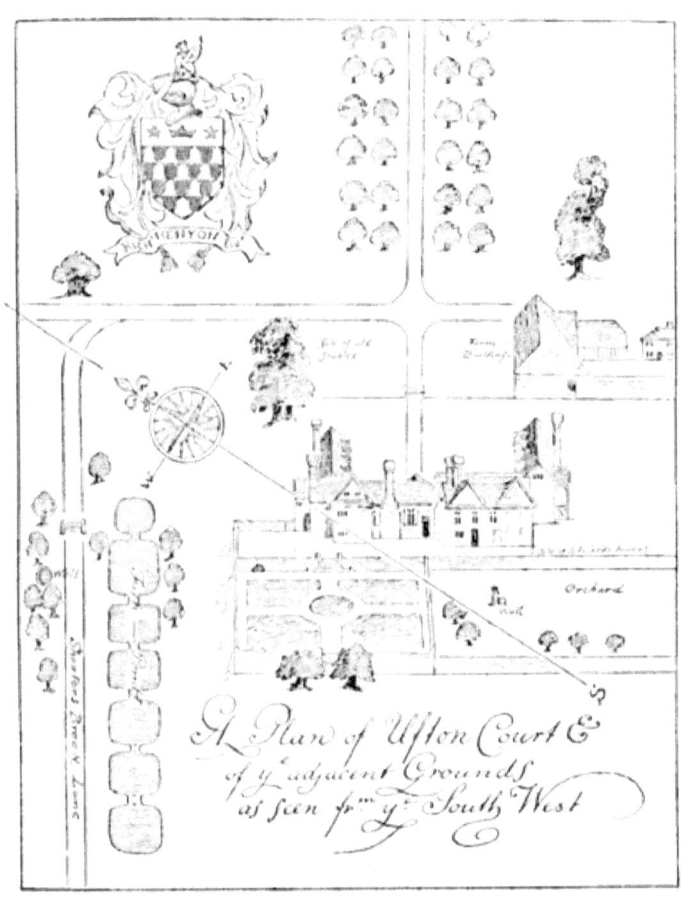

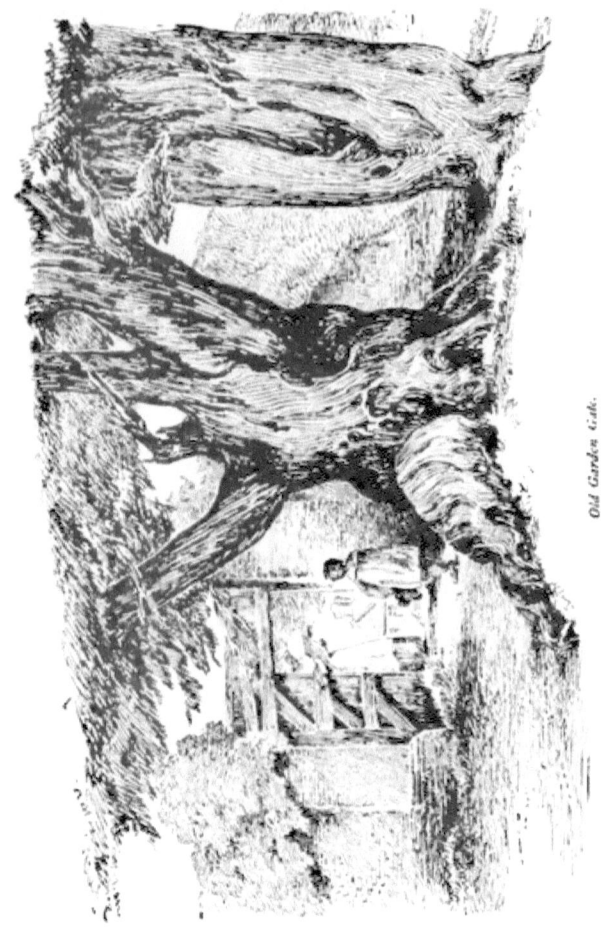

Old Garden side.

addition—boil the liquor with the other ingredients, but oysters only just simmer up after the butter is put in.

Adjoining the garden was the orchard, and beyond that again the hop-garden, still so called. Hops seem to have been much grown in this neighbourhood formerly. They are among the crops that are said to have suffered in the hail-storm in 1762. Probably, when most families brewed their own ale, it was convenient to grow them on the premises. They have now quite ceased to be cultivated in this part of Berkshire.

Beyond that, again, is a tract of land, about 146 acres in extent, planted with wood, but still known as Ufton Park, which extends as far as the limits of what was formerly common land, now planted with fir woods. In the park the ground is very undulating and pretty. Everywhere the steep valleys and sloping banks are clothed with a thick growth of young oak-trees and brushwood. A little stream, dammed up near its source so as to form a good-sized pond, runs through the whole width of the enclosure, and is known as Shooter's Brook. The trees are all about the same age, having been planted about the beginning of this century to replace the older timber then cut down. Among the few survivors that remain of earlier forest generations, one venerable pollard oak stands within sight of the Court, as though still keeping guard over the old house of whose varying fortunes of prosperity and decay it has been for centuries a silent witness.

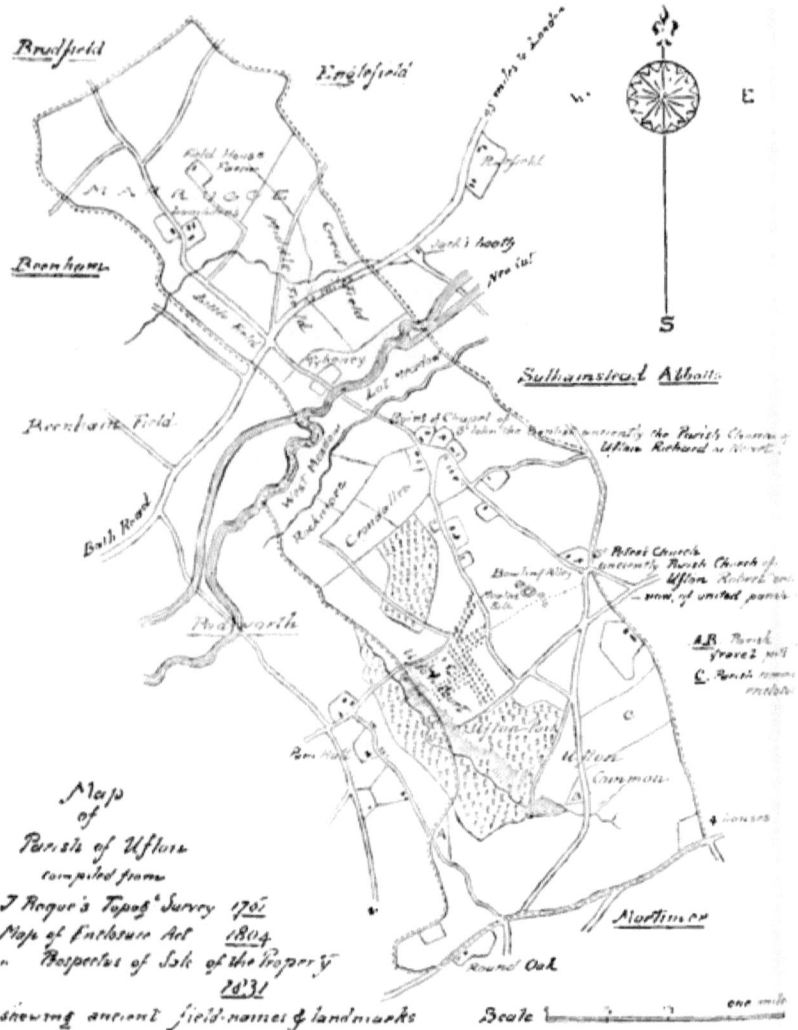

Chapter ix.

Of The Parish.

HE parish of Ufton, in the county of Berks and the hundred of Theale, is a long narrow strip of land, lying in a south-easterly direction across the valley of the river Kennet, by which it is divided into two unequal parts. It is about four miles long and a mile and a half broad in its widest part, and contains 2,122 acres, and at the last census, in 1881, its population numbered 315.

With the rest of Berkshire, Ufton was formerly included in the diocese of Salisbury, but by a redistribution made at the time of the appointment of Bishop Wilberforce the county was transferred to that of Oxford. An interesting record of the earlier ecclesiastical connection was to be seen till a few years ago on a doorway of the church of St. Lawrence, in Reading, where a carved scutcheon, bearing the episcopal arms of Salisbury—a Virgin and Child on a shield azure—formed one of the corbels; it disappeared when the church was restored. _{Diocese of Salisbury.}

The soil of Ufton is various, consisting of Woolwich clay and Reading beds in the northern part of the parish, of alluvial deposit by the river banks, and of London clay on the southern slopes of the valley, while the high lands still further south are covered with the flinty gravel of the lower Bagshot _{Soil.}

CHAP. ix. beds—most healthy for human habitation, but rather depressing to the agricultural interests.

To the north Ufton is divided from the neighbouring parish of Bradfield by a little brooklet called the Bourne. The hilly district lying between this stream and the river Kennet bore in early days the name of Marrugge, or Marrige, a name still preserved in connection with the lane that now passes through it. It has been suggested that the word is possibly the same as Mere-ridge, a term still used in this part of the country to denote the low turf ridges, or banks, which formerly divided the different portions of the common meadows.

The Bath Road.

The old coaching road from London to Bath runs through the parish of Ufton, along the low land parallel to the river Kennet, and is still known by its old name, though so many years have now passed since anyone has thought of travelling to Bath that way. Whether the main road always at this point passed along the valley has sometimes been disputed; the river-meadows were in early times, and before the improvement of the drainage system, constantly flooded, and it is probable that travellers on horseback or in the clumsy waggons in use before the seventeenth century would often have followed in preference the higher ground. Leaving Theale, there was a choice of roads on either side; to the north of the valley there was the old road which, till not long ago, passed through an archway close behind Englefield House and under the long gallery, built, as it is said by Sir Francis Walsingham, to receive the visit of his royal mistress and benefactress, Queen Elizabeth; this road follows the ridge of the hill by the beautiful avenue of oaks at Chapel Row— also a memorial of the same royal progress—and does not descend again to the level country till just before reaching Newbury. On the opposite, or southern, side of the Kennet an alternative road led behind Aldermaston by Brimpton and Crookham Common. Whether either or both of these routes were more usually followed, it is certain that there must always have been some roadway very much where it now is, along the valley. In the record of a Manor Court, held at Aldermaston in 1550, the road is incidentally alluded to as *the King's highe waye, called Harrowe Waye, leading from Newbury to Reddinge*, and is described as crossing the stream called Holbrook (Holy Brook), and bordering on the property of the heirs of Edward Yelsley (Hildesly), of Beenham, thus fixing its locality much where it now is. In 1751 we have the testimony of Defoe that it was very much frequented. He says that Thatcham, Woolhampton, and Theale were noted for being great thoroughfare towns, full of inns. These quiet villages have shrunk in size and importance since the time when they could be so written of; but, at any rate, the description goes to prove that then, as now, the great Bath road passed through that way. Not, however, by any means such as it existed later on, for Defoe says that the road just beyond Woolhampton was so narrow and inconvenient that in some places there was not room for two carriages to pass.

CHAP. IX.

THE BATH ROAD.

Defoe, Description of Berkshire.

In the *Gentleman's Magazine* of 1752 great complaint is made that English roads were far inferior to those in France, and that, moreover, *Englishmen of sense were so senseless as to justify themselves*. "*God be praised*," say they, "*that we have not such roads as are in France! Who would take the French roads & Government together?*" Agreed, but why must good roads be the effect of despotism? One has need to rub one's eyes and recall the fact that this was written in the time of the "ancien régime." The author goes on: *The last tour I made was from London to Falmouth. After the first 47 miles from London you never set eyes on a turnpike for 120 miles. The respective parishes either can or will do nothing; nor have the inhabitants abilities to make or mend a road, though one gave them the resources of the Exchequer.*

Severe reflections these on the waywardens of the day! Mann, in his "History of Reading," 1713, says that a great impediment to the improvement of the borough in his day was the miserable state of the high roads leading to it. These had been suffered to be worn down by carriages driving a long number of years without the least attempt being made towards their improvement till they had become almost impassable, so

CHAP. IX.
THE BATH ROAD.

much so that nearly within the limits of the borough a single carriage could seldom proceed on its journey till others came up to its assistance.

Waylaring Life in England.

Somerset House Register.

History of Newbury.

Pat. Roads, Editions 1771, 1781, 1792, 1822, 1826.

In 1714 the gentlemen of Reading had petitioned the House of Commons for leave to bring in a Bill to repair the highway between the borough and Puntsfield (a point on the Bath road just outside the confines of the parish of Ufton). It was something that road making and mending were already recognised as duties of the community. In early times, as M. Jusseraud has shown, such necessary works were left to the chance bounty of individuals encouraged thereto by spiritual blessings and indulgences which were often granted in acknowledgment of this act, as it was then considered, of charity and piety. Henry Kelsall in 1493 thus earned for himself virtue's own reward by leaving in his will certain sums *for the mending of the way between Reading & Thele*.

It was in 1774, or thereabouts, as Mr. Money says, that the new Bath road was finally altered and improved. In August, 1752, the Flying Coach was started, which made the journey from London to Newbury in twelve hours. From that time forward reference to various succeeding editions of Paterson's Roads shows that the highway followed the same line as now, passing by Theale and Puntfield, through the parish of Ufton to Woolhampton and Thatcham; between Englefield and Beenham on the right, and Sulhampstead, Ufton Court, Padworth, and Aldermaston on the left.

The Great Western Railway to Bath was opened in June, 1841, and the branch line from Reading to Hungerford soon afterwards, in 1847. Then coaches ceased to run, and the glory of the Bath road departed. The railway and the road pass through the parish of Ufton side by side.

The Kennet and Avon Canal.

Almost parallel with these flows the river Kennet, as Pope calls it, *Kennet swift for eels renowned*. On its course between Reading and Newbury its many bends are connected by a series of short canals or cuts, by which the navigation between the two towns is very much shortened. The first Act of Parliament to authorize the improvement was passed in 1714, in spite of great opposition from the citizens of Reading, who fancied that their road traffic would suffer in consequence. It was no sooner completed than they found themselves mistaken; but then the millers in their turn complained that their water-supply was in danger, and the farmers that floods would ensue and their crops be damaged. The work, however, was carried on, and in 1810, by the opening of the Kennet and Avon Canal beyond Newbury, complete water communication was established for the whole distance between London and Bristol. The prosperity and utility of the scheme was, however, shortlived. In 1852 the Great Western Railway Company purchased the Kennet navigation property, and since that time the river and its canals have quietly gone to sleep together.

By the river banks are extensive osier beds, whose value has much decreased of late, since Free Trade has enabled the foreigner to undersell their produce.

A long meadow on the south side of the Kennet, in the parish of Ufton, still retains the name of Tydney, or Tybeneye, by which it was known in 1394, when it formed part of the jointure of Joan, widow of Sir John Langford, of Bradfield.

The Common Fields.

Till the beginning of this century at Ufton, as elsewhere, a great part of the land of the parish was common land; almost all the level tract in the valley was so appropriated. To the north of the river it was divided into three fields, viz., Little Field, Middle Field, and Great Field, and to the south there were West Meadow and Lot Meadow. The fields were

CHAP. IX.
THE COMMON FIELDS.

the common arable lands of the parish; the meadows were for the pasture of the flocks and herds, each landowner and leaseholder having a right to send out a certain number of beasts, according to the size of his holding. Lot Meadow, however, was shut up during springtime and devoted to hay, to be thrown open again for pasture when the crop was carried. This, and the arable lands, were divided by the low turf ridges which have been before alluded to, called "mere ridges," and the several strips were apportioned to the parishioners each year in rotation, the order being decided by lot.

From some curious old lotting books, which have been preserved in the adjoining parish of Sulhampstead, we learn something of the manner in which this very ancient custom of our village communities was carried out. In this case the rotation of allotments was for five years, at the end of which period, as it is expressed in the heading of one of the books, *each lot returns & is the same as it was the five years before, & so continue changing forever.* This book is dated 1778.

At Sulhampstead the lord of the manor had 14¾ lots, the rector had 1 lot, and several of the neighbouring squires had their portions in right of being owners of land in the parish. Paulet Wright of Englefield had 8 lots, Christopher Griffith of Padworth had ¾ of a lot, and John Jones, at that time the owner of Ufton Court, had 1 lot. Mr. Money says, in an article in the *Archæological Review*, December, 1889, that the parishes of Sulhampstead, Beenham, Padworth, and Ufton inter-commoned with each other over a tract of about three miles, from the 46th to the 49th milestone along the Bath road.

The enclosure of common fields began in some places as early as 1700; but it was no doubt the pressure of high prices, after the long war at the end of the century, which induced the completion of the change. A separate Act of Parliament was required for the enclosure in each parish. That for Ufton was passed in 1804, when the open lands were awarded to the several landowners and leaseholders in proportion to the amount of property they held in the parish. Dr. Beke, the then Rector of Ufton, bears witness to the immense improvement that was brought about at that time in the value of the land and the increase of the crops produced. Of the agricultural condition of the parish he says, in some notes written for Oriel College, Oxford: *The parish of Ufton is in general very well cultivated. I have good reason to believe that the whole produce, including all kinds, is nearly twice as great as it was 60 or 70 years ago, when it was much more sub-divided; that is, before the general introduction of the four-course system of turnip husbandry. Before this system was adopted there were more horses, nearly the same number of cattle, & seldom more than 150 or 200 sheep; but of late years* (that is, since 1804) *near 2,000 have often been maintained during the whole winter, & the crops of grain have been much improved by their manure. This improvement has been materially assisted by an inclosure of the arable fields & meadows by the river Kennet.*

The waste tract of land on the south side of the parish, on the hill, called Ufton Common, covered with gorse and heather, and dotted over here and there with the huts and enclosures of squatters, was enclosed by virtue of the same Act of Parliament at the same time. There were here, however, certain reservations. Two plots were set aside *for public gravel-pits, for getting gravel and other materials for repairing public and private roads.* Also, a part of the common, thirty-one acres in extent—that is, about equal to one-fifteenth of the whole—was vested in the hands of the lord of the manor, the rector and the churchwardens as trustees, to be for the free use and enjoyment of the poor of the parish. Some little time later this plot was let to the lord of the manor as tenant at will, and at a vestry meeting it was arranged that the rental money should be spent in coals to be distributed once a year to the poor and resident parishioners. This arrangement still continues. The greater part of the enclosed common has been planted with fir-trees. Through these woods there runs a remarkable fosse and bank. It begins about a quarter of a mile to the south of the church, and can be traced straight across the parishes of Ufton, Padworth, and Aldermaston. The ditch is on the north side of the bank. It goes by the name of Grimmer's Bank, perhaps from the word "grim," meaning a giant, and it is supposed to be of ancient British origin.

A little way from it, in a part of the woods called Ufton Park, is a round knoll with some signs of fortification, probably either British or Roman. In later times it seems to have been occupied by some Roundhead soldiers as a camping place, as pipes and coins of the period have been found there.

The Chapel of St. John the Baptist, Ufton Nervet.

It has been explained in an earlier part of this work (see p. 6) that Ufton formerly consisted of two separate parishes, called severally Ufton Richard, or Nervet, and Ufton Robert. Roughly speaking, it is probable that Ufton Nervet comprised the district of Marrugge north of the river, the low lands of the valley, and the lower slopes of the hill on the southern side; while Ufton Robert included all the high lands still further to the south. The parish church of Ufton Robert occupied the site of the present church of St. Peter. The ruins of the other church, the parish church of Ufton Nervet, dedicated to St. John the Baptist, are still to be seen standing on a little eminence just above the valley, and the rectory house was close by. It existed, degraded into two very bad cottages till 1886, when it was pulled down and finally disappeared.

See Appendix. A list of the institutions to the living from 1297 to 1434 is given in the Appendix.

The patronage was in the gift of the prior and brethren of the Order of St. John of Jerusalem in England, whose central priory was in Clerkenwell. It was founded by one Jordan Bresset in Henry I.'s reign, and its gateway, now known as St. John's Gate, still stands to mark the site of its buildings.

Extenta Terrarum Hosp. St. Johna in Anglia A.D. MCCC., tricissimo octavo. A curious document relating to the order, and dated 1338, has been lately found in Malta and published by the Camden Society. It contains a list of their possessions in England, and it is there stated that amongst the endowments of the preceptory of the order at Greenham were the ecclesiastical emoluments of the parishes of Speen, Ilsley, Wallingford, Wasing, Catmore, and Ufton. It appears that a very considerable income accrued to the brothers from the appropriated funds of churches or chapels in their gift, to which they appointed vicars or chaplains at the reduced rate then usual.

The order was suppressed by Henry VIII., but its connection with Ufton had terminated before that time.

In 1434 a deed of union between the two parishes of Ufton was executed, a copy of which exists in the Diocesan Registry of Salisbury. It runs in the name of *Robert, by Divine Permission Lord Bishop of Sarum;* and after a greeting *to all the sons of Holy Mother who shall see or hear these present,* it sets forth that whereas *the parish churches of Ufton Robert & Ufton Richard, otherwise Nervyte, founded aforetime by faithful servants in Christ . . . are very near to one another . . . & that the fruits & income of each are by themselves so small & meagre that to the support of one priest in charge they scarcely suffice,* and in consequence of a petition on the part of Master William Fishburne, Rector of Ufton Robert, and with the *full consent of the venerable men, the Prior of the Hospital of St. John of Jerusalem in England & his Brethren, the patrons of the church of Ufton Richard, & of William Parkyns armiger, patron of the church of Ufton Robert, & of all others interested in this respect. . . . We of our ordinarial & pontifical authority annex & unite the said churches of Ufton Richard & Ufton Robert, & we declare that the said church of Ufton Richard, alias Nervyte, shall be for the future not a church, but a chapel, dependent on the parish church of Ufton Robert.*

He goes on to provide that the said chapel, with its burying-ground attached, should be kept decently and in good repair, and that Mass should be said there three times a week by the Rector of Ufton Robert, and that the said rector should also pray for the souls of those buried in the disused churchyard, and that he should pay to the Prior and Brethren of St. John of Jerusalem in London the yearly sum of 4s. on the feast of St. Martin the Bishop, in the winter (November 11), in addition to another 4s. which they had always hitherto received from the church (the whole equal to about £4 of our present money). In witness hereof the Bishop's seal and the seals of the Prior of St. John's of Jerusalem and Mr. William

CHAP. IX.

CHAPEL AND CHAPEL CLOSE, UFTON NERVET.

Parkyns' seal were appended on the 26th day of March in the year of our Lord 1435.

We may suppose that the provisions for the preservation and sanctity of the chapel and its surroundings were observed during the next succeeding century; but in Henry VIII.'s reign few things were sacred and nothing safe by which any gain, however small, could accrue to the King or his favourites.

At that time the proprietorship which the Brotherhood of St. John's had retained over the chapel and its endowment had passed into the possession of the Augustinian Priory of Goring.

Wilder MSS.

We find that after the suppression of this latter establishment, Henry VIII., by a deed dated June 17, 1543, granted to Richard Andrews, of Hayle, in Gloucestershire, and Leonard Chamberleyn, of Woodstock, Oxfordshire, the manor of *Sulham*, alias *Nunhyde*, in Berkshire, with appurtenances, consisting of lands in the adjoining parishes of *Tilehurst, Ufton, Miggels* (Michael's), *Sulhamsted, & Burfield*, late *belonging to the monastery of Goring, now dissolved*. For this grant the recipients paid the very moderate sum of 12s. 11¼d.

These lands in Ufton, or, as it is here sometimes called, *Ufton Robert or Rabette*, are very particularly and carefully described in various deeds, as they passed, always with the manor of Sulham, through the hands of different owners. They are said to have been *that parcell of meadowe in Ufton, Co. Berks, conteyninge by estimacion two acres, lieinge & beinge in a certeine meade there comonlye called Ufton West-meade, adjoyninge on the east & west parts to the land or meadowe now or late of Frauncys Parkyns, Esquior, & also all that close called the Chappell Close & the Chappell thereupon standing*. There seems to be no doubt that this description refers to the former parish church afterwards called a chapel, and to its burying-ground, here called the chapel close, where lay the forgotten dead of past generations, for whose souls no one now any longer cared to pray. The portion of the common meadow which went with the chapel was probably the endowment from the proceeds of which the yearly rent to the Brotherhood of St. John's had been paid.

The original receivers of this small property in Ufton, attached to the manor of Sulham, only kept it long enough to make profit out of it. The grant is dated June 17th, 1543, and on June 19th, two days later, they obtained from the King leave *to give, concede, enfeoff, and alienate the whole to Thomas, Robert, and Bartholomew Burgogne, for which license they paid* £5 14s. 1¼d. On June 21st, in consideration of the sum of £342 6s. 8d., the transfer actually took place, and the Burgognes were acknowledged as holding the manor and its appurtenances *in capite* from the king.

Men's heads were turned in those days by the sudden flooding of the country with landed properties, the possessions of the suppressed monasteries, then granted or sold to private individuals, and manors and estates changed hands almost as rapidly as counters across a gaming-table. After an interval of only two years the Burgognes in turn parted with Sulham Manor. They obtained the royal license to alienate it for the same sum of £5 14s. 1¼d., and sold the property to one Richard Bartlet, of London, Doctor of Physycke, who, as lord of the manor, held a court at Sulham in the first year of his possession, 1545. He, at all events, intended to be a *bonâ-fide* landowner, and, if possible, to found and settle a family on the estate.

With a pathos which is sometimes found even in yellow parchments, thickly covered with long lines of court-hand writing, he says, in a deed of settlement, that *for as much as he hath no children of his bodye begotten, & therefore intending the preferment & advancement of Thomas Richard & John Bartlet, sonnes of his brother, Edmund Bartlet, deceased*, he gives over the Sulham property to trustees for their benefit. However, the younger Bartlets did not care for the inheritance. Some time before 1587 the doctor died, and on May 4th in that year Richard Bartlet the younger, as he calls himself, *of Lyons Inn, co. Middlesex, granted, bargained, & sold unto Sir Humfry Forster, of Aldermaston, all that his manor of Sulham, alias Nunhyde, with all its appurtenances . . . in Ufton & elsewhere, some tymes in the possession & use of Richard Bartlet, of London, Doctor of Physycke, deceased, for the sum of* £500.

CHAP. IX.

MANOR OF SULHAM.

Meanwhile another family, already settled in the neighbourhood, had acquired an interest in Sulham. Ten years before Richard Bartlet had *granted & farme letten* all his manor of Sulham, with the land in Ufton and elsewhere, to John Wilder, of Sulham, and in 1598 Sir Humphry Foster confirmed John Wilder's lease for a longer period.

Sir Humfrey Foster, the new *tenant in capite*, was a large landowner in the neighbourhood. He was a man of great wealth, but of still more magnificent tastes. He it was who built the stately manor-house of Aldermaston, which was standing till within fifty years ago, when it was accidently destroyed by fire. The staircase which still exists, having been incorporated in the new house, gives some idea of the style of rich decoration of carving and ornament in which it was built. It is said the expense of the building seriously crippled the family fortunes ever after. At any rate, it is certain that when William Forster succeeded his father Humfrey he sold off much outlying property to free the estate of encumbrances.

Wilder MSS.

Amongst other portions of his father's property he parted with Sulham Manor and the land attached to it to a lady, Jane, one of the daughters of Francis Winchcombe, of Bucklebury, who in 1607 acquired it to herself and her heirs for ever. The license to alienate cost £3, and is signed *Bacon*.

Two years later, in 1609, the property is described as in the hands of Anthony Blagrave, Richard Libbe and others; these were probably trustees for the marriage settlement of Jane Winchcombe, who about that time became the wife of Edmund Perkins, the second son of Francis Perkins, of Ufton.

See p. 166.

In 1633 Sir John Blagrave, of Southcott, and Richard Libbe, of Hardwicke, *granted, bargained, sold, alyned, enfeoffed, released, & confirmed, for the sum of £950, unto Thomas Wylder & John his sonne* the manor of Sulham and its appurtenances, of which they were already in occupation as tenants, guaranteeing them against any future claims that might be made by their heirs or the heirs of Jane Perkins, now deceased.

As far as the manor of Sulham, or Nunhyde, was concerned the changes here had an end; but one more deed remains to be quoted, referring to the small property in Ufton. It is dated 1634, September 29th, and in it Thomas and John Wylder, for the sum of £276, grant, bargain, and sell to Wm. and John Parre, various lands in Tilehurst and Englefield, with all that parcell of meadow in Ufton,

conteigning by estimacion two acres ... in Westmeadow, and also all other meadow grounds belonging to Thomas and John Wylder, in the Ufton Westmeade; by this last clause was no doubt intended the chapel close of Ufton Nervet. In 1804, at the time of the enclosure of the common fields, the plot was in the freehold possession of one John Bearfoot. Surviving all these changes, the western wall of the ruined chapel still stands, built of flints and covered with ivy, as shown in the sketch, and is an object easily recognised in the village.

In modern times the parish, which has ceased to exist, has

CHAP. ix. given its name to the united parish now known as Ufton Nervet, while the name of Ufton Robert is quite forgotten.

The Church of St. Peter.

The present parish church is an entirely new building, having been erected in 1861 by Mr. Benyon, the lord of the manor. The old church, as far as one can judge of it from the description of those who remembered it and from existing drawings, had no very good architectural features. A sketch of it, taken by Mr. C. Buckler, is here reproduced, by the kind permission of his son, Mr. C. A. Buckler, *Surrey Herald*.

It will be seen from this careful drawing that the side windows were in the Tudor style; these windows have been built into the present school-house. The porch, and perhaps also the brick tower, were still more modern. If, therefore, one can feel any regret for it, it must be from the fact that, in spite of lack of beauty and accumulated alteration and disfigurements, it was still the old church in which successive generations who have preceded us had continued to worship.

The Rev. Alfred Suckling, in a collection of MS. notes preserved in the British Museum, dated 1838, says of the interior that it possessed few attractions, and that the font was modern; probably the one he saw was the plain round bowl, shown in the illustration at the end of this chapter as lying on the ground. He also says that the windows were unfurnished with stained glass, but mentions one exception. In a window on the north side was a shattered escutcheon of arms: the bearing of the right hand impalement was, according to him, *argent, a chevron between three horses' heads caboshed gules, on the chevron, a crescent of the field for difference*; but he must have been wrong about the heads, for beasts with horns are represented in a sketch in Powell's "Topographical Collections for Berks," here reproduced, as also in Ashmole's MS. Church Notes, Bodleian Library. They are probably intended for oxen. A similar shield with oxen was borne by Sir John Ipre, as described in an ancient roll of arms of the time of Richard II.

A complete list of the furniture of the old church was made by order of King Edward VI., in the year 1553, and is as follows (I quote from Mr. W. Money's *Inventories of Church Furniture in Berks*):

James Russell & Walter Butler, Churchwardens; one chalice waying ix. unces, one olde alter clothe, one whyte vestment of Sattene of Brydges, two olde vestmentes, one Bawdkyne, the other Dornyxe, one front of Satten of Brydges, one olde horse clothe & banner clothes, iiij. olde towelles, one olde napkyne, one olde redd Damaske vestment, one surplice, iiij.⁽ᵉ⁾ lytle candlestyckes, one Byble & a paraphrasis of Erasmus, three olde crosses of laten, one broken payer of Sensers, one oyle bosa, one Ketell, one sakering belle, iij. lytle belles hanging in the belfrey, one lytle belle hanging in S⁽ᵗ⁾ John's Chapel, one lytle sakering belle, three corpores w⁽ᵗʰ⁾ their cases, two cructes, & all the foresaid percelles safely to be kepte & preserved.

The chapel alluded to as St. John's Chapel was on the

CHAP. IX.

ST. JOHN'S
CHAPEL.

north side of the chancel. Its east window and gable are seen in Mr. Buckler's sketch; it contained the Perkins monuments.

The materials named in the inventory are satin of Bruges, and brocades with silver and gold inwoven called bawdkyne and dornyxe; laten is an alloy of copper. The sakering bell, it is perhaps needless to explain, is the bell rung during mass-time at the consecration of the elements; the other little bell may have been for ringing before the sermon, in the manner prescribed in the Injunctions of Edward VI., dated 1549, which also enjoins the use of the candlesticks, that two lights shall be set before the high altar, which was *for the signification that Christ is the true light of the world*, and that the Paraphrasis of Erasmus upon the Gospels in English should be set up in some convenient place in the church that the parson might diligently study the same.

<small>CHAP. IX.
INVENTORY OF CHURCH FURNITURE.</small>

Again, in 1784, another inventory was taken of the church furniture at Ufton. The church is then described as *an ancient building, 87 feet by 19 feet, with a steeple 37 feet high with 4 bells; the chancel 21 feet by 14 feet. To the chancel is annexed a building of the same size, the burial place of the family of the Perkinses, maintained by their heirs.*

<small>Sarum Reg.</small>

There was in the church *an old green pulpit cloth, green baize on the Reading Desk, a very old Bible & a folio Prayer book, twelve hassocks, a surplice, bier, a bason in the font & in the church a green cloth on the communion table & an old coffer; for the communion, a silver cup with a cover, a pewter plate & a pewter flagon, a white cloth & napkin.*

The old church contained many monuments, inscribed brasses, and gravestones. Such inscriptions as are still in existence in the present church are given in the Appendix.

The monuments of the Perkins family in the chancel aisle are described elsewhere in connection with the individuals to whose memory they were erected. Formerly in the same aisle, but now placed in the floor of the tower, is a brass representing the figures of William Smith, who died 1627, aged 70, and his wife, Constantia, daughter of George Tettersale, who died 1610, with the arms of both families. It will be remembered (p. 63) that the widow of William and mother of Francis Perkins married again, in 1562, a Mr. George Tatershale. The age of Constantia Smith is not given; but if she was about 37, she may well have been the daughter of

<small>For inscription see Appendix.</small>

William Perkins's widow and half-sister of Francis Perkins, who himself died in 1616, which would account for her interment in the family chapel.

The present church is larger by a north aisle than its predecessor. It has stained glass in all the windows; those of the nave represent the miracles of our Lord in grisail with a very good effect. The east window of the chancel is of German glass, and was contributed by Dr. Fraser, the then rector, who also gave the reredos of encaustic tiles. The families of the late rectors, Mr. Christie and Mr. Erskine, presented the stained glass of the side chancel windows. One small window at the east end of the aisle, both stonework and glass, was preserved from the old church. It is not very good in style, but has a value as a link left in the broken continuity of Ufton Church. The present font is of the same date as the church. One previously presented by Mr. Christie's family stands in the churchyard (see illustration, p. 198).

On two boards at the west end are recorded the benefactions to the parish. That of Lady Mervyn and of Dr. Fraser, a former rector, and the late Bishop of Manchester, these will be found in full in the Appendix. There is a handsome brass eagle, which was subscribed for by the parishioners to Dr. Fraser's memory. Just outside the church door a splendid old yew-tree overshadows the path, having outlived the chances and changes of many centuries. It measures 15 feet 9 inches in girth, at three feet above the ground. Unfortunately a heavy snowstorm during the winter of 1886 rent away nearly half its branches, though its tall, straight stem still remains.

Of the Parish.

CHAP. IX
THE
REGISTERS.

The Registers.

The registers are preserved from 1636. Though in other respects, complete from this date onwards, there is a marked omission in them which must strike everyone inquiring into the history of the parish; no record of any marriage in the family of the lord of the manor is to be found there. From the time of the Reformation marriage ceremonies of the Old Catholics were in all probability performed in their own private chapels, and as the law did not then require public registration, it is seldom that any written record of these events can be found. In times of persecution no priest would have dared to sign a register, nor any householder to keep such a document in his possession. It was not till the year 1745 that an Act of Parliament was passed obliging all Nonconformists, Roman Catholics, and others to be married and to have their marriages registered in their respective parish churches, all other marriages being declared null and void in the eyes of the law. But this change came too late to affect the present history.

The Rectors.

A full list of the rectors, as far as they have been ascertained, is given in the Appendix. The earliest of whom any mention has been found is one *John, parson of the church of Uffington*, who in 1248 brought an action against the Abbot of Reading concerning a certain pond in Sulhamstead. It was the first of many such disputes; indeed, the history of Ufton affords ample confirmation of the well-known fact that much animosity existed between the secular and regular clergy; irritation being the more easily excited when, as in this case, the monks were landowners connected by obligations and duties to the parish priest, though often divided by separate interests.

In 1255 possibly the same Rector of Ufton claimed from the *Abbot & religious men of Reading certain tithes issuing from lands called Marruge, in the parish of Uffinton, formerly belonging to Simon, son of Nicholas of Bradfield, which the said religious men had brought into proper culture*. The rector maintained that the *small tithes which his predecessors had fully received* therefrom had been unjustly withheld—*to wit, wool & lambs & cheese & young pigs & St Peter's pence*; therefore he demanded restitution. The decision, given by the Archdeacon of Berks, before whom the matter was brought, was that *although the same religious men, by apostolic letters & other muniments, are free & absolved from payment of tithes of the land which they cultivate by their own hands, or cause to be cultivated, nevertheless for the good of real peace* a composition should be made between the parties; that the rector should renounce all claim to the tithes, but that the *religious men, with a view to piety, & lest anything of the question hereafter should be moved by any rector of the church of Uffinton, should pay annually* 2^s. *sterling* (about equal to £2 of our present money) *at the feast of St Michael,* by the hand of their chamberlain, to the said church & its rectors forever.

In 1284 Master Thomas Abberbury was parson of Ufton. He was owed money by a certain William de Cobeham, whereof he was to receive 23 *marks on the Feast of S. Thomas the Apostle next to come, &* 23 *marks on the Feast of the Nativity.* This Thomas may have been related to the family of the same name who were at the time lords of the manor of Donnington, near Newbury.

From 1305 a fairly complete list of the rectors exists in the Diocesan Register at Salisbury. The appointments to the living, first of Ufton Robert alone, and then of the united livings of Ufton Richard, or Nervet, and of Ufton Robert, were, from very early times till the Reformation, generally made by the lords of the manor of Ufton Robert.

The first rector on this list is Walter de Ufton. It seems probable that he was a relative of his nominee, the lord of the manor, William de Ufton. Thomas, son of William de Ufton, was appointed in 1339, after his father's death, by Thomas Paynel, the succeeding landowner. With the exception of these two names and that of Thomas Abberbury above mentioned, there is but little in the surnames of the rectors to indicate from what rank of life they came— whether connected with the land-owning class, or whether, as is still the case in some continental countries, they belonged rather to the peasantry. Evidence seems somewhat to favour the latter view.

It is to be remarked that in early days at Ufton the succession was almost always by exchange. Possibly it was in accordance with the ecclesiastical system of the time that parish priests should not remain long in one place. Three or four years seems to have been a usual length of incumbency. One rector is mentioned as having been dismissed, but for what cause is not divulged.

At the time of the Reformation the Parkyns family, who owned the advowson, remained of the old faith, and henceforth the exercise of their inherited right of presentation was in forced abeyance.

The last nomination to the living made by a member of

CHAP. IX.

THE RECTORS.

the family was in 1566, when Lady Marvyn, widow of Richard Parkyns, acting in accordance with the provisions of his will, instituted one Thomas Presse as rector. A gap then occurs in the list, perhaps accounted for by the fact that at the time there was often great difficulty in finding priests to serve the churches, and to understand and carry out the frequent changes of ritual. The succeeding entry is a complicated one (translated) :

On the 9th August, 1614, the Ven^{ble} Robert Wright, for this turn, as is alleged, by reason of the consignment of the right of patronage by Francis Parkins, Esquire, the real patron, as is alleged, of the said Rectory, to a certain Thomas Elston, one of the ordinary grooms of the chamber to the Lady Elizabeth, lately Queen of England; that concession being duly made, was transferred by the same Elston to the above named D^r. Wright.

Dr. Wright nominated John Wright.

On January 25, 1616, the patronage was retained by the Crown. King James I., *by lapse*, appointed Robert Goode.

The succeeding rector, Marmaduke Goode, is missed out of the register, no acts of institution having been recorded at Salisbury during the Commonwealth—that is, between October 6, 1645, and June 21, 1660.

During his time, which, as has been said, covered the period of the rebellion, there is a corresponding break in the entries made by him in the parish books. He was, in fact, dispossessed for the time, certainly of his office of registrar, and probably also of his functions as parish priest. In 1645 the Prayer Book had been abolished, a new *Directory for Publique Worship* was compiled, and its observance enforced by an Act of Parliament, which further ordained that every minister who should continue to use the Book of Common Prayer should be fined £5 for a first and £10 for a second offence, and afterwards should suffer a whole year's imprisonment.

Acts of Parlt., Scobell, p. 37.

In 1653 a law was passed for the appointment of lay registrars throughout the country, and for the civil registration of births, deaths, and marriages, all other marriages being declared invalid. The registrar was to be elected by the parishioners. In accordance with this legislation, an entry appears in the Ufton parish-book as follows:

John Wickens, of the Parish of Ufton, in the Countie of Berks, is nominated by the paryshioners & approved by one of the Justices of the Peace in the said Countie, to be Tyth Registrar, according to an Act of Parliament bearing date the 21st August, 1653; & hath taken his corprall oath for the trew registeringe of all marriages, births & burials, according to the sayde Act. In witness whereof I have hereto sett my hand the 28th November, 1653. James Phipps.

This description of the office held by John Wickens, as *Tyth Registrar*, seems to imply that the rector, Marmaduke Goode, was not only disestablished, but also disendowed as well.

During the few years following, marriages at Ufton were performed, as directed by the Act, before laymen; in one case a Mr. Humfrey Dolman and in another Mr. James Phipps. Baptisms are not recorded at all; births are simply entered thus: *James, sonne of James Potter, was borne 30th January, 1654*. But in 1660 this double entry appears: *Richard Eagust, sonne of Richard & Mary his wife, borne* ^{bapt} *June 19 1660*. Between those four days the rector had returned or resumed his functions, and the parents of the new-born child had hastened to take advantage of their restored spiritual privileges.

The intimation, as given in the register, is a dry one, but surely something may be read between the lines of the excitement, religious and social, which must then have disturbed the community of this quiet country village.

The Acts of Parliament above alluded to were, together with nearly all, passed during the Commonwealth, rescinded shortly after the restoration of Charles II., and are not enrolled among the statutes of the realm. They may be found, however, among the Parliament Acts of 1640 to 1656, edited by the great lawyer of the time, Scobell.

Thomas Wilson succeeded Mr. Goode in 1678. He also held the living of Coylie, in Glamorganshire, where he died and was buried in 1721. He owed his preferment to the

CHAP. IX.

SALE OF ADVOWSON TO ORIEL COLLEGE, OXFORD.

nomination, as it is said, *for this turn only* of *Elizabeth Aldridge, widow & executrix of Thomas Aldridge, late of Beenham, in the County of Berks.*

Thomas and Elizabeth Aldridge are both buried at Beenham.

In the year 1720 Mr. Perkins, the lawful patron, despairing of the return of a good time and of the old faith, and very much impoverished by the many fines to which his family had now been subjected during more than a century, sold his right of patronage, for the sum of £701 5s., to the Provost and Fellows of Oriel College, Oxford, in whose possession it still remains.

DR. BEKE.

Dr. Beke, who was appointed rector in 1789, says of his two immediate predecessors, Mr. Cooper and Mr. Reade, that they were neither of them residents. He himself took a great interest in the parish, and has left some valuable notes relating to its topography and agricultural condition, from which some quotations have been already made. He was Dean of Bristol, and had been Professor of Modern History at Oxford; he is the author of some well-known works, among them a treatise on the Roman Roads of Berkshire. He was a man of very wide intelligence. The late Provost of Oriel used to say of him that he was consulted by Vansittart when Chancellor of the Exchequer. His soubriquet at Bristol is said to have been *Omniscient.* He was buried at Torquay.

MR. BISHOP.

William Bishop succeeded him in 1819. His name is deservedly remembered in connection with the liberal endowment of £1,000 which he made *for the education of boys & girls of the parish of Ufton, without respect to the religious opinions of the parents,* a benefaction which is still enjoyed. He was the intimate friend of the Spaniard, Joseph Blanco, usually known as Blanco White, whose best known work *Letters from Spain,* by Don Leucalion Doblado, was written during a visit at Ufton Rectory. This remarkable man attracted much attention at the time. He began life as a Spanish Jesuit. Having adopted the reformed faith, he came to England in 1810, took orders in the English Church, and resided for many years as a member of Oriel College, Oxford, of which college Dr. Bishop was then a Fellow. After a time he avowed himself a Unitarian, and gradually passed into rationalism, sacrificing thereby the friendship of many of his former Oxford associates. Archbishop Whately and Mr. Bishop were among the few who remained faithful to him to the end of his life. He died at Liverpool in 1841, aged sixty.

The memory of Dr. Fraser is still too fresh among us to require much notice here from me. He was appointed to the living in 1860. A most kind and liberal heart, a singularly charming and sympathetic manner, and a brilliant eloquence, endeared him both to his parishioners and his neighbouring friends. Nor was he unknown beyond this circle.

In 1862, soon after he had been settled at Ufton, he was offered a residentiary canonry in Salisbury, on condition of his deciding to live there, and in 1866 Lord Cranbrooke offered him the bishopric of Calcutta, but he declined both appointments. Shortly afterwards he undertook a mission to America, under Government, to examine into the educational system of the United States and Canada. He was also desired to report on the state of education in the agricultural districts of England. The lucidity and excellence of his memorandum made a great impression on Mr. Gladstone, who in 1870 offered him the bishopric of Manchester, which he accepted. But during his twelve years of episcopal service Dr. Fraser never ceased to look back at the time he spent at Ufton as the happiest period of his life, and continually sighed after and made plans for a day when he might retire from active work and find a home and rest here. Alas! his untimely death cut short all such plans, and the rest he found here was the grave in the churchyard he himself had chosen in the parish that he had loved so well. Not long before, he had given a last proof of the attachment he felt to the place by the bestowal as a free gift to the parish of an annual sum of £20, to be laid out in the purchase of warm clothing for twenty poor and respectable parishioners, to be chosen by the Rector. He directed that the donation should be distributed yearly in the first week of November, that it might come as a seasonable gift at the beginning of winter. Dr. Fraser, also at his own expense, built the present school-house on glebe land. It will be seen, therefore, that succeeding Rectors have been very liberal out of their private means in contributing to the education of the children of Ufton.

The rectory is a good and comfortable house, part of which is undoubtedly very old; but many additions have been made to it at different times, the last being during the incumbency of Mr. Erskine, 1870-78, who added about one-third to the original buildings. In the garden is a beautiful over-arching yew hedge, at the end of which is a stone arbour, built up by Dr. Fraser out of the fragments of a monument taken from the church, which is described elsewhere (see page 59).

Ufton Common.

At the southern extremity of the parish, where was formerly the highest and most conspicuous part of the common, bordering on the public road which here divides Ufton from Mortimer, is a plot of ground, now planted with fir-woods, still known by the unenviable name of *Gibbet Piece*. There, almost within living memory, stood two gibbets, on which, hanging in chains, and shaking and waving with the wind, were the mortal remains of two criminals executed on the spot within their parish boundary, and in sight of their homes. The printed account published at the time, and the chains themselves, were preserved by some lover of horrors, and are now in the Reading Museum.

The murderers were Abraham Tull and William Hawkins, idle and dissolute lads of 19 and 17 years of age respectively. On February 2, 1787, prompted only by want of money, they conspired to waylay and kill an old man, a labourer like themselves—one William Billimore. They took his silver watch, and, too frightened to search for the money they had hoped to find, they made their escape, but were soon followed and taken, tried at the Reading Assizes, and condemned. After the fashion of the day, a long ballad was added to the printed account of their execution, as follows:

Sorrowful lamentation while in confinement.

> To all young men whose sinful hearts
> Are wickedly inclined,
> These mournful lines are now addressed,
> With anguish in our mind.
> Our parents once did little think
> They nursed us for the tree;
> A warning take, both high & low,
> By our sad history.

And so on *ad libitum*.

These ghastly remains hung on the spot for many years, it being unlawful to remove them, till, as I have been told, the last Mrs. Brocas of Beaurepaire, then residing at Wokefield Park, having been much annoyed and shocked by them during her daily drives, gave private orders that they should be secretly taken down one night and buried, and they were seen no more.

The Hailstorm.

Of the recent history of the parish there is not much to record. On Thursday, June 25, 1762, a terrific hailstorm devastated Ufton and the neighbourhood. It laid waste more than 700 acres of wheat, oats, peas and beans, and, strange to add, hops, which are no longer grown at all in the district. The damage was estimated at £1,143, and so great was the feeling excited by the disaster that, on the representation of the justices of the peace for the county, letters patent were issued by George III. authorizing the parish authorities to make a collection for the relief of the sufferers in all the counties of England, and the town of Berwick-upon-Tweed, and the counties of Flint, Denbigh, and Radnor, in Wales. The King is not said to have subscribed himself to the fund, but he doubts not *but that when these present shall be made known to our loving subjects, they will readily & cheerfully contribute to the relief of their poor suffering brethren.* The money collected was to be paid over to Bernard Brocas,

CHAP. IX.
RECENT HISTORY.

Christopher Griffith, Charles Perkins, Ralph Congreve, James Morgan, Henry Lannoy Hunter, and others, for distribution.

Parish Feasts.

In 1815 a parish feast was given in honour of the Battle of Waterloo. Tables were spread on the green in front of Ufton Court. One parishioner, Mary Bolton, is still living who remembers the event.

Again, in 1863, on the occasion of the marriage of the Prince of Wales, a feast was held, this time in the big barn opposite the Court. It was subscribed for by Mr. Benyon, the lord of the manor, and Dr. Fraser, the Rector of the parish, and his family. Three hundred people were entertained.

Once more, on June 16, 1887, to celebrate the Queen's Jubilee, the whole population of the village sat down in the barn to a good meal of beef and plum-pudding, and spent the rest of the afternoon in sports and dancing. This time the farmers and others contributed, as well as Mr. Benyon and the Rector.

Improved Condition of Parish.

Looking back to the beginning of this century, an examination of the parish books and other records proves beyond a doubt that the population of Ufton is much more prosperous now than formerly. From a book of the topographical details of the county of Berkshire, by J. Marshall, published in 1830, we learn that in 1821 the inhabitants numbered 350, and that the amount expended annually for the maintenance of the poor of the parish, on an average of three years ending Easter, 1825, was £307, and the number of persons receiving relief on the same average was 38. In contrast with this, I have the authority of the late Mr. Bland Garland, Chairman of the Bradfield Union, for stating that, with a present population of 315, the average amount spent on the relief of the poor in our parish for the three years ending in 1888 has been £58.

The reduction of the population is probably caused by the changes that have been lately introduced in the system of agriculture, the use of machinery, and the fact that far less land is now under the plough than was the case fifty years ago. Corn can no longer now be so profitably grown as formerly, and the Ufton farmers have taken largely to producing milk for the supply of the London market.

As to the great difference between the cost of relieving the poor of the parish now and then, it is owing, no doubt, in part to the rise in wages and the cheaper cost of food, but also, in part, to a wiser administration of the poor laws.

We are able, to some extent, to fill in the picture here sketched of the state of our rural population a generation or two back by consulting the parish account books. In the days of John Ballard, *overseere of the Pore,* or, as he elsewhere writes himself, *overseare of the Paris,* his position was not altogether a desirable one; the only wonder is that he was found to undertake it at all, considering the fees of five shillings for which he was liable upon *goin out or quitin offis.* The outgoing expenses which he had to administer came under two heads : *monthly paiments* and *casualties,* sometimes spelt *cacelties* or *colstis.* The first of these were to the paupers of the parish, and apparently a large proportion of the population came under that head, and depended without shame upon the rates for their subsistence. No sooner does one often-recurring name disappear from the list, its owner being laid in the grave, than his son and successor takes his place, whole families thus continuing an hereditary claim to live in poverty and idleness.

And not only necessaries of life were supplied to the pensioners of the parish, but washing and mending was done for them, and such articles as *hankerchefs, apperns, shous* and *stokins, shourtes* and *shifts* were also abundantly provided.

Wages were very low. The parish clerk's yearly "salourrey" was £1 3s ; a waterman for two days' work got 5d., and the cost of *Horshire* (horse-hire) for a day was 1s. *The parish money was widely if not wisely spent,* says Mr. F. Cornish, to

CHAP. IX.
RECENT HISTORY.

whom I am indebted for these extracts from the old church books. The rates were very heavy, though, as the accounts were badly kept, it is not easy to ascertain accurately their amount. In 1781 they seem to have been as much as 7s. in the pound; in 1788 they were 4s.; and in 1801 they rose to 14s. After 1815 they had sunk again to 6s. and 4s. At present they average about 5¾d. in the pound.

As far, then, as money statistics can be taken as a gauge of prosperity and civilization, it must be allowed that the present state of things in Ufton is an improvement on the past; since changes, social and political, though perhaps not always unmixed with evil, have yet brought with them more self-respect and independence, as well as a larger share of the profits of their labour, to the members of our village community.

Appendix.

TABLE OF DESCENT OF THE [
COMPILED FROM HERALDS' VISI[

Peter Morley, *alias* Perkins,
votus to Lord Hugh Desp[
Shipton, co. Oxon; living

Henry Perkins.

John Parkyns, seneschal to Thomas Despenc[

William Parkyns, Lord of Ufton   Robert, M[
Baillieu to Humphrey, Duke of
Gloucester: living 1411-1447.

Thomas Parkyns, living 1452-1479.

John Parkyns,   Margaret Collee, heiress of
living 1495.   -stead and Padworth.

Thomas Parkyns,   Dorothy.
living 1495-1524.

Richard Parkyns,   Elizabeth,   2nd husband,   William Parkyns—Anne, dau. of T[
living 1500-1560.   daughter of   Sir J. Marvyn.   died 1558.   of Bambridge, c[
                    Sir J. Mompesson.

(1st) Francis Perkins,—Anna, dau. of Edmd.   Dorothy.   Gertrude.   Henry Perkins, of [
living 1558-1615.   Plowden, of Ship-   Katherine.   Mary.   Ilsley, co. Berks. of
lake, co. Oxon.   Elizabeth.   Suzanne.
See Perkins of [

(2nd) Francis Perkins,   Margaret, daughter of   Edmund Perkins,—1st, Jane, dau. of
born 1586;   J. Fyston, of Cat-   living 1660.   of Bucklebury, c[
died 1661.   more, co. Berks.   2nd, Elizabeth, dau[
A daughter.   3rd (?), ... Keny[

Francis Perkins,—Frances,   2nd hus-   John Per-   Mary=John Hyde,   Eliza-   Ann[
born 1622; died   dau. of H.   band,   kins, died   of Hyde   beth,   died
1660, before his   Winchcomb, of   James   before   End, co.   died   1078
father.   Bucklebury.   Hyde.   1660.   Berks.   1677

(3rd) Francis Perkins,=1st, Katherine, dau. of Augustus Belson, of Dorking, co. Surrey.
born about 1654;   2nd, Anne, dau. of Richd. Perkins, of Beenham, co. Berks.
died 1694.

(4th) Francis Perkins,=Arabella, dau. of Henry Fermor,   Eleanor,   Mary,   F[
died 1736.   of Tusmore, co. Oxon.   died 1681.   died 1691.   die[

(5th) Francis Perkins,   Arabella,   Henry Perkins,   James Perkins,   Charles Perkins,   John
born 1716;   died 1723.   died 1724,   died 1755.   died 1762.   last o[
died 1750.   aged 7.   died

OF PERKINS OF UFTON
AND OTHER DOCUMENTS

Agnes Taylor.

...living 1307-14...

Edward More, of Wich-
wood, co. Hants.

children: Thomas More — Mary.

                    Sons.   Elizabeth—1st, Scoteville.
                                        2nd, Hobson.

Francis — Anne, dau. Alice Elizabeth — Bartalmewe Christopher Mar-
Parkyns.   of ...   garet.
                                                    Daughter.

William   Frances   Arthur   Elizabeth   Anne   Margaret
Perkins. Perkins. Perkins.

                              Katherine — George Tatter- A daughter   ... Aly...
                                          sall.
... James, of London.
...tation Pedigree, p. 205.   See p. 111.

Edward Eliza-—William   Mar- 1st, John St. George, of Winn—Arthur Main-
Codring beth.   Blunt, of   garet. Hadley, co. Cambridge fred. waring, of
...on, of   Felhouse,   2nd, Col. Butler, of   Bisseth Hill,
...Wilts   co. Berks.   ....   co. Berks.

                    Dorothy.   Katherine, John Wyborne, of Hawkwell,
                    died 1692.   born 1695. co. Kent.

...y 1st husband.   John   Anne Robert   Katherine Philip Jones, of Llan-
                    Wyborne,   Berkeley.   arth, co. Monmouth.
                    died
...beth Mary.   unmarried.   John Jones, of Llanarth,
                                                      succeeded to Ufton
                                                      estates in 1769.

Appendix.

SECTION I.

Note on Chapter I., Page 1.

Paragraphs relating to Ufton in Domesday Book.

In Radinges Hᵈ.   Domesday Book.

Wᵐᵘˢ filius Ansculfi tenet in Offetune, et quidam miles de eo. Herling tenuit de Rege Edoardo. Tunc se defendebat pro quinque hidis, nunc pro quatuor et dimidium. Terra est quinque carucatarum. In dominio est una et octo villani et quinque bordarii cum quinque carucis. Ibi unus servus et 44 acræ prati et silva de 1 porc.

De hac terra tenet alter miles tres virgas et ibi habet caruca. Totum tempore Regis Edoardi valebat 100 solid : et post et modo 60 solid :

Ghilo frater Ansculfi tenet Offetune. Saulf tenuit de Rege Edoardo. Tunc se defendebat pro quinque hidis modo pro tribus hidis et demidium. Terra est quinque carucatarum. Ibi sunt quinque villani et quinque bordarii cum tribus carucis et 36 acris prati. Valuit 100 solid ; modo 60 solid :

Note on Chapter IV., Page 44.

Of the Manors of Finchampstead, Sulhamstead and Padworth.

Manors of Finchampstead, Sulhamstead & Padworth.

Robert Achard, who received from Henry I. a grant of the manor of Aldermaston as *tenant in capite*, had by the same grant received, together with several other manors, that of Finchampstead, and, as it would appear, included with it, Sulhamstead also. It must have been between the years 1118 and 1135 that Richard Achard, son of Robert, enfeoffed two knights, Alard and John Banastre respectively, with these two manors. In Henry III.'s reign a second Robert Achard, the great-grandson of the original receiver of the grant, was chief lord of the fee, and in his time, about the year 1229, Finchampstead was held under him by William Banastre, and Sulhamstead by John Banastre. The name of this latter tenant has been preserved to the present day, attached to the parish of Sulhamstead Bannister.

Charter Roll, 13 Henry III., Part I., No. 22.
Escheq. Black Book, No. 12 f. 38.

Testa de Nevil, pp. 121, 122.

The original deed by Henry I. does not now exist, but it is referred to in a charter, 13 Henry III., in which the King renewed to the second Robert Achard, *son & heir of William Achard*, the grant of *the manors of Aldermaston, Finchamsted, Coletop, Spereshott & Chawelowe, with all their appurtenances, which King Henry, the grandfather of King Henry our grand-*

father, gave to Robert Achard, grandfather of the aforesaid William, father of the aforesaid Robert.

<small>Sarum Reg.</small>

About the year 1290 a second William Banastre, Kt., held Finchampstead, and at his death the estate was divided between his two daughters, who had married two relatives. Agatha, the wife of Peter de la Hoese, inherited the half-manor afterwards known as West Court, and Constance, who married John de la Hoese had the other half called East Court. In 1369 Thomas de la Hoese, grandson of Peter, died without sons, and his daughter Joan, married to John de Colneye, of Padworth, succeeded to the half-manor of Finchampstead (West Court), and bequeathed it to her son, also John de Colneye. He died in 1385, and as his son John was only six years old at the time, the chief lord of the fee, Thomas de la Meere, the then owner of Aldermaston, *by reason of the minority of the said John, son of John Colneye, took the profits of the moiety of the manor of Finchamsted.*

<small>Rot. Fin., 35 Ed. I. (30), v. 307.

Inq. P.M., 43 Ed. III. (51).

Inq. 10 Ric. II., No. 110. Chancery suit.

Feet of Fines, Berks, 2 Hen. VI., No. 4. P.R.O.

Sarum Reg.

Deed of trust quoted in Inq. P.M., 17 Hen. VIII., No. 33.

21 James I., E. 13. No. 63.</small>

This John de Colneye, or Collee, of Padworth, was the same who afterwards, in 1424, with his wife Elizabeth, was party to an agreement with William Parkyns, of Ufton, concerning a settlement of the manor and advowson of Ufton Robert (see p. 41). After him Stephen Collee, presented to the living of Finchampstead as lord of that manor; then the property came to an heiress, Margaret Collee, perhaps the daughter of Stephen, who married John Parkyns, of Ufton Robert. She was possessed in her own right of the fee tail and advowson of Finchampstead, and she bequeathed them to her son Thomas Parkyns and his heirs, who retained the property in their possession till about 1615. In a Chancery proceeding (Tattershall v. Harrison) some years later, Sir Richard Harrison says that *the manor of West Court was anciently the inheritance of Francis Parkins, & that by mortgage or some indirect means it came into the possession of George Tattershall, the said reputed manor being formerly conveyed to some persons in trust for the benefit of George Tattershall's wife and children.*

The other half-manor of Finchampstead, known as East Court, passed by female descent from John and Constance de la Hoese to the Pagenham or Pakenham family. In the sixteenth century the family was represented by the two daughters and co-heiresses of Sir Edmund Pakenham, one of whom, Elizabeth Pakenham, married a Sir Edward Mervyn or Marvyn. He was the uncle of Sir John Marvyn, who had married Elizabeth, daughter of Sir John Mompesson and widow of Richard Parkyns of Ufton. Thus two Elizabeths, Ladies Mervyn or Marvyn, were living at the same time—one, Elizabeth née Pakenham, was heiress of East Court, Finchampstead, in her own right; and the other, Elizabeth née Mompesson, had owned West Court, Finchampstead, by the right of her first husband, Richard Parkyns. They have sometimes been mistaken one for the other.

Appendix.

NOTE ON CHAPTERS IV., VI., AND VII.

Pedigree of Perkins of Ufton (Visitation of Berks, 1623). William Camden, VISITATION Clarencieux, by his deputies Henry Chitting, Chester herald, and John PEDIGREE, Philipot, Rouge dragon, with later additions in italics. Coll. Arms, c. 18, p. 44.

```
           Petrus Morley alias Perkins,=Agnes Taylor, uxor ejus.           Coll. Arms,
   de Com. Salopiæ servus Dni Hugonisde                                    c. 18, p. 44.
   Spenser Dni de Shipton in Com. Oxon.                                    Harl. MSS.,
                                                                           1532, fo. 80;
                                                                           1673, fo. 72;
   |                                                                       Add. MSS.,
   Henricus Perkins, filius Petri=                                         4061, p. 17.
   |
   Johannes Perkins Ar., filius Henrici,=
   seneschallus Thomæ Comiti Glouces-
   triæ 21 R. II. Vixit. p'mo H. IV.
   |
   Will'm Perkins Ar., filius Johannis super-=
   stes 7 H. V.—5 H. VI.
   |
   Thomas Perkins Ar., filius Will'mi=
   38 H. VI., ob ante 18 Ed. IV.
   |
   Johannes Perkins, filius Thomæ=
              |
              Thomas Perkins Ar.,=uxor ejus filia et hæres .... More.
              filius Joh'is
   _____|_____
   |                                   |
   Richardus Perkins, p'mus filius    Willmus Perkins=uxor ejus filia Wells
   obijt sine exitu ux ejus filia                    de Com. Southton.
   Mompesson.                          |
              Franciscus Perkins de Ufton=Anna filia Plowden.
                in Com. Berks Armiger.
       _____|_____
       |                           |                      |
   Franciscus Perkins, - Margaretta, filia Joh.   Edouardus=filia ...
   filius et hæres modo   Eiston de Catmore       Perkins,  Kenyon.
   superstes 1623.        in Com. Berks, Ar.      2 filius.
                                                     |
                                          Edward. James. Francis=Mary, dau. of John.
                                                              John Powell.
   _____|_____
   |                      |              |              |
   Franciscus unicus filius et   (1) Maria.    (3) Anna.    (5) Elizabeth.
   unius anni 1623.              (2) Jana.     (4) Francisca. (6) Margaret.
                                                        FFRAUNCIS PARKYNS.
```

I, George Underwood of Ufton did sett down this name, ffrauncis Parkyns, and I testifie this latter pedigree to be true.

206   *The History of Ufton.*

VISITATION PEDIGREE.

Pedigree of Perkins of Ufton (Visitation of the County of Berks). Elias Ashmole, Windsor Herald, 1664-1666.

Coll. Arms.
C. 12, p. 146.

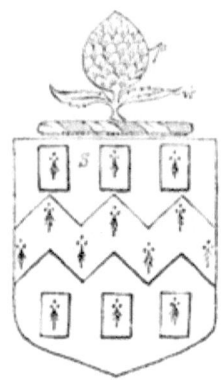

Francis Perkins of Ufton = Margaret, dau. of John Eston, of
in Com. Berks, Esquire. | Catmore in Com. Berks, Esquire.

| (6) Mary, wife to John Hide, of Hide End in Com. Berks. (3) Frances, wife to Edward Codrington, in Com. Wilts. | (5) Winifred, wife to Arthur Maynwarling, of Beech Hill, Esquire. | Francis Perkins, ob. anno 1660. | = Frances, youngest dau. to Hen. Winchcombe, of Burghlebury in Com. Berks. | (1) Anne. (2) Elizabeth, wife of Wm. Blunt, of Felhouse in Com. Berks. | (4) Margaret, wife 1st to John St. George, of Hatley in Com.Camb.; 2ndly to Edward Butler, of . . . . |

Francis Perkins of Ufton,
æt. ij. annors, 25 Mar., 1665.

Copied by Francis Hildesley, on the behalfe of Francis Perkins, now in minority.

Note on Visitation Pedigrees.

It will be seen by a reference to the facsimile drawings from Ashmole's notes (page 56) that the representation of the arms given in these pedigrees is incorrect. In the first quartering the Perkins' arms (see p. 205) are given with six billets. William Parkyns' shield (1411) bore eight, but in after-times ten is the number always given (see also representation of seal, p. 134). The second quartering should have a mullet on the chevron for difference; in the third the cross should be wavy, and not engrailed; and in the fourth there should be nine martlets, 3, 3 and 3.

In the shield attached to the pedigree of the second Visitation the tinctures are wrongly given. They should be or, a fess dancetté ermine between ten billets ermines.

It may be noticed that at neither of the Visitations did the head of the family appear personally to sign the pedigree. On the second occasion he was a minor; but in 1623 the reason may have been that Francis Perkins, being a recusant, was not allowed to go more than five miles from his home without special license.

NOTES ON CHAPTER IX.

List of Institutions to the Rectory of Ofton or Offeton Robert, otherwise called Ufton Robert, Berks; and also to the Rectory of Ufton Richard, Berks. Extracted from the Registry of the Lord Bishop of Salisbury.

INSTITUTIONS TO LIVING OF UFTON ROBERT

Date.	Patronus.	Clericus.
Kalends November, 1305.	Wills de Ofton	Waltus de Ofton per resig Laurentii de Ufton
Kalends November, 1331.	Not mentioned	Hugo de Tychewell per exchange of his church of Hemstede Mareschal with Waltus de Ufton of his church of Ufton Robert
Kalends May, 1339.	Ric Paynell	Thomas son of Willi de Ufton, a priest of the diocese of Sāry to said church vacant
9 Feb., 1380.	Thomas de Cateway	Per exchange
21 July, 1388.	Roger Atteffelde	" "
2 March, 1391.	Thomas Paynell	Robtūs Marchall per exchange with Ric Barbour
24 November, 1402.	Thomas Paynell donzell	Johēs Melham per exchange with Robūs Martall
13 May, 1403.	Thomas Paynell donzell	Johēs Inglewode per exchange with Johēs Matham
15 October, 1403.	Thomas Paynell donzell	Johēs Boteler per exchange with Johēs Inglewode
10 October, 1406.	Thomas Paynell donzell	Johēs Wyrsall per exchange with Johēs Boteler
26 June, 1410.	Alicia Paynell de Ofton Robert	Ric Shabourne per exchange with Johēs Wyrsall
June, 1411.	The honourable man Wm Perkyn Esquire	Ric Fygge per exchange with Ric Sheborn

Date.	Patronus.	Clericus.
23 October, 1414.	Wm Perkyn, Esquire Patron	Thomas West per exchange with Ric Fygge
11 May, 1417.	Wm Perkyn	Radulphus Crowe per exchange with Thomas West
24 March, 1422.	Wm Perkyn, Dominus de Ufton	Johannes Webb
11 November, 1424.	Wm Perkyn donzell, true patron	Nichs Thorp
21 March, 1432.	Wm Perkyn, Armiger	Henricus Couper
8 March, 1434.	Wm Perkyn, Armiger	Willms Fishborne

INSTITUTIONS TO LIVING OF UFTON RICHARD.

List of Institutions to the Rectory of Ufton Richard, Berks.

Date	Patronus	Clericus
Kal February, 1297.	W. de Tothale Prior of the Hospital of St John of Jerusalem England	Michael de la Slane
Kal May, 1306.	Ditto	Rogs de Caumpeden per resig Michās de la Slane
October, 1341.	Philippus de Thame, Ditto	Willm de Churchulle per exchange with Wills Kyng
September, 1342.	Ditto	Walter Poul
13 March, 1361.	Johannes Pavely, Ditto	Johēs Giles per demissionem Walteri ultimi Rectoris
28 July, 1409.	Walter Grendon, Ditto	Johēs Grenelane per exchange with Johēs Housebonde
9 July, 1423.	Henricus Cromvale Preceptor de Tytle & locum tenens of Wills Hulles Prior, etc.	Johēs Caldecott per resig Ricardi Lytilman
13 March, 1424.	Ditto	Wills Reve
20 August, 1429.	Wills Hulles Prior, etc.	Wills Aleyn per exchange with Wills Reve
23 November, 1433.	Robertus Malorie Prior, etc.	Robertus Ros per resig Wills Allen
14 July, 1434.	Ditto	Johēs Wheleton per resig Roberti Rose

INSTITUTIONS TO UNITED LIVING.

List of Institutions to the Rectory of Ufton Robert with Ufton Richard Chapelry.

Date	Patronus	Clericus
12th April, 1452.	Thoma Perkyns, Armiger	Robertus Bolton per mort Fysheborne

Appendix.

Date.	Patronus.	Clericus.	Institutions to United Living of Ufton.
20th June, 1474.	Thoma Perkyn de Ofton Armiger	Willm Clibburn per resig Bolton per proc. Jeromini Hyde alias Sparkeford	
15th December, 1504.	Johēs Perkyn, Armiger	Wills Lee per resig Robert Resum	
23d July, 1507.	Ditto	Robert Halding per resig Willi Lee	
7th April, 1511.	Johēs Perkyns, Generosus	Willm Atkynson per resig Roberti Haldyng	
29 August, 1552.	Johēs Duke	Willus Robertson per mort Incumbent	
22 October, 1566.	Elizabeth Marvin Relict John Marvin Militis under will of Ric. Perkyns Arm., formerly the husband of the said Elizabeth	Thomas Presse per mort Hollwatt	
9 August, 1614.	Venerable Robtus Wright pro hac vice (ut dicitur) Patroni ratione advocationis juris patronatus ejusdem per Franciscum Perkins Arm. Verum dictæ Rectoriæ (ut dicitur) Patronum quidam Thoma Elston uni ordinar. Valetorum cameræ Dominæ Elizabeth nuper Regina Angliæ, etc., et assignatis ejus fact et concess et per eundem Elston prefato Doctori Wright fact et concess	Johēs Wright per mort Nichi Danlow	
25 January, 1616.	The King James I. by lapse	Robertus Goode	
15 November, 1678.	Elizabeth Aldridge Relict and Executrix of Thomas Aldridge, late of Beenham, Berks, deceased, for this turn	Thomas Wilson per mort Marmaduke Goode	

The following list is taken from the records of Oriel College. The advowson of the living of Ufton was bought by the Provost and Fellows of Oriel College A.D. 1720. The price was £701 5s. The presentations by the college have been as follows:

1721. Nicholas Rogers, M.A., loco Wilson defuncti.
1736. Edward Rayner, M.A., loco Rogers defuncti.
1742. Thomas Myddleton, M.A., loco Rayner cedentis.
1756. John Cooper, M.A., loco Myddleton defuncti.
1779. Thomas Read, M.A., loco Cooper defuncti.
1789. Henry Beeke, M.A., loco Read defuncti.
1819. William Bishop, M.A., loco Beeke cedentis.

1846. John Frederick Christie, M.A., loco Bishop defuncti
1860. James Fraser, M.A., loco Christie defuncti.
1870. Thomas Erskine, M.A., loco Fraser cedentis.
1878. Thomas Brooking Cornish, M.A., loco Erskine defuncti.

EXTRACTS FROM UFTON PARISH REGISTERS.

ENTRIES CONCERNING THE PERKINS FAMILY EXTRACTED FROM THE DIOCESAN REGISTER AT SALISBURY, AND FROM THE UFTON PARISH REGISTER.

FROM THE DIOCESAN REGISTER.

Elisa the wyffe of Edmund Perkins was buried the xiijth of September, 1615.
ffrancis Perkins, Esquire, was buried the xxvijth of January ffollowinge.

FROM THE UFTON REGISTER.

Mrs. Margaret Perkins was buried March 5th, 1641.
Winifred Perkins, of Beenham, was buried June 3rd, 1652.
Jane Perkins, of Beenham, was buried Sept. 23, 1652.
Ann Perkins, of Beenham, was buried July 17th, 1654.
ffrancis Perkins, Junr, eldest son of ffrancis Perkins, Esqr, was buried Oct. 9th, 1660.
ffrancis Perkins, Senr, Esqr, was buried Sept. 29th, 1661.
George Perkins, Gent, of Beenham, was buried May 9th, 1662.
John Perkins, of Beenham, Gent, was buried April 21st, 1665.
Elizabeth Perkins was buried May 31st, 1677.
Ann Perkins, Gen^e, was buried May 28th, 1678.
John, the son of Richard & Ann Perkins, of Beenham, Gent, was buried March 31st, 1680.
Eleanor, the daughter of ffrancis Perkins, Esqr, was buried April 28, 1681.
Elizabeth, the daughter of Richard Perkins, of Beenham, Gent, was buried ye S/w under ye window, February 9, 1681.
Frances, the wife of James Hyde, Gent, & mother of Francis Perkins, Esqr, dyed y^e 26th, was buried March 29th, 1686.
Katherine, the wife of Francis Perkins, Esqr, was buried June 6th, 1690.
M^{rs}. Mary Perkins, daughter of Francis Perkins, Esqr, was buried March 22nd, 169$\frac{1}{2}$.
Mrs Frances Perkins, daughter of ffrancis Perkins, Esqr, was buried June 25, 1692.
Mrs Dorothy Perkins, daughter of ffrancis Perkins, Esqr, was buried Jan. 21, 1692.
Francis Perkins, Esqr, dyed Feb. 21, was buried Feb. 27, 1694.
Richard Perkins, of Beenham, Gent, was buried July 23, 1700.
Francis Perkins, of Beenham, Gent, was buried March 25, 170$\frac{0}{1}$.
Ann Perkins, wife to Richd Perkins, of Beenham, was buried May 9, 1701.
Arabella, daughter of Francis Perkins, Esqr, was buried May 22, 1723.
Henry, 2^d son of Frn Perkins, Esqr, was buried March 23, 1724, in the 7th year of his age.
Francis Perkins, Esqr, was buried April 9th, 1736.

Appendix. 211

Mrs Arabella Perkins was buried March 9th, 1737.
Francis Perkins, Esqr, was buried April yᵉ 16, 1750.
James Perkins, Esqr, was buried January 5th, 1756.
Charles Perkins, Esqr, was buried June 1, 1762.
Mrs Mary Perkins was buried August 13, 1768.
John Perkins, Esqr, was buried November 7, 1769.

ENTRIES IN BEENHAM PARISH REGISTER CONCERNING PERKINS FAMILY.

Extracts from Beenham Parish Registers.

John Perkins, Churchwarden, 1658.
Mr Perkins was buried 1676.
Catherine, daur of Francis Perkins, Esqr, and Anne, his wife, was born 1695.

WRITTEN ON THE FLY-LEAF OF BEENHAM REGISTER-BOOK IS THE FOLLOWING (probable date about 1650).

Memorand. There is one Acre that Lyeth in Ufton ffield next to an Acre of Thomas Aldridge on the west side. It is Mr Perkins land, which whole piece is 5 Acres; the Meadow Banke is plowed up which did separate Padworth Tyth Acre from the other ffour. It concerns, that which Padworth clayms for an Acre to the ffarm is more than a fifth part. Measure it.

EXTRACT FROM REGISTER AND NOTES WRITTEN BY F. MADEW, PRIEST AT UFTON COURT.

Extracts from F. Madew's Register.

Francis Perkins Grandfather Died Febᵞ yᵉ ij, 1674.
Francis Perkins, his son, died April yᵉ 5th, 1736.
Mrs Perkins, alias Arrabella Fermer, died Febᵞ 19th, 1737.
Francis Perkins, their son, died April yᵉ 16th, 1750.
James Perkins, Bt, died December ye 25, 1755.
Charles Perkins died May the 21, 1762.
John Perkins, yᵉ last of yᵉ Family, died October yᵉ 30, 1769.

CONFIRMATION AT UFTON COURT SEPT. 2nd, 1749, BY BISHOP CHALONER.

Whitens 3 children, Mary, Elizabeth & Martha.
Jn Marshall's 4 children, Hanna, Mary, Ann & John.
Sarah Parats son Nicolas.
Jane Cowdrays two sons, Francis & William.
John Quine, wife & 4 children, Mary, William, John, Hanna.
Wm Buss's son William.
Rd Danil's children, Martha, Mary, Ann, Charles, George.
Mary Brundels children, Mary, Francis, William.
Total 24.

The Names of Persons belonging to the Ufton Congregation about the Year 1749.

Extracts from F. Madew's Register.

Mrs Prior and her son	... 2	Lewis & George Ham	...	2
Joseph Hannington, wife & son	... 3	Eliz. Newman	...	1
R^d Daniels, wife & six children	... 8	Thos. Whiten, wife & 3 childⁿ	...	5
Mary Brundels & 8 childⁿ	... 9	Jⁿ Marshall, wife & 5 childⁿ	...	7
Mrs Ireland & her nephew	... 2	Jⁿ Peace	...	1
Wm Gosling, wife & 3 childⁿ	... 5	Sara Parrat & 2 childⁿ	...	3
Charles Pearce, wife & 4 childⁿ	... 6	Johana Cowdray & son	...	2
Y^e widow Harle & 3 childⁿ	... 4	Jⁿ Quince, wife & 4 childⁿ	...	6
Ann Amall	... 1	Jas. Quince & wife	...	2
Mrs Berrington & maid	... 2	Humph Buss sen^r	...	1
Fran Alloway & wife	... 2	Wm Buss & child	...	3
Jⁿ White, wife & 5 childⁿ	... 7	Humph Buss jun^r	...	1
Mrs Hocley & maid	... 2	Fran Aldridge	...	1
Sara Leatis or Leaches & 4 childⁿ	... 5	Ann Brown	...	1
Phe Webb, wife & daughter	... 3	Jas. Whiton	...	1
J. Wickens	... 1	In all		...098

INVENTORY OF CHURCH ORNAMENTS IN USE IN UFTON PARISH CHURCH IN 1889.

Church Ornaments.

1 Bible, 1 Prayer-book, 2 Communion-books, 1 book of offices,
1 altar frontal of crimson velvet, 1 ditto of violet cloth,
and 1 ditto of white brocade,
3 pulpit hangings, and 3 pairs of alms-bags,
and 3 sets of book-markers to match.
A brass eagle lectern, 1 alms dish,
1 plated flagon, 1 chalice, 1 paten,
2 fair linen cloths, 2 veils, 1 credence cloth,
1 Bethlehem shell for baptisms,
1 pall, 1 bier, 4 bells and 1 oaken chest, 8 lamps.

There is, besides, an ancient silver Chalice with a cover, which formed the foot for a paten, now broken off. The workmanship is very rough. There are no Hall marks, but the style appears to belong to the eighteenth century.

MEMORIAL INSCRIPTIONS IN UFTON CHURCH.

In a Window in the Perkins Aisle.

✠ Edward, 4th son of Thomas Christie, Esqr, M.D.,
of Cheltenham, and Mary Isabella, his wife.
Major in the Bengal Horse Artillery, wounded
at Chilianwallah 13th Jan., died 15th Jan., 1849.

In a Window in the South Wall of the Chancel.

M.S. Johannis Frederic Christie
Hujus Ecclesiæ Rectoris Posuerunt amici.

In Another Window in same Wall.

✠ To the glory of God & the dear memory of
John Frederic Christie, Rector of Ufton,
and late Fellow of Oriel College, Oxford,
who died Sept. 25, 1860, aged 54, this window,
erected by his widow, brothers and sisters.

On a Brass Plate on the South Wall of the Chancel.

To the honoured memory of
James Fraser, D.D.,
Formerly Fellow of Oriel
College, Oxford, for 10 years
Rector of this Parish,
Afterwards for 15 yrs Bishop of Manchester.
Two of his nephews, Edward Alexander
and Henry Pole Fraser, place this tablet
in grateful recollection of the unfailing
generosity and kindly watchfulness
which ruled his private no less than
his public life. He lies at rest near
the western wall of this church, which
he loved. Born Aug. 18, 1818, died Oct. 20, 1885.

He fed them with a faithful and true heart, and ruled them prudently with all his power.—Ps. lxxviii. 73.

Monumental Inscriptions. MONUMENTAL LATIN INSCRIPTIONS TO MEMBERS OF THE PERKINS FAMILY AND OTHERS.

To Francis Perkins.

(Figure in armour with his wife Anna Plowden, two sons below and arms of the Perkins and Plowden families.)

Hic jacet Fran. Perkins
Si genus a pro-avis spectas (pie Lector) ab illis
Bissenus fuit hic, quem lapis iste tegit
Si virtus candorque parent encomia terris
Hic habet, aut cœlis præmia, certus habet
Jungitur hoc Tumulo, quem struxerat Anna marito
Corpora divisit Mors sociabit Amor
obijt ille 1615 et illa 1635.

To William Smith and Constantia his Wife.

Hic jacet corpus Gulielmi Smith generosi
qui ex hac vitâ migravit decimo
tertio die Novembris Anº
Dñi 1627, ætatis Septuaginta
annorum. Et hic jacet p illum Constantia uxor ejus filia
Georgii Tetershall armigeri illa defuncta anº Dñi 1610.

To Francis Perkins.

(A brass plate in the floor.)

Franciscus Perkins, filius Francisci
et Margaretæ, patre vivente
mortuus, & hic sepultus, anº Dñi
1660 ætatis vero suæ 38.

To Francis Perkins.

(On a marble slab now placed under the altar, formerly in the Perkins Chapel.)

Hic jaceo Franciscus Perkins filius et
hæres Franc. & Annæ qui supra jacent
duxi Margaretam filiam Johis Eyston
de Catmer Armigeri, ipsa genuit mihi
Sex filios, filiasque decem, Amboque sub
hoc Marmore contegimur
Viximus Unanimes Tumulo Sociamur in uno.
Una sit ut requies, det Deus una salus
Obiit decimo nono Septembris anno 1661
ætatis suæ 79.

Appendix.

TO MARGARET, WIFE OF FRANCIS PERKINS.

(On a brass plate formerly fixed on the north side of the above.)

Fr: Perkins, Margaretam uxorem
Alloquitur, In Pace requiesce (dilectissima Conjux) et paulisper
expecta adventum meum, quod si
diutius mansero, hoc divino obsequio
non vitæ desiderio concessum obtestor
obijt primo die Martij an⁰ 1641
ætatis suæ 55.

TO KATHERINE, WIFE OF FRANCIS PERKINS.

(On a stone slab in floor of the chancel aisle.
With armorial bearings.)

Hoc mærens posui
Franciscus Perkins in memoriam
Katherinæ
sub hoc marmore jacentis Filiæ
Augustini Belson
Armigeri et conjugis meæ dilectissimæ
Quæ 18 annos amoris mihi et religionis vinculo
Vincta cœgit, novemque mihi congenuit proles
Fide Felix
Spe Felicior
Vitam hanc utcunque sustinuit meliorem expectans
Quam post diuturnam et asperam ægritudinem
plangente terrâ
Lætante cælo
Obtinuit 1ᵐᵒ Junij Anno Dom̄ 1690
Ora pro ea   Ætatis suæ 37.

Primogenita et in Primis dilecta
Maria Perkins
Genitore abrepta ut cum Genetrice luceat virtutum
Hæretrix tumuli particeps
Filia dilectam sequitur dilecta parentem
Corpora bina lapis non duo corda tegit
Virginitate Candida cœlos decoravit
12 Martii Anno Dom̄ 1691.

TO FRANCES, WIFE OF JAMES HYDE.

(On a small brass slab in floor of aisle.)

Memoriæ Sacrum
Francesceæ Filiæ Henrici Winchcomb de
Bucklebury Armigeri, relicta Francisci Perkins
Subter jacentis cui Unicum edidit Filium. Post hac
connubio juncta Jacobo Hyde Generoso quem

MONUMENTAL INSCRIPTIONS.

Liquit 21 Martii 1686 ut conjugis primæui
tumulo requiesceret
Franciscum sequitur charum Francisca maritum
in cinere ad cineres nil nisi cogit amor
Ætatis suæ 63.

TO FRANCIS PERKINS.

(On a slab in the floor of aisle.
With armorial bearings.)

Sub hoc marmoreo Tegmine placide
occumbunt cineres
Francisci Perkins Armigeri.
Hujus Manerii dominus, qui nondum
Annis preteritis quinque venit ad
Tumulum primæ conjugis Katherinæ
Prope jacentis ex qua unico tantum
filio superstite tam vertutum quam
Patrimonii hærede ; maturæ indolis
Minervæ fecundæ omnique mentis et
Corporis pulchritudine ornato
Relicta vidua Anna filia Richardi Perkins
de Beenham Armigeri ex qua una
Superest filia posthuma
Pulchritudinis et spei maximæ
Justus Pius et Castus
Deo Cæsari et Proximo
Debita cuncta fideliter reddidit
et animam cœlis die 21
Februarii 169$\frac{1}{3}$ anno
Ætatis
Ora pro eo.

LIST OF BENEFACTIONS.

A LIST OF BENEFACTIONS TO THE PARISH OF UFTON.

BENEFACTION OF LADY MARVIN.

Lady Marvin in 1581 Gave 10 Bushels of wheat to be made into good household bread, 12$\frac{1}{2}$ ells of canvass at 1ˢ per Ell for shirts and smocks, and also 12$\frac{1}{2}$ yards of narrow blue cloth at 1ˢ 8ᵈ per yard for coats and Cassocks. She did by her Will charge divers lands and Hereditaments at Ufton and elsewhere with the payment of A sufficient Sum of money to purchase the said Wheat,

Appendix. 217

Canvass and Blue Cloth,
To be annually
Distributed about
the middle of Lent.

THE BENEFACTION OF THE REV. W. BISHOP.

The sum of £1,000 Three per cent consols, bequeathed by the Rev. W. Bishop, formerly Rector of this Parish. The interest of which is annually to be paid to the Rector for the maintenance of the Parish School, A.D. 1847.

THE BENEFACTION OF DR. FRASER, LORD BISHOP OF MANCHESTER.

The sum of £500 in the four per cent. debenture stock of the London and North West'n Raily Company, placed in their hands by the Right Rev. James Fraser, Bishop of Manchester, formerly Rector of this Parish. The interest of the same to be annually expended in the month of November in purchasing warm clothing for 20 poor & respectable people of the Parish. To be chosen by the Rector at his discretion, A.D. 1884.

ON THE FLORA OF UFTON.

The flora of the parish of Ufton is, of course, very much the same as that of the immediately surrounding district. Owing, however, to the great variety in the soil, altitude, and cultivation, or absence of it, within its limits, a considerable number of plants more or less uncommon elsewhere are to be found here. The following is a short list. In the valley of the Kennet: Iris pseudacarous (yellow fleur de luce), the Saggitaria sagitifolia (arrowhead), Eupatorium rapunculus (hemp agrimony), Gentian pneumonanthe (marsh gentian), Lathyrus palustris (blue marsh vetchling), Geranium pratense (meadow cranebill), Campanula rapunculus (rampion bell-flower). In the woods on the high land: Polygonatum multiflorum (Solomon's seal), Epilobium angustifolium (rose bay willow), Galanthus nivalis (snowdrop). Mosses and ferns: Sphagnum moss, Lycopodium selago and inundatum (fir and marsh club mosses), and the Osmunda regalis (royal fern).

RECIPES WRITTEN BY FATHER MADEW, SOMETIME CHAPLAIN AT UFTON COURT.

A Syrup for Consumption.

Take sage, maidenhair, colsfoot, hysop, penny rial, wild time, harts tongue, mousear, oaklungs, of each 4 handfuls, horehound, ground ivy, of each 1 handful, 2 oz. of Pyany root, bruised Elicampane roots, comfrey roots sliced, of each 4 oz.; lickrish stick, enseeds, of each 2 ounces. If the person is far gon put in one p^t of shell snails bruised. Boyl all these in 12 quarts of water till one half is boyl'd away. Then strain it off and put to every quart of liquor, one p^t of good sugar either Lisbon or powder'd, which sutes best with the patient. Then boil it again and scum it—when cold botle it and cork it close, it will keep good a whole year. By this rec^{te} many have been cured when taken in time, and by taking it, many other lives have been prolong'd, though far gone in a consumption.

A R^t to Cure ye Bite of a Mad Dog.

Of ye Leaves of Rue pick'd from ye stalks, six ounces, garlic pick'd and bruised four ounces, Venice treacle four ounces, scrapings of Pewter four ounces, methidate four ounces. Boil these ingredients over a slow fire in 2 quarts of strong Ale till one Pinte is consum'd ; then keep it in a Bottle close stop'd and give of it 7 spoonfuls to a man or woman, warm, seven mornings fasting and six to a dog.

This, the Author believes will not, by God's blessing fail, if it be given within 9 days after ye bite of ye dog. Apply some of ye ingredients from wch ye liquor was strained to ye bitten place.

N.B. This Rec^t was taken out of Cathorp Church in Lincolnshire ; many of ye Inhabitants being bitten by mad dogs. All who took this medicine did well and recovered. The others died mad. It has likewise been found effectual when applied to other animals.

An Infalible Cure for Ague.

Take a point of best brandy, one ounce of best Peruvian Bark, mix them together for any time before ; take of this mixture half a gill every two hours, beginning first an hour before you expect the Fitt, cease taking it while ye fit is on, w^n off take it as above. Keep yourself warm in bed all ye time ; repeat half ye same in ye space of 7 days in ye same manner as before.

SECTION II.

Notes concerning various families of the names of Perkins, Parkyns, and Parkins, of whom records or pedigrees exist as living in England during the 16th & 17th centuries, of which the following is a list :

Perkins of Beenham, Co. Berks.
,, of Wokingham, Co. Berks.
,, of Winkton, Co. Hants.
Parkyns of Madresfield, Co. Worcester, and of Nottinghamshire.
Sir Christopher Parkins.

(The above only, are known or assumed to have been connected with the Ufton family.)

Parkins of Ashby, Co. Lincoln.
,, of Grantham, Co. Lincoln.
Perkins of Llandogo, Co. Monmouth.
,, of Norfolk.
Parkins of Sheffield.
,, of Marston Jabet, Co. Warwick.

DESCENT OF FAMILY OF PERKINS, OF BEENHAM, CO. BERKS.

Henry Perkins, of Ilesley, co. Berks; = Margaret, dau. of William Wayte, of Wymeringe, co. Hants. died before 1591.

Children:
- **Richard Perkins**, of East Ilesley and Beenham, died 1605.
- **John Perkins**, of Beenham, living 1606.
- **Thomas Perkins**, living 1599.
- **Susan** = **Thomas Meysey**, or Meauca, of Ciconebors, co. Worcester.
  - John Meysey, bachelor, aged 80 in 1682 (Visitation Worcester).
- **Ann** = **John Bolney**, of Titehurst.
  - Francis Bolney and others.
- **Mary**, mentioned, as well as her sister Ann, in the will of her grandmother, Ann Wayte, in 1571.

Children of Richard Perkins of East Ilesley:
- **John Perkins**, of Beenham, buried at Ufton 1665.
- **John Perkins**, alias Jennings (perhaps Mr. Perkins buried at Beenham 1676).
- **Richard Perkins.**
- **Francis Perkins** (perhaps F. Perkins, of Thatcham, died 1671, in St. Clement Danes, Midlx. Letters of admon. granted to Margery Nash, alias Whittington, niece, by sister).
- **Katherine.**
- **Christian.**
- **Winifred**, buried at Ufton 1652.
- **Jane**, buried at Ufton 1652.
- **Anne**, buried at Ufton 1654.

Next generation:
- **George Perkins**, bachelor, buried at Ufton 1662; letters of admon. granted to sister Katherine.
- **Elizabeth**, letters of admon. granted to sister Katherine in 1663.
- **Anne**, letters of admon. granted to sister Katherine in 1663.
- **Jane**, letters of admon. granted to brother Richard in 1665.
- **Katherine**, died at St. Clement Danes; letters of admon. granted to brother Richard in 1672.
- **Richard Perkins**, = **Ann**, dau. of John Eyston, buried at Ufton 1700. of Lye Farm, co. Berks.
- **Francis Perkins**, buried at Ufton 1701.

Next generation:
- **John Perkins**, buried at Ufton 1680.
- **Mary**, buried at Brill 1715. = **Maurice Belson**, of Brill.
- **Ann** = **Frances Perkins**, of Ufton.
  - Catherine, born 1695. See page 114.
- **Elizabeth**, buried at Ufton 1681.
- buried at Kemsey 1721. = **Margaret**, = **Wm. Acton**, of Little Wolverton.
  - William Acton. Vincent Acton. Perkins Acton. Barbara.

220

OF THE FAMILY OF PERKINS, OF BEENHAM, CO. BERKS.

The immediate ancestor of this branch of the family was Henry Parkyns, or Perkins, living 1558-1581, who was nephew to Richard Parkyns, of Ufton Robert. He married Margaret Wayte, daughter of William Wayte, of Wymeringe, in Hampshire, and of Ann Mompesson, one of the sisters of Elizabeth, Lady Marvyn. Richard Parkyns, in his will (1560), bequeathed to *my Neve, Harry Perkyns, my manor & firme & tenementes, lands arrable, &c., &c., in Woolhampton, Brympton, Aldermaston & Mygeham, &c., &c.* . . . *& a pasture called Kystlande, & a tenement & certayne messuages with land in Bughulburye*, to be exchanged, however, at the pleasure of his heir, Francis Perkins, for *all my purchased landes in Fynchamsted*. Also he left him *my young trotting colte & the bridell & sadle that was my brother William Parkyns.*

Lady Marvyn in her will, dated 1581, left to him and his wife Margaret a reversionary claim to the property in Wiltshire, which she had settled on Francis Perkins, of Ufton, in case the latter did not fulfil the conditions of the settlement. She also left to Margaret, and her two sons Thomas and John, a life interest in her *farme called Hanginge Langforde in Wiltshire*, and a small legacy of five pounds a year to the other son, Richard. As Henry Perkins is nowhere styled *of Beenham*, the property that his descendants held there was probably acquired after his death.

In 1589 his son Richard was in the Recusant Rolls called *of Ilesley in Berkshire*, and it was stated that he owned *one messuage, &c., called Gardiners Ferme in Beenham & Bradfield*, and also *one virgate of land called Admores*, 8 acres of common meadows, 30 acres of pasture, and 23 acres *in the common fields* (probably of Beenham), *& one tenement & 2 acres in Bucklebury*, all in Berkshire. In 1591-92 he was fined £240 by virtue of the Act of Parliament passed on October 28, 1586, for not having attended his parish church within the preceding twelve months, and another £20 because he had not made submission and become conformable. This Richard Perkins died in 1605. In his will he called himself *of Beenham*, and bequeathed *to the mother churche of Sarum twelve pence, to the poor people of Brympton* (in Berkshire) *twenty shillings*, and some small sums to his sister Ann Bolney and to her children. He mentioned *his loving cosyn, William Wollascott, Esq'., & Ann, the wife of William Wollascott*, and his brother Thomas Wollascott, of Tidmarsh; (his mother's sister, Susan Wayte, had married William Wollaston, of Wollscott, sen'); and he left to his youngest brother Thomas all his goodes not otherwise disposed of. Thomas Perkins was the same who, in 1599, was called *keeper* of Ufton Court on the occasion of the search made there by Sir Francis Knollys' party.

John, the second son of Henry Perkins, and elder brother of Thomas, who is not mentioned in his brother Richard's will, inherited from him the landed property in Beenham and elsewhere. In 1606, just after the death of Richard, he claimed exemption from the fines hitherto levied from his family as Recusants, on the score of his having *conformed*, that is, given in his adhesion to the reformed faith. It was probably his son, also John, who in 1658 signed the Beenham parish books as churchwarden, showing that he, too, accommodated himself to the established religion. John Perkins of Beenham, the second of the name, appears to have had a son, John Perkins, or Jennings. He died in 1665, leaving the main part of his property to his younger brother Richard, and a small, outlying estate in Kent for the use of his other brother and sisters.

Close Roll., 17 Chas. II., Part I., 703.

This estate, consisting of some lands in the parishes of Ivechurch, Old Romney, and St. Martin's Pountney, and of a moiety of the manor called Serry's, or Seare's Court, in the same parishes, had been purchased in 1627 from William Smith, of Pangbourne, and Thomas Purcell, of Okefield, by Francis Perkins, of Ufton, and William Eyston, of Catmore, the parties on both sides probably acting as trustees. The same property of Serry's, or Seare's Court, as it will be remembered, was bequeathed by Sir Henry James to his granddaughter Elizabeth, who had married Edmund, the younger brother of the Francis Perkins mentioned above. In accordance with the will of John Perkins of Beenham this property was sold after his death in 1665 by his younger brother Richard, and the proceeds were divided between his brother Francis and two sisters, Katherine and Christian.

Close Roll., 2 Chas. I., Part XII.

See p. 106.

There is much uncertainty as to the generations of this family, but it seems probable that the Francis here named was the same who died unmarried in the parish of St. Clement Danes, London, and who, in the letters of administration taken out by his niece, Margery Nash, is called *of Thatcham in Berkshire.*

Richard Perkins, the last holder of the property in Beenham, died in 1700. He was buried in the family burying-place in Ufton Parish Church. The following inscription is to be seen on a slab in the pavement:

> Here Lyeth ye bodys of
> Richard Perkins, of Beenham,
> Esqr, who dyed ye 18th of July,
> 1700, and Anne his wife,
> daughter of John Eyston,
> Of Lye Farm, in ye County of
> Berks, Esqr, by whom he left
> Four daughters. She departed
> This life ye 6th of May, in y^e
> yeare 1701.
> Requiescant in pace.

His son had died before him, and his four daughters were co-heiresses of his estates. Of Anne, who married Francis Perkins of Ufton more has been said elsewhere (see page 117). The youngest sister, Margaret, married William Acton of Little Wolverton, in the parish of Kemsey, in Worcestershire, where a monument exists to her memory. With the subdivision of the small property between the sisters, the connection of the family with the parish of Beenham ceased.

OF THE FAMILY OF PERKINS OF WOKINGHAM.

Edward Perkins, of Wokingham.

- **Edward Perkins**, matriculated at Mag. Hall, Oxford, 4 Dec., 1629, aged 17; exo^r to his brother 1671-76. Styled in his will *as of Wokingham, Gent.;* proved 21 Oct., 1687.
- **Other children**, mentioned in will of Ed^d Perkins, senior.*
- **Rev. Benjamin Perkins**, matriculated at Wadham Coll., Oxford, 6 Dec., 1639, aged 16. Styled in his will (proved 10th Nov., 1676) *as of Wokingham, Berks: minister of the Gospel of Christ.*

Children:
- **Edward Perkins, Junr**. Styled in will (nuncup.) 11 April, 1687, *as of Wokingham, co. Berks, gent.* Aff^t of *Edward Hyde, of Wokingham, gent.*
- **Benjamin.**
- **Rebecca.**
- **Martha** = **Henry Savage.**
- **Mary** = **Thos. Simmons.** She admin^d to her father 14 June, 1689.
  - Son, Perkins Symonds.

It will be remembered that a manor in Finchampstead, in the near neighbourhood of Wokingham, had belonged to the Perkinses of Ufton from the time of the marriage of John Parkyns and Margaret Collee (about 1470) till about 1610, when it passed to the Tattersalls. It seems likely, therefore, that the family afterwards found settled at Wokingham were in some way descended from a younger branch of the same family.

* Edward Perkins' will mentions *cousin* (great nephew), *Perkins Symonds, son of my cousin* (niece), *Mary Symonds;* also *my cousin* (niece), *Martha Savage;* also *brother-in-law, Richard Haws, gent.,* and his wife, *Sister Haws;* also brother-in-law, *Henry Haws,* and *Alice Haws, daughter of brother-in-law, Richard Haws;* also to *Margaret Haws, widow, & John Haws, gent., cousin,* are left certain furniture in the testator's house and some chairs in the house of *Mr. Thomas Haws;* also cousins *William, Elizabeth & Alice Haws, son & daughters of my sister, Margaret Haws;* also *cousin Robert Avelin & his sister Abigail Avelin, &* a *cousin, daughter of cousin John Wallis, deceased.* Three of his sisters seem to have married Haws.

DESCENT OF THE FAMILY OF PERKINS OF WINKTON, CO. HANTS.

Edmund Perkins, Esqr, of Winkton, d. 1697. =
- 1st, Barbara, d. of . . . ; died 1686.
- 2nd, Elizabeth, d. of . . . Rivington, widow of . . . Fortescue; died before 10th June, 1696.

Edmund Perkins, Junr, Esqr, over 21 y^{rs} of age 10th June, 1696. =

James Perkins, Esq., of Winkton, living 15th March, 1744; died 1772. — Martha, dau. of . . . ; died 1749.

(The shield on their tombstone in the parish church of Christ Church is as below, showing the same arms as of the Ufton family:)

Edmund Perkins, son of James, arm^r of Winkton, co. Hants; matriculated at St. Mary's Hall, Oxford, aged 18, 15 March, 1744; died 1773.

Thomas Perkins, died 1722.

Two others, who died young.

OF THE FAMILY OF PERKINS OF WINKTON, CO. HANTS.

Edmund Perkins, Esq., styled *of Winckton, Co. Southton*, was living in 1686, when his name appears as trustee to a deed of settlement. In 1696, on the death of his wife Elizabeth, letters of administration were granted to Edmund Perkins Junr, Esqr, son and attorney of Edmund Perkins Senr, husband of the deceased, *now in parts beyond the seas*, during his absence. The cause of his absence beyond the seas is found explained in his epitaph, which among the sepulchral inscriptions in Latin at the Augustine Nunnery, Canonesses Regular, in Paris, Rue des Fossés St Victor. It is as follows (translated):

Here in peaceful sleep from which he will bye & bye be awakened & raised to a life which knows not death, rests a man of distinguished family descent, wisdom & piety, Edmund Perkins of Winton in the County of Hampshire in England. But when the Father of his country was exiled, he too was summoned by him to share his banishment & undertake a most delicate office, that of vice-Guardian & Director of His Serene Highness the Prince of Wales. With what fidelity, industry, care & zeal he discharged the duties of that distinguished & most important office, the singular graces of mind & body which distinguished that most excellent Prince, are a proof which cannot be gainsayed. That young man, His Serene Highness, most miraculously perfect in all respects, is an honour to him who is dead, & invests him with a glory to which nothing can be added to augment it.
He deceased 13 August, 1697.
Rest in peace.

Elizabeth, who died before 1696, must have been a second wife, for, in the parish registers of Sopley, to which parish the manor of Winkton belonged, there is this entry: *Mrs Barbara Perkins wife of Mr Edmund Perkins was buried Oct. 30th 1686.*

The name of Edmund, so persistently preserved in this family, suggests a connection with Edmund, the second son of Francis Perkins of Ufton, and of his wife Anna, daughter of Edmund Plowden of Shiplake. This Edmund is last heard of, in 1660, as living in the parish of Bramshaw, in Hampshire, where, however, he does not appear to have been buried. He had married two wives when still young, who both died before 1616, and he had only one daughter by his first wife; but, according to the Visitation pedigree, where his name is wrongly given *Edward*, he must afterwards have married a lady of the name of Kenyon, by whom he had an elder son Edward (more probably Edmund) and a second son James. These names and the dates correspond very well with the supposition that he was the ancestor of the Winkton family. The expression made use of by his elder brother when he settled a reversion of the estates on Edmund and on his sons *to be begotten* (see p. 111), need not necessarily imply that at the time (1660) he had no sons. It may merely be an accidental abbreviation of the usual form, *begotten, or to be begotten*.

The old manor-house at Winkton, once inhabited by the Perkins family, and called *Akers*, stood not far from the weir, before the building of Winkton House, which now belongs to John Mills of Bisterne.

OF THE FAMILY OF PARKYNS OF MADRESFIELD AND NOTTINGHAMSHIRE.

The arms of Richard Parkyns, as displayed on his tomb 1603.

Thomas Parkyns,=Ellen, sister of John Tompkin, of Knappend, Herefordshire. of Madresfield.

William Parkyns (perhaps trustee to Ufton Settlement 1495, and ancestor of Marston Jabet family).

Humphrey Parkyns.

William Parkyns,=Joan, dau. of —— Reade, of of Madresfield. ——, near Coventry.

James Parkyns, of Shropshire.

Richard Parkyns.

Lawrence Parkyns, twin of Richard.

Humphrey, died 1552.

William.

Humphrey.

Richard.

Christopher.

Richard Parkyns=Anne, daughter of Walter Twymborrowe, of Woodmenton, Hertfordshire.

Richard Parkyns, of Fenny Park,=Elizabeth, daughter and co-heir of Aden Beresford, of Fenny Bently, Nottinghamshire, died 1603. Derbyshire, and widow of Humphrey Barley, of Stoke.

Sir George=Mary, dau. Parkyns, of Ed. Isham, of Kt., died Walmer, 1626. Kent.

Adrien Parkyns.

John Aden=Mary. Parkyns, Parkyns, died 1630.

Frances=John Penruck, of Torlaston, co. Notts.

Anne=Henry Plumtre, of Nottingham.

Eliza.=Geoffrey Pole, of beth. Heage, co. Derby.

Mar—Brether, garet. of Newcastle.

Henry, Eliz., born died born 1608. 1608. 1617.

Richard George Parkyns. Parkyns.

George. Richard. Anne.

3rd son, John, killed at Ashby 1644.

Col. Isham=Mary, dau. of Parkyns, Henry Cave, died 1671. of Barrowe.

Henry Parkyns=Rebecca. Katherine, born 1645.

Edward Parkyns.

Mary=Sir Richard Mynshull.

Penelope, a nun.

Amy, died 1613.

Isabel=——Lloyd. Mary.

Richard Parkyns, born 1633.

Henry Parkyns, died 1637.

George Parkyns, died 1648.

Theophilus Parkyns,=Jane, dau. of Nathan died s.p. 1671. Wright, of London.

Sir Thomas Parkyns, =Ann, dau. and heir of Bart., died 1684. Thomas Cressy, of Berkyn, Yorkshire.

Cressy, died s.p.

Sir Thomas Parkyns, Bart.

Beaumont.

Catherine.

Anne.

OF THE FAMILY OF PARKYNS OF MADRESFIELD AND NOTTINGHAMSHIRE.

In addition to the usual sources of information, there exists concerning the early descent of this family a record of some importance and authority in a grant of an Heraldic crest made in 1559 to *Richard Parkins*, in it styled *of Mattisfelde in Berkshire*. After the usual preamble, *William Herry Esquire als Clarencieux* states that *beinge required of Richarde Parkins of Mattisfelde in the countie of Berks gentleman, sonne & heire to Richard Parkins, sonne & heire, to William Parkins, sonne & heire to Thomas Parkins of Mattisfelde aforesaid, gentleman, to make searche in the Registers & Recordes of myne office for the auncient armes unto hym descended from his auncestors. . . . I could not but allow the same acordinglie & . . . I have ratified & confirmed unto the said Richarde Parkins gent & his posteritie & to all the posteritie of the said Richarde Parkins his father, his said auncient armes, as hereafter followeth: That is to saye, Argent, an eagle displayed sables, in a canton golde, a fess dauncette between seven billettes sables, on eche an ermines. And forasmuch as I found no creaste unto the same (as comonlie to all auncient armes there belongid none), . . . I have given unto hym by waye of encrease for his creaste & cognisaunce, on a wreath argent & sables a pine aple braunche verte, the aple in his proper coullor mantled gules, doubled argente. . . .*

Here it is stated that Richard Parkins, the receiver of the grant, was descended from a great-grandfather, Thomas Parkins of Mattisfelde in Berkshire. This appears to be an error, as there is no place now in Berkshire of that name. However, in a pedigree of early date, preserved in the College of Arms, which is added to Richard Mundy's copy of the Worcestershire Visitation, the same descent is found traced from Thomas Parkins of Mattisfelde in Worcestershire, which place may be supposed to be the same now called Madresfield in that county.

The allusion to Berkshire may be explained by the fact that a descent from the family of Ufton was always accepted as authentic by the Nottinghamshire branch, and that Thomas, their immediate ancestor, was in other deeds actually styled of Ufton as well as of Mattisfelde, suggesting the idea that he may have been one and the same person with Thomas Parkyns of Ufton Robert who died in 1478.

It may be remembered that a John Parkyns had in 1390 acquired a small property in Madresfield, and if, as there seems no reasonable doubt, he was the same as John the grandfather of Thomas of Ufton, he, inheriting his grandfather's estate, would be rightly styled of Ufton in Berkshire and of Madresfield in Worcestershire. It is true that the Berkshire Visitation mentions only an eldest son of Thomas, John, who inherited the manor of Ufton Robert, but the pedigree at this early date makes no mention of any but the son who carried on the direct descent. The Worcestershire pedigree here gives the clue that the same Thomas had other sons, and that to his next son he bequeathed his land in Madresfield, who thereupon became the founder of another branch of the family.

PARKYNS OF NOTTS.

This seems the more probable because the arms originally borne by the Nottinghamshire descendants were identical with the Ufton shield, and not the same as described in the grant by Clarencieux. In Guillim's "Display of Heraldry," 1721, it is stated that the arms of Richard Parkins' descendants were, *or, a fess dancetté between* 10 *billets ermines* (exactly those of the Ufton family), *but of late times, argent, an eagle displayed sable, on a canton or a fess dancetté between* 10 *billets ermines*. Richard Parkins of Madresfield himself treated the shield, described in the Deed of Grant, as a modern one, and on his tomb it is borne in the second quarter (see pedigree, p. 226).

The device adopted for the newer shield, *an eagle displayed sable*, was evidently taken from the first of the Ufton quarterings namely, that of the heiress wife of William Parkyns (living 1411)—showing that the Madresfield family claimed descent from that early ancestor, but not from his grandson John, son of Thomas, whose descendants quartered also the wavy cross of Collee.

Although Clarencieux describes the compound arms as *duly registered and recorded in the registers & recordes of myne Office*, it is certain that this was only an official form. There was no record at that date in the Heralds' College, nor is there now, of those or of any other arms belonging to any family of the name. The practice of the heralds was to require some proof of arms having been used, and then to allow them as *found registered*.

Thomas Parkins, of Madresfield, the ancestor of the family, had three other sons besides William ; James, who was the probable ancestor of the numerous families of the name afterwards found in the district between the borders of Shropshire and Gloucestershire ; Richard, who was the father of a William, probably the same who appears not far south as the ancestor of the Monmouthshire family, who claim to be descended from Perkins of the north, and who had a grant of similar arms and crest ; and Lawrence, a twin-brother of Richard (see pedigree, page 226).

Richard, the grandson of William, and great-grandson of Thomas Parkins, of Madresfield, was a barrister of the Inner Temple, London. He married, about the year 1570, Elizabeth, the widow of Humphrey Barley, of Stoke, in Derbyshire, and daughter of Aden Beresford, of Fenny Bentley, Co. Derby. By an agreement with her late husband's brother, who succeeded to his estates, she had one of the manors of Bunny, in Nottinghamshire, for her life in lieu of her right of dower, the reversion of which manor her husband afterwards purchased, as also the other two manors in Bunny and that of Bradmore, so becoming the owner of the two entire parishes.

He was recorder of Nottingham, and probably owed the appointment to local influence or to his great professional reputation, for the post was much sought after in those days, and he was preceded and succeeded in the office by members of two powerful ducal families. He was also, in 1575, chosen recorder of the borough of Leicester ; he was justice of the peace and *custos rotulorum* for the county of Nottingham, and for many years of his life member of Parliament for the town.

In 1600 Richard Parkyns made a settlement of his estates on the occasion of the marriage of his eldest son, by which, in default of his own children, they were to go to a cousin, Christopher Parkyns, with a remainder to Francis Parkyns, of Ufton, who was also appointed trustee under the deed.

In 1603. *Queen Anne* (wife of James I.) *& Henry, her son, the young Prince, in their travel from Newstead to London, came through the town of Nottingham, & on their entryment at Cow Lane, Richard Hurt, the Mayor, & Richard Parkyns, Esq*, then Recorder, the Aldermen, Council & Clothing, all in their scarlet gowns, & forty of the best commoners carrying Halberts, Her Majesty was received with an oration by the Recorder, expressing the most happy benefits of Her Highness' presence & delightful aspect of the Royal Issue, which being ended, M*r* Mayor presented unto the Queen a large Cup, with a cover of silver, & of the value of £22, & likewise gave to the young Prince a purse with 20 double sovereigns in it, the purse being of value 20. This done, the presents were carried by the Mayor & a gentleman before the Queen into the town. On Thursday 23*rd* of June: The Queen & Prince Henry came from Ashby to Leicester. Memo: that there was no oration made to the Queen, for the Recorder, for that purpose, came that Thursday morning from Boney, fell sick at Leicester, where he remained sick till Sunday next after, then went home sick.* He died on the 3*rd* July, 1603.

PARKYNS OF NOTTS.

Nichol's Progresses.

In his will, dated January 14, 1603, he directed that his body should be buried in the chancel at Bunny, *with some monyment*. After devising his estates, he bequeathed to his wife, among other legacies, *all the pales, waynscot, & glass* in the manor house for her life, and that after her death they were to go as heirlooms to the family. From this it would seem that wainscot, or carved panelling, was often not a fixture, but could be taken down and put up again like tapestry, and left away from the immediate heir. *Pales*, which were probably the carved balustrades of the staircase, and the glass (stained glass) appear to have been regarded in the same way. He left a gold ring, which was his mother's, and three bed-testers, *one of purple velvett embroidered with gold, another of green velvett, & another of blewe velvett, with their curtains & vallances*, to his eldest son, George.

Sir George Parkyns, Knight, the eldest son of Richard, was admitted to the Inner Temple, November, 1587. He was Member of Parliament for Leicester in 1597, and was knighted at Whitehall on July 23, 1603, at the same time with his relative Sir Christopher Parkyns, both being described as *of Kent*. His connection with Kent was in right of his wife, Mary Isham, who had inherited the manor of Walmer through the families of Fogge of Ashford, De Criol, and Auberville, which last-named family had held it from the Conquest. Sir George Parkyns was styled *Captain of Walmer Castle*. He was Sheriff of Nottingham in 1613, and died in 1626.

A True & Perfect Inventorie of the Goodes, debts, & chattels of this Sir George Parkyns, now existing, contains some curious items illustrative of the manner of living of the day and the money value of property.

The wearing apparel and three trunks are valued at £120; while all the horses in the stable—three old horses, three of the best geldings, three mares, three of the worst geldings, five young colts and fillies, and two other *nagges* and a mare, are all together only valued at £61; and of the cattle, *two greate bulles & three heffers* were worth £12. *All the fixtures about the walls in the dyninge Parler, one pair of verginalles & two other instruments*, are priced £3 6s. 8d. Other musical instruments are mentioned—a *rvall* and a *cytheron*. There was a very good supply of linen for the table and beds, and also of pewter dishes, basins, candlesticks, and pots. *All the books in the*

PARKYNS OF NOTTS.

Studdie, with other implements of household, were worth £2. There were *paycocks* in the yard, and of coal, which had not then been long in common use, there was £10 worth in the *colehouse*.

Isham Parkyns, the eldest son of Sir George, was born on October 27, 1601.

After his father's death he had much trouble and dispute with his mother, who was *inveigled to be a Popishe Recusant,* her daughters and younger sons following her, under the influence of her son-in law Sir Richard Mynshull, *an eminent Popishe Recusant, & most active in that Religion & in the enlargement of the Professors thereof;* and there followed a complete estrangement between them and the eldest sons, Isham and Richard, who remained staunch Protestants. George, the youngest son, declared that before he or his mother knew of the father's death Isham had entered the house at Bunny, made away with his father's will, and removed £6,000 in gold, besides jewels and other property; and he, on the other hand, petitioned Parliament against the sale of lands belonging to his grandfather, Edward Isham, which should have been his. He declared that Sir Richard Mynshull had *gotten most parte of the monie by the sale, & of the residue is parte sent over beyond the seas to the Seminaries & Nunneries of the English there, & parte bestowed upon Jesuites & Seminary Priestes within the Realme.*

Isham Parkyns was High Sheriff of the County of Nottingham in 1629-30. He was commissioned captain to command the horse forces of Nottinghamshire, and afterwards was made colonel in the Royal Army, and appointed governor of the castle of Ashby-de-la-Zouche. He held this fortress against the Parliamentarian forces till the last, when its surrender was arranged between Lord Hastings, then commander-in-chief of Royal Armies, and the Parliament.

Nichol's Hist. of Leicestershire.

Whitelock, p. 162.

20 June, 1645. *Sir Thomas Fairfax's army marched from Leicester & sate down before Ashby, which for several months was closely besieged. In September the town was much visited by sickness, & the garrison reduced to* 60 *men. . . . In the following January this garrison made several successful sorties, but on the 7th, at night, a strong body of horse came from Leicester undiscovered, surprised the sentinels, fell in at the turnpike, broke the chain, took much pillage, & returned to Leicester without opposition. After this, the following articles of Surrender of this " Maiden Garrison"* (*so styled from never having been actually conquered*) *were sent up to Parliament; and after a debate whether the sequestration of the Earl of Huntingdon, the Lord Loughborough, & Colonel Perkins, the Governor, should be taken off, were agreed to by both Houses.*

The terms were that *they were to march out with all the honours of war, with horses, arms, & ammunition, bagg & baggages, trumpets sounding, drums beating, colours flying, matches lighted at both ends, muskets loaded, &c., &c.*

Isham Parkyns' cousin John Plumtre was killed in one of the fights near Ashby.

Theophilus, the eldest son of Isham, married Jane Wright, spinster, aged twenty, *orphan of the City of London, daughter of Nathan Wright, late of the said City, with consent of the Court of Aldermen,* but died without children before his father, in April, 1671.

Isham Parkyns died in 1671, aged seventy; and Thomas, his second son,

Appendix.

succeeded, and was created baronet by Charles II. on account of his father's services in the defence of Ashby.

Sir Thomas Parkyns, the son and successor of the above, was the author of a book on wrestling called ΠΡΟΓΥΜΝΑΣΜΑΤΑ, *The Inn Play or Cornish Hugg Wrestler*, of which art he was a great proficient. In Thornton's History of Nottinghamshire it is recorded that he studied physic for the benefit of his neighbours, and had a perfect and complete knowledge of all parts of mathematics, especially architecture and hydraulics. He died in 1741, and was buried in Bunny Church, under a monument, still existing, which he himself had designed, representing his own statue in a wrestling posture with Time.

<small>Parkyns of Notts.</small>

<small>Thornton, Hist. of Notts., vol. i., pp 95-97</small>

OF SIR CHRISTOPHER PARKINS.

This man's remarkable career may be summed up in the words of John Chamberlain, when, in writing to his friend, Dudley Carleton, and recording his death, he described him as *Jesuit, Doctor, Dean, Master of Requests, & what not*. He was one of the clever instruments chosen by the astute Lord Burleigh and his still more talented son, Secretary Cecil, afterwards Lord Salisbury, to do the work of the Government, of which they took the credit and their royal mistress reaped the glory. A great number of his letters are extant, preserved at Hatfield, in the Record Office, and elsewhere, showing that in all questions of foreign policy, especially connected with trade, his advice was sought and his diplomatic skill employed, though he himself was generally in the background, or occupying a subordinate position.

The exact relationship which he bore to the Perkins of Ufton is not clearly ascertained—in fact, his parentage has been hitherto an unsolved riddle, baffling the researches of more than one genealogist. He was probably more nearly related to the Parkyns of Bunny, in Nottinghamshire, themselves descended from the Berkshire family (see page 227). In a deed of settlement, dated 1600, Richard Parkyns, of Bunny, gave a reversion of his estates, after entailing them on his own children, to Christopher and his sons, if there were any, and, failing them, lastly to Francis Parkins, of Ufton. The widow of the same Richard also calls him in her will *her worshippful cosen, Sir Christopher Parkins*.

He was born about 1557, and went up to Oxford when he was probably about 14, where he took his degree as Bachelor of Arts on April 7, 156?. Then he abruptly left England, and on October 21, 1566, when he was 19, he joined the Society of Jesus, which at the time was gaining very numerous disciples among young men of birth in the country. He is next heard of at the Jesuit College in Rome; then he seems to have gone to study divinity at Dillingen, in Bavaria, where a Jesuit College had been founded in 1552, that he might be assistant to Jac de Valentia, at Ingolstadt, and he continued there till 1580. He afterwards went to Cologne and many places in Germany, and finally returned to Rome. He was still there, when there arrived in the city Mr. William Cecil, afterwards Lord Exeter, grandson to William Lord Burleigh, with whom he made great friends. Foley says that Mr. Perkins was very useful to the young nobleman in various obliging offices; and even, according to an account given by Anthony Wood, he saved his life by giving

<small>Sir Chris. Parkins</small>

<small>Foley's Records, vol. ii., p. 240.</small>

<small>Oxoniensis, f. 94.</small>

SIR CHRIS. PARKINS.

him warning that there were whisperings in the English College of doing him some mischief, in revenge for what his grandfather had done in apprehending several priests and putting them to death. When Mr. Cecil had seen the monuments, therefore, *Mr. Perkins did conduct him out of the City, & being a man of very great understanding, & Mr. Cecil delighting much in his company, he persuaded him to accompany him to England.*

Strype's Annals, vol. iv., p. 1.

Landsdown. MSS. No. 61, p. 58.

It is clear that Christopher Parkins had at that time broken with the Jesuits, but it does not appear equally certain that he actually then returned home, for in June, 1589, he was still abroad; and Sir Edward Kelly reported from Bohemia, judging him no doubt from his antecedents, that he was suspected to be a Jesuit, and to have spoken treason respecting a plot to murder the Queen. In August of the same year Dr. Dee, from the Low Countries, reported the same thing, having heard from Kelly that Perkins was returning to England *viâ* Dantzic in disguise. It gives some idea of the condition of danger and precaution in which Elizabeth lived, for fear of plots against her life, that his journey home was so watched and reported on. On his arrival he seems to have been at once arrested, and kept in confinement in a private house, Alderman Ratcliffe's, which was called *the Three Cranes*, and was near the Exchange, under suspicion of his possibly treasonable intentions.

Dom. State Papers, Elizabeth.

From there he wrote letters to Sir Francis Walsingham in March, 1590, and also to Sir Thomas Hennedge, of the Privy Council, urgently pleading his innocency, and imploring that he might be set at liberty, and employed abroad in the service of his *Prince & Countrye, where,* he says, *I may do much good & no harme, rather than that I be here, contrary to all desert, consumed with sorrowfull Idelness.* Especially he suggested that he should be employed to help the Lords of Elbinge and the Company of Merchants concerning their residence in Poland; the merchants of York had also desired his help with the Duke of Russia, for which missions he would be the more useful, as he had horses and coaches and other necessaries of his own in those parts in readiness. He intimates that he owes his imprisonment to the ill-will of Sir Edward Kelly, himself influenced *by his friends & ghostly Fathers, the Jesuits, who had vowed theyr endevor to troble thys estate & all its well willers.* Very soon afterwards, perhaps owing to the favourable interest of his former acquaintance, Mr. William Cecil, he obtained his desire, and on May 9, in the same year, was entrusted with a mission to Poland and Prussia, with an allowance of £300 for the charges of his journey. From that time forward he was constantly travelling to and from the continent on the queen's service; sometimes on matters of shipping interest, as when an English barque, the *Salamander*, had captured a Danish vessel and brought it to Cork and afterwards to Kinsale, where the goods not being found *just prize*, compensation was offered to the captain, who most inconsiderately refused to accept it, pretending he had been *greatly damnified* by being brought there.

While negotiating on another occasion, also with the Court of Denmark, concerning the evil doings towards England of a certain Mons. Hennison, he gives an account of an uproar in Copenhagen. He had demanded of Wolkendorf, the Minister, in the name of Elizabeth, not only that restitution of certain losses should be made, but that Hennison, *as likely to do much mischief, should be cut off.* Accordingly he was put to death. But the nobility of Denmark had been *so wrought upon by a licentious tumult in the last Parliament, that Lord Wolkendorff was faine to leave his offices of Treasurer & Governor.* Then a great multitude met in triumph, took up Hennison's body, & buried it with great pomp, restoring him his honours with a favourable golden Inscription.

In August, 1594, he writes to Lord Burghley commenting on letters written in Elizabeth's name to the Margravine of Anspach and his wife, and encloses one written by himself in another form for approval. In November, to Sir Robert Cecil, he sends a letter he has written in Latin for *certayne hyr Maties service in Moscowe, the which, my lo: y^r father thoght too good for that countrye.* The signature of this letter is here reproduced.

SIR CHRIS. PARKINS.

In 1596 he was apparently sent to Venice as bearer of a letter from Elizabeth on certain matters of dispute between herself and the Republic. She specially wished them to forbid to their own ships all intercourse with Spain, and on such conditions she expressed herself willing to assist in capturing and sending back to Venice one Ottavio Negri, who, it seems, was being prosecuted for embezzlement of money by a Venetian senator of noble birth, Joanno Bassadona. Several letters on this subject are preserved among the archives in Venice; from the last, dated 1599, it appears that as the Venetian Government had declined, though politely, to interfere with the freedom of their commerce, Elizabeth, on her side, had refused to give up the criminal whom they claimed. He was then in prison in England, and she represents that the Republic should certainly provide for his maintenance. He being so poor as to be in debt for 180 *mine* to the keepers of the prison for his maintenance, *who cease not,* she adds, *daily to clamour to her for payment.*

Venetian Archives. Lettere di Principi.

In a letter dated Nov. 10, 1595, Christopher Perkins mentions a pamphlet which he had written from Venice about the Jesuits, and also concerning the pope and his religion, of which, he says, he wrote with the respect and caution necessary for his safety.

But in nearly all these letters, besides treating of public affairs, he deals largely with his own claims for further remuneration. In December, 1591, he had received an annuity of 100 marks, but this, he repeatedly urges, was quite insufficient for his wants; and, as he says in one place, *I, who do whollie attend to hyr Maties service, yet am not able therebye to mayntain myself with gode Order, but I am faine to relie oppon good Mr Alderman Ratcliff for comons & lodging oppon grownde of his courtisie.* He appears to have lodged habitually whenever he was in London with his host of former days, and from Alderman Ratcliff's house all his home letters are dated. From other notices of this person elsewhere, it seems that, either he kept an open hostelry or that,

SIR CHRIS. PARKINS. at all events, his house was a usual lodging-place for persons engaged on the queen's service. For the unseemly state of things which he described Christopher Parkins suggested many remedies. His well-wishers thought that he might be placed among the Masters of Requests and Chancery; or, as he said, *Their lack no livings in commonwealles fit for men that spend their tyme in learning & applie themselves to serve.* He had now, in 1594, for five years —the tenth of his life—been in probation attending to the occasions of the queen's service; and *Iff the Deane of York, of Eton, or some like, might be preferred to some better place to their content, some such living without cure would be as fitt for me as another.* Elsewhere he asks for the promise of St. Cross or of the Deanery of Durham. Or that, *as it hath been usuall to have two latine Secretaries, the Elder I thinck for Countenance, the other for labr, who now is in place seemeth willing to be eased. So that the Simples, Promicion, Title of Service, & the man are at hand, there only wanteth some happy hand to make the Composition.* So *in summe* he earnestly beseeches Lord Burghley to favour and recommend his promotion.

In 1596 the death of Sir John Wooley, also a layman, made a vacancy in the Deanery of Carlisle, and Christopher Parkins was appointed his successor. In 1599 he was admitted to Gray's Inn, and also to Doctors Commons and the Freedom of the Clothmakers' Company. In 1600 he was already one of the Masters of Requests, the others being Sir Sydney Montague, Sir Lionel Cranfield, and Sir Ralph Freeman; in 1601 Elizabeth appointed him her Latin Secretary, and in 1603 he was knighted by James I. It was probably then, that he obtained a description of his arms by Mercury Patten, Blue mantle. They are as represented in the accompanying drawing. The three

shields are in the original on three separate pages of a small vellum book, and are described as follows: *He beareth or, a fess counter indented between nine byllets ermines. His crest is a pine-apple or, leaved vert, mantled gules, doubled argent. He beareth sable, a chevron, between three eagles argent, membered or.* The shield, which is here wrongly attributed to Gervace, is the same as that quartered with the arms of William Parkyns, of Ufton, on the monument (see page 56), showing that Christopher claimed a descent from the Ufton family before the time when the latter had taken the Collec arms also into their shield. SIR CHRISTOPHER PERKINS.

Meanwhile Sir Christopher had been employed on many missions. In 1598 he went in company with Lord Zouch as ambassador to Denmark, to assist him with his advice and experience; and when the Danish Commissioners came afterwards to London, he, with Dr. Herbert and the Bishop of London, was appointed to receive them. He was, later on, spoken of as likely himself to be sent as ambassador to France, but whether he actually went there does not appear.

A contemporary writer, Dr. Goodman, said of him: *Truly he had a great understanding; & I have sometimes sate by him when he hath read his petitions & epitomised them,* as Master of Requests, *& therein he had an excellent faculty.* Goodman's Court of James I., vol. i., p. 329

Besides all his other gifts he was a very good Latin scholar, and the author of some Latin plays, etc.

In 1608 he was named as one of the supervisors of the will of Elizabeth Parkyns, of Bunny, the widow of Richard, and the mother of Sir George Parkyns, the other supervisor being one of the Beaumonts of Leicestershire; and it may have been partly in this way that he made acquaintance with his future wife. In 1617, when he was above sixty and still a bachelor, he was married in the Church of St. Martins-in-the-Fields to Anne, widow of James Brett, of Hoby, in Leicestershire, and daughter of Anthony Beaumont, of Glenfield, in the same county. She was sister to the Countess of Buckingham, the mother of George Villiers, first Duke of Buckingham; and her daughter by her first husband had married Sir Lionel Cranfield, as it will be remembered, one of the four Masters of Requests, and who was afterwards made Earl of Middlesex. She was, in fact, a very highly-connected lady. Perhaps Sir Christopher hoped by her means to have gained further promotion; but if so he was disappointed, whether, as has been said, because Buckingham was scandalized at the breach of his vows of celibacy, or because he feared his rivalry with the king, or from other causes. Certain it is that Sir Christopher Parkins rose no higher. Nor did he in any way apparently add much to the happiness of his declining years by his marriage. Anthony Wood records that he had made it a condition with his wife that he should not be expected to pay her old debts; but that after marriage they did not agree about money matters, and that out of revenge he, in his will, bequeathed all his estate to an old servant, only leaving his wife 100 marks. He died September 1, 1622, and is buried in Westminster Abbey, without a monument, on the north side of the long aisle.

In his will, after giving directions that he is to be buried in St. Peter's, Westminster, he bequeaths £25 yearly to the University of Oxford, "*where I was sometime bred,*" for the increase of the stipend of the professor of divinity. To his wife, all the goods that she brought, also some silver plate,

SIR CHRIS- and, at her own choice, either the third of the estate usually awarded to the
TOPHER widow, or 100 marks, or an annuity. He mentions his sisters' children and
PERKINS. their grand-children. "*And forasmuch as I was admitted, first to Gray's Inn,
then to Drs Commons, & lastly to the Company of Clothworkers,*" he bequeaths
to each of these £10, to be paid within six months after his death.

His manor of Paddington and his house in Channon Row is to be for the enjoyment of A. Bright, also all rents due from Carlisle, Henham, and *Paddingdeane*. He appoints the Archbishop of Canterbury to be the supervisor of his will, and in consideration "*I give his Grace the greatest gilt Cup I have, with the cover shutting thereunto.*"

PARKINS OF ASHBY, PARISH

[Ric... of Ashby, par. of Bottesford, co. L... dated 2 Oct., 1539; proved 27 Ma...

[William, under 21 in 1539.]   Richar... under 21,

[... Elizabeth Parkins, w... co. Linc., April, ...

Visitation of Lincoln, 1634.

Richard Parkins, eldest son, s.p.

William Parkins, of Ashby, co. Lincoln; 2nd son; descended out of Yorkshire. [Buried at Bottesford 7 March, 1608-9.] [Son and h., William, aged 18 and over, 1609.]

Edith, d... at Bar... Feb., co. Li...

William Parkins, of Ashby, eldest son in 1634. [Proved mother's will 12 Feb., 1633-4; will, as of Ashby aforesaid, gent., dated 20 Aug., 1658; proved 14 July, 1660; "my sister Parkins of Hull." (W. P. aged 18, 1609.)]

Elizabeth, dau. and heir of John Good, of Ounby, co. Lincoln. [Buried at Bottesford 21 June, 1653.]

John Parkins, 2nd son. [Died before 18 Feb., 1632-3.]

[William. Edith. Elizabeth. All under 21 in 1632-3.]

.... [? widow, " of Hull," 20 Aug., 1658.]

Mary, youngest daughter.]

2

Richard Parkins, son and heir, 18 years old (in 1634). [Matriculated at Oxford from Lincoln Coll. 13 December 1633, aged 17; proved father's will 14 July, 1660.]

William, 2nd son in 1634. [Not 21 in 1632-3; died before 19 July, 1637.]

[John, baptized at Bottesford 30 October, 1619, and buried there 26 Sept., 1621.]

3

Edward Parkins, 3rd son in 1634. [Married at Messingham, co. Linc., 15 Jan., 1654-5; was of Ashby, gent.; buried there 19 Jan., 1666-7.]

[Anne, wid. of Godard Gravenor, Esq., of Messingham, co. Lincoln.]

=[Thos. Marshall (3rd husb.), of Reasby, co. Linc., gent.: married at Bottesford 9 July, 1672.]

[John, baptized at Bottesford 3 Nov., 1625; buried there 14 Dec., 1625.]

[Dorothy Caster (1st wife), of Bottesford; married there 30 Sept., 1690; buried there 15 Dec., 1692.]

[Edward Parkins, baptized at Bottesford 23 July, 1664; buried there 30 March, 1701.]

[Hester Hill (2nd wife), married at Lilyborough, co. Lincoln, 2 Feb., 1694-5.]

[Anne, baptized at Bottesford 31 March, and buried there 1 April, 1692.]

[Richard, baptized at Bottesford 4 Feb., 1695-6, and buried there 23 Feb., 1696-7.]

[Matthew, baptized at Bottesford 21 Sept., 1697.]

Visitation of Lincoln, 1634 (Coll. Arm., C. 23, fol. 74).
With additions in [ ]

Parkyn . . . . . dau. of John Atkinson;
dn; will he living in 1539.]
1541.

Katherine,   Anne,
not 21, 1539. not 21, 1539.]

, buried at Bottesford,
(P. R.).]

d Edmund Morley, of Holme, co. Lincoln. [Baptized   John Parkins, 3rd son.
by R. Beck, co. Linc., 26 April, 1574; will dated 18   [Living 18 Feb.,
3; proved 12 Feb., 1633-4; buried at Frodingham,   1632-3.]
, 18 May, 1633.]

Richard Parkins, 3rd son. [Susanna . . .] [living   William, official of Ashby.   Elizabeth [married at Bot-
iving, youngest son, 1632-3.] 1632-3; ? "of Hull."] [Living 18 Feb, 1632-3.]   tesford 4 Aug., 1614, and
                                                                                buried there 3 July, 1651.]

        [Elizabeth. Susanna. Editha.   See Parish Registers of Bottesford
        All under 21 in 1632-3.]   and grandmother's will.

	[Henry,	[Robert,	Francis, 5th	[Thomas,	[William,	[Arthur,	Alice [baptized at
e, 4th	baptized at	baptized at	son in 1634.	baptized at	baptized at	baptized at	Bottesford 22
1634.	Bottesford	Bottesford	[Baptized at	Bottesford	Bottesford	Bottesford	Aug., 1621; mar-
ed at	4 Oct.,	29 Sept.,	Bottesford	21 July,	10 July,	13 Aug.,	ried there 26 Oct.
esford	1629;	1631; not	24 May,	1635; living	1637; not	1639, and	1640, to Ralph
Nov.,	buried	named in	1634; living	20 Aug.,	named in	buried there	Johnson, gent.;
, living	there 18	father's	20 Aug.,	1658, as	father's	May, 1640.]	both living 20
Aug.,	July, 1630.]	will.]	1658.]	youngest	will.]		Aug., 1658,
58.]				son.]			with issue.]

[OTHER NAMES FROM PARISH REGISTERS OF BOTTESFORD.]

Married. 1610, July 10, John Parkins and Katherine Mauger.
    „   1618, Aug. 2, John Parkin and Katherine Warde.
    „   1652, April 23, Richard Kirke and Mary Parkins.
Baptized. 1604, July 2, Beatrice, dau. of Edmund Perkins, gent.
    „   1605, Sept. 2, Katherine, dau. of Edmund Perkins, gent.
    „   1610, Aug. 1, Henry, son of Richard Parkin.
    „   1611, Dec. 9, Francis, son of Richard Parkin.
Buried. 1633, May 18, Edyth Parkyns, of Ashby, buried at Frodingham.
    „   1639, Aug. 31, Elizabeth, dau. of William Parkins, gent.

PARKINS OF GRANT

Parkins of Yorkshire.

[Joan (2nd wife), dau. of .... buried at Grantham 6 April, 1602.] = Robert Parkins, of ..., co. Linc., Esq., J.P. ... odd years old. [... Grantham 11 Dec., ...]

Robert Parkins, of Grantham. = Gertrude, dau. of Geor... Barrowby, co. Linco... at Grantham 21 July, ...

[Dorothy (2nd wife), dau. of .... buried at Grantham 27 June, 1653.] = William Parkins, son and heir [signed Pedigree in 1634]; of Grantham. [Living 31 Dec., 1655; buried at Grantham 9 Jan., 1667-8.]

Elizabeth, dau. of William Marshall, of Bottesford. [Buried at Grantham 29 Oct., 1643.]

[John, baptized at Grantham 4 Sept., 1603.]

[A child, buried at Grantham 27 Sept., 1604. ? son John.]

[Anne, baptized at Grantham 2 Feb., 1605-6, and buried there 29 Aug., 1607.]

[Gertrude, baptized at Grantham 1 Aug., 1607.]

[Christian, a dau., buried at Grantham 29 April, 1610.]

William Parkins, son and heir apparent; 5 years old in 1634. [Living 31 Dec., 1655; baptized at Grantham 5 July, 1629; buried there 25 Jan., 1692-3.]

[Mary, dau. of ...., buried at Grantham 21 Jan., 1674-5.]

Eliza beth.

Gertrude [baptized at Grantham 1630; married there 24 Sept., 1653, Mr. Thos. Hurst.]

Sarah [baptized at Grantham 27 April, 1634, and buried there 13 Aug., 1655.]

[Sarah More, of Boston, married 18 June, 1661.] = John (2nd wife), dau. of .... Thompson, married at Grantham 7 Aug., 1673.] = (Anne),

[Robert Parkins, baptized at Grantham 13 March, 1637-8; Town Clerk of Grantham; buried there 25 March, 1685.]

[Dorothy, d... of .... Wort, of L... don, wid... of Richar... Thorold, ... Grantham ... buried the 6 Nov., 16...]

Robert Parkins, baptized 9 Dec., 1670; buried 28 May, 1672, at Grantham.]

[William Parkins, baptized at Bourne 20 April, 1660; Rector of Colsterworth, instituted 5 June, 1690; also Rector of Boothby Paynell, instituted 1692; died 17 June, 1720, aged 60; buried at Colsterworth.]

[Faith, dau. of .... buried at Grantham 12 Jan., 1731-2.]

[James, baptized at Grantham 27 Dec., 1667.]

[James Perkins, died 8 Oct., 1695.]

[Henry Hopkinson, M.A., Rector of Pattrington, co. York.] = [Faith, married at Grantham 4 Aug., 1731.]

CO. LINCOLN.

Visitation of Lincoln, 1634. With additions in [ ]
from Parish Registers, etc.

m,─[Anne], (1st wife), dau. of . . . .
Wright, of Swinstead, in Holland.
[Buried at Grantham 19 March, 1590-1.]

. . . . Graves,─Alice,
of co. Notts.

| | 2 Robert Parkins, [baptized at Grantham 20 Dec., 1601; living 31 Dec., 1655.] | [George, baptized at Grantham 29 April, 1613; buried there 23 May, 1614.] | 3 Wyatt Parkins [(signed Pedigree 1634); baptized at Grantham 20 Dec., 1611; will as of Spalding, co. Lincoln, gent., dated 31 Dec., 1655; proved 13 May, 1656.] [Buried at Spalding as Wyatt Parkins, Esq., 3 Jan., 1655-6; mentions "Sister Pedder," "my son-in-law, my nephew, Wm. Offer."] | [Joanna, dau. of William Slater, of Pinchbeck, co. Lincoln; proved first husband's will 13 May, 1656, and daughter Anne's will 26 April, 1660.] | =[Edward Sturton (2nd husband), gent.; married at Spalding, co. Lincoln, 11 July, 1658; living 25 Nov., 1659.] |

| 3 Wyatt Parkyns, [baptized [at] Grantham [ ] Oct., 1640.] | [Slater Parkins, baptized at Pinchbeck 8 June, 1645; buried at Spalding 19 Aug., 1675.] | ─[? Catherine . . . . ? 26 May, 1676; mar. licence, Vicar-General, for Catherine Perkins, of Pinchbeck, widow (aged about 25), to marry Michael Lister, of Burwell, co. Lincoln, Esq., widower, about 38.] | [Gertrude, buried at Pinchbeck 16 April, 1651.] | [Anne, not 18 in 1659; buried at Spalding 7 March, 1659-60. [Will, 25 Nov. 1659; proved 26 April, 1660, unmarried.] | [Joanna, not 18 in 1659; marr. at Spalding 9 May, 1667, to Edw. Tilson, of Boston, gent.] | [Constance, not 19 in 1655; died before 25 Nov., 1659.] | [Bevill Wimberley, gent.] | Isabella, born 14 and baptized 20 Oct., 1654, at Spalding; married at Pinchbeck 30 May, 1673; her admon. 31 May, 1686; granted to her husband.] |

| , baptized , 1661 ; 1 Jan. -3, at tham.] | [Robert Parkins, of Grantham, attorney, baptized there 18 Jan., 1664-5.] | ─[Mary, dau. of . . . .] | [Elizabeth, baptized 22 March, 1662-3, at Grantham.] | [William, baptized at Grantham 1 Oct., 1666.] |

PERKINS OF PILSTON, PARISH

Visitation of Monmouthshire, 1683 (Coll. of Arms, K. 6,

* By a pedigree produced by Mr. Pe[rkins]
is made to be the eleventh in descent fr[om]
paternally descended from Kynedd Av[...]
who was paternally descended from B[...]
Britain, and the arms underneath are [the]
arms of Perkin ; but although it be an[...]
seem to deserve much credit.

*William Perkin, of Pilston, in parish of Landogoe, in co. Monmouth. === .... dau. of ....

    Richard Perkin === Marian, dau. of Thomas Catchmay, of Michell Troy.

    Christopher Perkin === Jane, dau. of Christopher Hall, of High Meadow, in co. ...., Esq.

William Perkin, of Pilston, living 1647. [Will, as William Perkins of Pilson, par. of Landogo, co. Monmouth, gent., dat. 16 Dec., 1647; proved 10 May, 1648; mentions grandchildren Sarah and Martha Perkins.] === Ellinor, dau. of George Catchmay, of Biggesware, co. Gloucester, Esq.

Children:

1	2	3	
Edward Perkin, living 1647; died about 1650; age about 66. [Will as Edward Perkins, of Pilston, co. Monmouth, gent., dated 16 May, 1653, and proved 6 Sept., 1654.]	Mary, dau. and heir of Roger Morgan, of Llanvrethva. [Proved husband's will 6 Sept., 1651; living 4 Nov., 1666, and apparently 17 June, 1667.]	George Perkin, of London. [Richard Perkins, of Pilstone aforesaid, but died at Whitehouse, Cwmcarvan, co. Mon.; a bachelor; admon. 3 Aug., 1672.]	Moor... co. Glamorga[n]... Dec., 1647; w[...] Edward's will administered to 3 Aug., 1672.]

1	2	3	4
Christopher Perkin, of Pilston, co. Monmouth, died June, 1667; age about 31. Will as of Pilstone, gent., dated 4 Nov., 1666; confirmed 17 June, and proved 11 July, 1667.	Cecill, dau. and co-heir of Wm. Morgan, of Pencraig, in the parish of Lanhanog, in co. Monmouth.	Elizabeth, m. Edw. Reynolds, of Llantrishan, co. Monmouth. [She living 1647; both living 16 May, 1653; he proved brother-in-law, Christopher Perkin's will 11 July, 1667.]	Margaret, m. 1st, Wm. Jeyne, of Brockware, co. Gloucester; 2nd, David Jenkins, of Mamlylad, co. Monmouth; 3rd, Henry De la Hay, of the family of Halteremmes, co. Hereford. [She living 16 Dec., 1647; she and husband William Jeyne both living 16 May, 1653; she proved brother Christopher's will as Margaret Delahay 11 July, 1667.]	Jane, m. 1st, Mr. White, of Huelsfield, co. Gloucester, gent.; 2nd, Robert Jones, of the Grony, co. Monmouth. [She living 1647; she and husband Edward White both living 16 May, 1653.]	.... = Edmond [...] (1st wife), dau. of .... Green, of Cardiff, co. Glamorgan, r.p.	St. Nila[s] Glamorg[an] about 40 [...] [Living 1647, not as of St... dated 8 [...] proved 5 [...] 1691.]

Edward Perkins, of Pilston, co. Monmouth, aged 23 years 1683. [Only son in 1667; not 18; to go to Oxford; will, as of Pilstone, Esq., dated 17 Sept., 1700; proved 11 March, 1702-3.]	Cecill, dau. of Richard Guillym, of Whitchurch, co. Hereford, Esq. [Living 17 Sept., 1700, and her mother Margaret.]	Mary, m. George Bond, of Redbrooke, par. of Newland, co. Gloucester. [Only dau. in 1667, and not 18 years old.]	John, died very young.	Cecill, died very young.	Margaret, died very young.	

Cecill Perkins, a daughter, only child, aged 1 year in 1683.	[Christopher Perkins, proved father's will 11 March, 1702-3.]	[Edward, living 1700, under 21.] [1716, Edward Perkins, of Landogo, and Elizabeth Catchmay, married 24 May.—From Par. Reg. of Hewelsfield, Harl. Soc., Visitation of Gloucestershire, note, p. 242.]	[Richard, living [...] 1700, under 21.]

.ANDOGO, CO. MONMOUTH.

8, 229]. With additions from Wills, etc., in ( )

his first William Perkin lt. Prince of Merioneth, King of North Wales, Great, King of Great lepicted as the paternal er pedigree, it does not

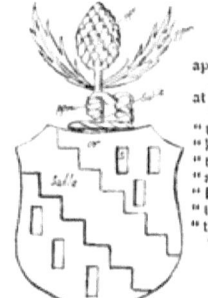

Arms.—Or, a bend indented between 6 billets sab.

Crest.—A right hand proper, ruffled sab. grasping a pine-apple and branch proper.

A scutcheon of these arms was produced by Mr. Perkins at Monmouth 8 Sept., 1683, thus attested.

"The armes and crest of William Perkins, of Pilston, in "the countie of Monmouth, gent., son of Christopher Per-"kins, of the same place, which Christopher descended from "the family of Perkins, of the North, who justly bear these "armes here depicted, which armes, together with the crest, "I do hereby ratify and confirm unto the said William and "to the several descendants of his body for ever, bearing "their due differences according to the Law of Armes.

"In witness whereof I do hereunto set my hand, A° 1634.

"(Signed),
"RI. ST. GEORGE CLARENCIEUX,
"Kinge of Armes."

| , of Silly, living 16 to brother y, 1653; Richard | ...., dau. of .... Matthews and sister of Humphrey Matthews, of St. Nihilt, co. Glamorgan. | Anne, wife of Richard Herbert, of Caldicott, co. Monmouth. [Living as Anne Herbert 16 Dec., 1647.] | Elizabeth, wife of Thomas Phillip, of Tal-y-van, co. Monmouth. [Living as Elizabeth Phillips 16 Dec., 1647.] | Mary, wife of David Edwards, of parish Cwmcarvan, co. Monmouth. [She living and married 16 Dec., 1647.] |

| s, of co. ed 83. will co. nt., and | Bridget (2nd wife), dau. of Captain ... Vaughan, of Bristol, s.p. [Admon. as of St. Nyll 27 March, 1673.†] | Elizabeth (3rd wife), dau. of John Walter, of Persefield, co. Monmouth, Esq. [Proved husband's will 5 Nov., 1691.] | William Perkins, of Silly, co. Glamorgan, Mon. [Living 16 Dec., 1647, under 21.] | ...., sister of Griffith Thomas, of Hendrey Skithan, co. Glamorgan. | Matthew, living unmarried in 1683. | Elizabeth, m. Griffith Thomas, of Heandry Skithan, co. Glamorgan. [Living 16 Dec., 1647, under 21.] | Frances, m. Edward White, of Huelsheld, co. Glamorgan, gent. | Anne, m. 1, Thos. Nicholls, of Llantwidd, co. Glamorgan, and after to John Wilkins, of same. | Jane, m. Edward Nicholls of Eglws Browise co. Glamorgan. |

| ibeth, very ing. | Christopher [eldest son in 1691; matriculated Jesus Coll., Oxon., 10 Oct., 1696; aged 18]. | John [youngest son in 1691]. | Moor Perkins. | A daughter. |

iving .]

† Admōn. 14 Dec., 1672, of Bridget Perkins, al' Vaughan, of St. Nyll, co. Glamorgan, widow, granted to her brother Herbert Vaughan. The later administration, 27 March, 1673, was probably to correct this mistake.]

OF THE PARKINS OF NORFOLK.

(From the Visitation of Arms, 1664.)

Arms, Or, a fess indented between 8 billets ermines.
Crest, a pineapple proper.

Gresham Parkins, of Butley, co. Suffolk. = Dorothy dau. of Sir John Gilbert, of co. Suffolk.   Coll. Arm, D. 20, p. 126.

|
Charles Parkins, of Coxford, in East Rudham, co. Norfolk, gent.; signed the pedigree in 1664. = Dionis, dau. of Thomas Tyrrel, of Gipping, co. Suffolk, Esq.

Gresham, son and heir, aged 12 in 1664. | William. | Charles. | John. | Dyonis. | Mary. | Selia.

OF THE PARKINS OF SHEFFIELD.

Coll. Arms.
Chaos I.,
p. 137.

Thomas Parkin, of Sheffield, = ... dau. of ... Bosseville, by Mary, dau. of John Rawson, of Walkley, near Sheffield.

- Thomas, died without issue at Sheffield.
- William Parkin, ironmonger in London, fined for sheriff; died without issue in London.
- John Parkin, of Bristol, = dau. of ... Worgan, of co. Somerset.

Elizabeth Parkin, died unmarried May, 1666; possessed of the manor of Ranfield, co. York, and a very great estate by purchase, left to her mother's sister's son, Walter Oborne.

A daughter, married ....

PARKYNS OF MARSTON

John Parkyns, seised of the manor of Marston Jabet, co. Warwick, in 1544; will dated 26 July, 1557; died 7 Aug., 1557. [Will, as of Marston Jabbet, parish of Bullington, Warwick, yeoman; proved 26 Oct., 1557.] = Emott, living 1569-70. [Proved husband's will 26 October, 1557. Will dated 12 Jan., 1568.]

[Richard Parkyns, will (dated 22 March, proved 13 Dec. Burton Hastings, co. Warwick, husbandman, mention...

[Thomas Parkyns, will (as of above) proved 1559. = Dorothy.

Joan = John Purefoy, of Ansley.
  |
  Elizabeth.

[Michael. John. Jane. Anne. Isabel.
These six children of Thomas P. all under age 22 M...

1 William Parkyns, of Marston Jabet, son and heir, aged 35 and upwards in 1557; died 31 July, 1582. = ...

2 John Parkyns [living 1557 at Marston aforesaid].

3 Alexander [living 1557].
  |
  (Elizabeth.)

5 Oliver Parkyns [living un... married 1557. Executo... to mother's will 1568.]

Thomas Parkyns, of Marston Jabet, son and heir, aged 24 and upwards in 1582; aged 65 in 1619; died 24 June, 1633. = Anne, ... Sutton ...

William Parkyns, son and heir, aged 28 in 1619; aged 42 and upwards in 1633; died about Aug., 1663. [Proved son Samuel's will 28 May, 1650. His will, as of Burton Hastings, co. Warwick, gent., dated 5 April and proved 4 July, 1661.] = Joane, dau. of Humphrey Staunton, of Longbridge, co. Warwick, gent. [Living 26 March, 1650.]

2 Valentine = Ellen, dau. Parkyns, of Thomas of Marston, aforesaid. Shilton, of co. Leicester.

Ri... [Will as of Nuneaton, 23 Feb., 1634-5.] Zacchæus Parkyns, son...

1 William Parkyns, son and heir, aged 3 years in 1619; in 1640 seised of manor of Marston aforesaid; aged 66 in 1682, and J.P. for co. Warwick. = Elizabeth, dau. and co-heir of Robert Reynes, of Stanford, co. Notts, Esq.; married 1640. [Living 26 March, 1650.]

2 Samuel Parkyns, aged 3 months, 18 Sept., 1619, ob. s.p. [Will, as of St. Saviour's, co. Southwark, woodmonger, dated 26 March, and proved 28 May, 1650; mentions uncle, Joseph Muston, and cousin, Anne Pierce.]

3 John Parkyns, of Atherstone, co. Warwick. [Proved father's will 4 July, 1661; living 9 Aug., 1666.]

4 Nathaniel, of Thames Ditton, co. Surrey. [Proved brother Thomas' will, 9 May, 1667.]
  |
  [Nathaniel, living 9 Aug., 1666, not 21 years old.

... (?) [living 9 Aug., 1666.]

5 Thomas, d. bach. [Will as of St. Giles', Cripplegate, London; living in Threadneedle Street, grocer, bach., dat. 9 Aug., 1666; pro. 9 May, 1667.]

Joseph = Venour, of co. War., gent. [Living 9 Aug., 1666.]

Ab... age... year... 16... [Li... 26... 16...

(Isaac, liv... 1661 an... 1666.]

Sir William Parkyns, one of the six clerks in Chancery; aged 32 in 1682. [In Mar. Lic. "of Inner Temple, Bachelor, about 24;" knighted 10 June, 1681; hanged and quartered at Tyburn 3 April, 1696, for conspiring to kill King William III.] = Susan, dau. and co-heir of Thomas Blackwell, of Bushey, co. Herts. Esq. [Mar. Lic. Faculty 26 June, 1673, of St. Giles-in-the-Fields; spr. about 22; consent of mother, a widow; living 23 April, 1721.]

1 2 Thomas, d. bach. married Hannah, dau. of Fran. S... of Bedworth, co. Warwick, by Mar... of Thomas Mill, of Polesworth, co. wick, and that she was living 168... 30.]

Blackwell Parkyns, aged 4 years in 1682. [Will, as of Leicester Grange, co. Warwick, Esq., dated 23 April, proved 8 Aug., 1721; d. 17 July, 1721; Mt. in Burbage Church. (See Nichols' "Hist. of Leicestershire," vol. iv., p. 465.)] = [Barbara, and siste... thwaite (... husband's...

[? Parkyns (not named in father's will)

[Joseph Parkins, of M... (Coll. Arm. MS., J.P. 9...

BET, CO. WARWICK.   245

Arms.—Sab. an eagle displayed argent, on a canton of the second a fesse dancettée of the first.
Crest.—Out of a ducal coronet or, a unicorn's head.
[The above arms granted to Sir William Parkyns, 11th July, 1682.] (v. Grants, vol. iii., 153.)
On the tomb of Blackwell Parkyns (son of Sir William Parkyns), in Burbage Church, Leicestershire, the above coat appears quartered as the "modern" coat.
1 and 4, Gules a chevron between 3 escallops, argent (ancient).
2 and 3, as above (modern).—Nichol's "Leicestershire."

Visitations of Warwickshire, 1683. Coll. of Arms, K. 3, pp. 100-1, with additions from Wills, etc., in [ ].
In the Visitation of Warwickshire, 1619 (published by the Harleian Society), the name is spelled Perkins.

57); as of . . . John. . . . =Henry Wise.]

gues.]
1557.

[Richard, proved father's will 1557.] [Thomas, living 1557.] [Elizabeth,=. . . Jerom, living 1557.] [Margaret,=Thos. Myles, living 1557.] [Agnes,=. . . Brodgate, living 1557.]

. . . William Roberts, of . . . ney, co. Leicester.   Anne=Barnaby Holbech, of Filloughley, co. Warwick.

Parkyns, living in 1619. Warwick, 1 Jan., proved . . . heir, aged 2 years 1619. (See below.)   Mary, dau. of John Wright, of Nuneaton, co. Warwick. [Proved husband's will 23 Feb., 1634-5.] Two other sons, living 1634-5.   Winifred, m. Sampson Wood, Rector of Fawsley. [Living, his widow 26 March, 1650.]   Mary, m. Thos. Wilmore, of Huningham, co. Warwick.   Sibill, m. George Pegge, of Burdesley, co. Warwick.

Richard Parkyns, of Burton Hastings, co. Warwick, gent., *ob. ante* 1682. [Will as of same, gent., dated 3 Sept., proved 17 Nov., 1658.] Rebecca, aged 4 years in 1619; d. before 1682. [Married *ante* 1650; proved husband's will; living 5 April, 1661; *ob. ante* 9 Aug., 1666.] [Joseph, living 26 March, 1650.] [Zacchæus Parkyns (1st husband, her cousin, son of Richard Parkyns, see above); living 26 Mar., 1650, and died before 1661.] [Mary, living 9 Aug., 1666.] [John Luntley (2nd husb.), living 5 April, 1661, and 9 Aug., 1666 (then called Luntby).] [Hannah, ux. Anna, living 26 March, 1650, then ux. Abraham Wright; both living 9 Aug., 1666.] [Peter Venour (1st husband) living 26 Mar., 1650.] Elizabeth, living 9 Aug., 1666. Arnold Stone (2nd husband), living 5 April, 1661, and 9 Aug., 1666.

. . . Robert, living 1682. Joseph, d. bach. Dorothy. Anne, living 1682, m. Matthew Smith, of the city of Coventry, gent. Susanna. Elizabeth. [Richard, living 1658, and 5 April, 1661, as eldest son.] [Other issue, in 1658.] Elizabeth, living 1650, and 5 April, 1661. Mary, living 1650.

of Thos. Micklethwaite, Joseph Viscount Micklearm. J.P. 90*). Proved 8 Aug., 1721.]   William, aged 2 years in 1682.   Susan.

[Barbara, living 1721, but cut off with 40s.]

Appendix.

SECTION III.

A ROLL OF THE PIONEERS OF NEW ENGLAND OF THE NAME OF PERKINS.

The account here given of the early settlers in America of the name of Perkins, offshoots from families living in England at the beginning of the seventeenth century, has been supplied by Mr. D. W. Perkins, of Utica, New York; as collected from the following authorities:

1. James Savage's "Genealogical Dictionary of the First Settlers of New England."
2. John Farmer's "Genealogical Register of the First Settlers of New England."
3. Dr. George A. Perkins' "Family of John Perkins of Ipswich, Massachusetts."
4. Augustus T. Perkins' "Private Proof of the Perkins Family."
5. Joseph B. Felt's "History of Ipswich, Essex, and Hamilton."
6. Miss F. M. Caulkins's "History of Norwich, Connecticut."
7. William B. Weeden's "Economic and Social History of New England."
8. E. De V. Vermont's "America Heraldica."
9. "The New England Historical and Genealogical Register."
10. "The Historical Publications of the Essex Institute, Salem, Massachusetts."
11. "The Records of the Governor and Company of the Massachusetts Bay."
12. "The Ipswich Antiquarian Papers."
13. "The Hammatt Papers."
14. James Savage's edition of John Winthrop's "History of New England."

Of the social status of the founders of New England, Mr. Vermont, in "America Heraldica," says: "The great emigration led by Winthrop included among its numbers a considerable proportion of gentry recognised as such prior to their departure from their early homes. The remainder were men of respectable position—yeomen, tradesmen, and mechanics, but most evidently not of the lowest class, for in those days colonists must have required a large sum of money to equip a vessel, or even to pay for a passage on so long a voyage, also to provide themselves with means of subsistence when arrived at their destination. A large majority of them, as witnessed by the early county records of New England, could read and write: they were capable of self-government, and were prompt to devise satisfactory solutions for the problems presented by their new life."

Among these men of pluck and decision there were at least twenty bearing the name of Perkins, who settled in New England before the eighteenth century began, all of whom are believed to have been of English birth, not having been identified as belonging to any family already found in the colonies. They were probably adventurers from England; but once arrived in the New World they made it their home, became heads of families, and no doubt performed their part in establishing the struggling colonies, which in after years were destined to become a great nation.

Their names are here arranged in chronological order; that is, in the order in which they are mentioned in the colonial and other authentic records.

It is quite unlikely that this is the order of their arrival in New England. Of only two among them is it known when they arrived there; the others may have been in the colonies for months, or even years, before making a permanent home; for until they had done this it is hardly probable that their names would be found on record.

The names of the twenty emigrants, the places where they settled, and the first year in which their respective names appear on New England records, are as follow:

1. 1631. John Perkins, of Ipswich, Massachusetts.
2. 1632. William Perkins, of Topsfield, Massachusetts.
3. 1653. William Perkins, of Roxbury, Massachusetts.
4. 1637. Isaac Perkins, of Ipswich, Massachusetts.
5. 1639. Abraham Perkins, of Hampton, New Hampshire.
6. 1639. Isaac Perkins, of Hampton, New Hampshire.
7. 1650. Edward Perkins, of New Haven, Connecticut.
8. 1662. William Perkins, of Dover, New Hampshire.
9. 1665. Thomas Perkins, of Dover, New Hampshire.
10. 1666. Luke Perkins, of Charlestown, Massachusetts.
11. 1671. Jonathan Perkins, of Norwalk, Connecticut.
12. 1674. Jacob Perkins, of Edgartown, Massachusetts.
13. 1675. Edmund Perkins, of Boston, Massachusetts.
14. 1677. James Perkins, of Exeter, New Hampshire.
15. 1678. Eleazer Perkins, of Hampton, New Hampshire.
16. 1682. Daniel Perkins, of Norwich, Connecticut.
17. 1684. Benjamin Perkins, of Newbury, Massachusetts.
18. 1686. William Perkins, of Easthampton, Long Island, New York.
19. 1688. John Perkins, of New Haven, Connecticut.
20. 1698. Joseph Perkins, of Norwich, Connecticut.

JOHN PERKINS, OF IPSWICH, MASS.

I. John Perkins, of Ipswich, Massachusetts.

He was the pioneer of the name in New England, and settled in Ipswich, in the colony of Massachusetts Bay, where he spent the remainder of his life.

Winthrop, in his Journal, mentions his arriving at Nantasket, February 5, 1630-31, on the ship *Lyon*. He says:

"The ship *Lyon*, Mr. William Peirce master, arrived at Nantasket. She brought Mr. Williams (a godly minister), with his wife, Mr. Throgmorton, —— Perkins, —— Ong, and others, with their wives and children, about twenty passengers, and about two hundred tons of goods. She set sail from Bristol, December 1."*

JOHN PERKINS, OF IPSWICH, MASS.

Deputy-Governor Dudley, in a letter to Lady Bridget, Countess of Lincoln, shows what was the state of feeling at home towards the Puritans of New England at the time of the departure of the *Lyon*, and also records some incidents of the ship's voyage, and what transpired on its arrival. He writes as follows:

"On the 5th of February arrived here Mr. Peirce with the ship *Lyon*, of Bristowe, with supplies of victuals from England, who had set forth from Bristowe the 1st of December before. He had a stormy passage hither, and lost one of his sailors not far from our shore, who in a tempest having helped to take in the spritsail, lost his hold as he was coming down, and fell into the sea, where, after long swimming, he was drowned, to the great dolor of those in the ship, who beheld so lamentable a spectacle without being able to minister help to him, the sea was so high, and the ship drove so fast before the wind, though her sails were taken down.

"By this ship we understood of the fight of three of our ships and two English men-of-war coming out of the Straits, with fourteen Dunkirkers, upon the coast of England, as they returned from us in the end of the last summer.

"By this ship we understood the death of many of those who went from us the last year to Old England, as likewise of the mortality there.

"Also, to increase the heap of our sorrows, we received advertisement by

---

* Winthrop enumerates the passengers who arrived "with their wives and children" in the *Lyon* as "*about twenty*," but Dudley expressly states they numbered "*twenty-six*." It is improbable that the names of *all* the twenty-six will ever be known; but, having followed up the clues to the four families mentioned in the text the following incomplete list has been made up; and it is believed to be correct, viz.:

Mr. Roger Williams.
Mrs. Mary Williams, wife of above.
Mr. John Throgmorton.
John Perkins.
Judith Perkins, wife of above.
John, Thomas, Elizabeth, Mary and Jacob Perkins, children of John and Judith.
—— Onge.
Frances Onge, wife of above.
Simon, aged 6, and Jacob Onge, children of —— and Frances Onge.

Thus accounting for fourteen out of the twenty-six.

It is unnecessary to mention any particulars concerning the Reverend Roger Williams, the founder of Rhode Island; they may be easily obtained elsewhere.

An account of Mr. John Throckmorton (or Throgmorton) can be found in J. O. Austin's Genealogical Dictionary of Rhode Island.

Henry Bond's History of Watertown, Massachusetts, contains an account of the Onge family. Savage says: "Mary Onge, aged 27, a passenger, in 1634, from Ipswich, county Suffolk, in the *Francis*, may have been sister or daughter of the above." On November 20, 1636, Edmund Peisley, citizen and grocer of London, brought an action for debt against Thomas Onge, of Bury St. Edmunds, in the county of Suffolk, grocer; according to Chancery Proceedings. Since Ipswich and Bury St. Edmunds are only about twenty miles apart it is reasonable to conclude that the Onge family was living at the latter place. Hence, it is doubtful if any relationship or connection existed between the Perkins and Onge families.

JOHN PERKINS, OF IPSWICH, MASS.

letters from our friends in England, and by the reports of those who came hither in this ship to abide with us (who were about twenty-six), that they who went discontentedly from us the last year, out of their evil affections towards us, have raised many false and scandalous reports against us, affirming us to be Brownists in religion and ill-affected to our State at home, and that these vile reports have won credit with some who formerly wished us well.

"Upon the 22nd of February we held a general day of Thanksgiving throughout the whole Colony for the safe arrival of the ship which came last with our provisions.

"The wheat we received by this last ship stands us in thirteen or fourteen shillings a strike [bushel], and the pease about eleven shillings a strike, besides the adventure, which is worth three or four shillings a strike; which is a higher price than I ever tasted bread of before.

"And everyone having warning to prepare for the ship's departure to-morrow, I am now, this 28th day of March, 1631, sealing my letter."

John Perkins, according to a family tradition, partly confirmed by known facts, was born in 1590, in Newent, Gloucestershire. His family at the time of his emigration consisted of his wife, Judith, and five children, viz.: John, aged sixteen; Thomas, fourteen; Elizabeth, twelve; Mary, ten; and Jacob, six.

He arrived in America at a comparatively early date in its history. Only 138 years had passed since its discovery by Columbus, 118 since Ponce de Leon had explored the coasts of Florida, and 107 since the Italian Verrazano entered what is now known as New York Bay.

The planting of the first permanent settlement at Jamestown, in the colony of Virginia, was effected in 1607, and it was two years later when Hudson sailed up the river that now bears his name. It was in 1615 that the Dutch established a trading post of a storehouse and fort, and four huts where New York City now is; and it was five years later that the Pilgrim Fathers sailed from England in the *Mayflower*; and a year had not elapsed since John Winthrop and his followers began the settlement of Boston.

On the 18th of May, John Perkins took the oath of freeman, which admitted him to all the civil rights of the colony. He resided in Boston during 1631-32, and his youngest child, Lydia, was born there, and baptized on June 3 in the latter year.

April 3, 1632. "It was ordered" by the General Court, "that noe pson wtsoeuer shall shoote att fowle vpon Pullen Poynte or Noddles Ileland; but that the sd places shalbe reserved for John Perkins to take fowle wth netts."

November 7, 1632. He and three others were "appoincted by the Court to sett downe the bounds betwixte Dorchester and Rocksbury."

In 1633 he removed with his family to the new settlement (subsequently called Ipswich) then being founded by the younger Winthrop and twelve others. In 1634, 1635, 1636, and 1639 he was granted land in Ipswich, aggregating 171 acres; and in 1637 he sold 40 acres to Thomas Howlett.

In February, 1636, he was one of the seven men chosen to order town business for the three months following, and in the same year was Deputy to the General Court.

June 21, 1637. He and his son John signed a petition to the Governor and Council of Massachusetts, asking that John Winthrop, junior, be permitted to remain with the Ipswich colony; which document is still extant, and in the possession of the Essex Institute, Salem, Massachusetts.

JOHN PERKINS, OF IPSWICH, MASS.

In 1645 he was appraiser of the estate of Sarah Dillingham, and the inventory then taken (which is still extant) also bears his signature. In 1648, and again in 1652, he was on the Grand Jury. In March, 1650, "being above the age of sixty, he was freed from ordinary training by the Court."

On March 28th, 1654, "being at this tyme sick and weake in body," he made his will, and died a few months later.

He was a typical representative man: and his inventory shows how small were the values and how limited the range of the possessions then necessary to everyday life in his station. His house and barn were valued at £40, and his 8 acres of land about the house at £12. Other lands, comprising 52 acres, were put down at £77. He had cows, horses, pigs, and sheep, in all 33 animals, valued at £93. His bed and furniture were put down at £4; his cash on hand at £10; his utensils, farm and kitchen, at £7; and his wearing apparel at £5. In all, there was a total of £250, or $1,250.

A genealogy of his family has been published by Dr. George A. Perkins, of Salem, Massachusetts.

The children of John and Judith Perkins were:

1. John, born 1614; married, 1635, Elizabeth ——; was a yeoman, innkeeper, and quartermaster; lived in Ipswich, Massachusetts, where he also died, December 14, 1686. His wife died September 27, 1684. Their children were:

    John, born 1636, died 1659.
    Abraham, born 1640, died April 27, 1722.
    Jacob, born 1646, died November 26, 1719.
    Luke, born 1649, died after 1694.
    Isaac,* born 1650, died 1726.
    Nathaniel, born 1652, died after 1703.
    Samuel, born 1655, died 1700.
    Thomas, born 16—, died after 1683.
    Sarah, born 16—, died after 1683.
    (Mary Perkins, who married Thomas Wells, January 10, 1669, at Ipswich, may have been his daughter.)

2. Thomas, born 1616; married Phebe Gould in 1640; was a farmer, deacon, selectman, tithing-man, and committee-man; died May 7, 1686. He

---

* It is from Isaac that both Dr. George A. Perkins and Mr. D. Walter Perkins are descended; the line of descent of the former being:

  (4) Jacob (born November 9, 1678; died March 28, 1754).
  (5) Francis (born May 5, 1732; died June 12, 1812).
  (6) David (born September 24, 1770; died April 22, 1859).
  (7) George A. Perkins, born October 15, 1813; resides in Salem, Massachusetts.

And the line of descent of the latter:

  (4) Abraham (born September 15, 1671; died after August, 1750).
  (5) James (born 1705; died September 27, 1789, at Lyme, Connecticut).
  (6) Isaac (born June 14, 1749; died in 1776).
  (7) David Lord (born July 4, 1776; died February 15, 1852, at Utica, New York).
  (8) David (born January 8, 1816; died June 20, 1877).
  (9) David Walter, born October 23, 1851; resides at Utica, New York.

wife outlived him, but the date of her death is unknown. They had nine children.

3. Elizabeth, born 1618; married William Sargent as early as 1642; lived in Ipswich, Newbury, Hampton, and in Amesbury, Massachusetts, where she and her husband permanently settled. She died in 1700, at the age of eighty-two. They had five children.

4. Mary, born 1620; married, in June, 1636, Thomas Bradbury; settled in Salisbury, Massachusetts, where she died in 1700, at the age of eighty. He died March 16, 1695. They had eleven children.

5. Jacob, born 1624: married, first, Elizabeth ———, about 1648; and second, after 1685, Damaris Robinson, widow; was a farmer, also sergeant of a military company; lived in Ipswich, where he also died, January 27, 1699-1700. His wife Elizabeth died February 12, 1685, and his wife Damaris in 1716. By his first wife he had nine children, but none by his second.

6. Lydia, born in Boston in 1632, and also baptized there June 3rd of that year; married Henry Bennet in 1651, lived in Ipswich, and died there about 1672. After her death Henry Bennet married Mary (Smith) Burr, widow; he died after October 3, 1707. She had five children, possibly one or two more.

WILLIAM PERKINS, OF TOPSFIELD, MASS.

II. Reverend William Perkins, of Topsfield, Massachusetts.

He was the son of William Perkins, merchant tailor, of London, and Katherine his wife, and grandson of George and Katherine Perkins, of Abbots Salford, in Warwickshire.

His grandfather was a yeoman of a class who were the owners of land of a stated considerable yearly value, and had various privileges.

His father's will—that of William Perkins, of the City of London, Merchant Taylor, of the parish of St. Dunstan in the West—supplies what few particulars are known concerning the family of his grandfather, George Perkins.

One of the latter's daughters married ——— Fosbrooke, of Bridgenorth, in Shropshire, and the testator bequeaths to her daughter Katherine, his niece, £5. Another married ——— Charlett, and Beatrice Charlett, probably her daughter, is given £50 by the testator, who styles her his "cousin." A third married ——— Parker, and each of her two daughters, Dorothy and Alice, is given a bequest of £5.

Nothing has been learned concerning George Perkins' son Thomas or his other two daughters.

The children of George and Katherine Perkins were:

(1) Elizabeth, baptized in 156-.
(2) Beatrice, baptized in 156-.
(3) Joane, baptized May 14, 1571.
(4) Anne, baptized February 28, 1573.
(5) Thomas, baptized February 14, 1576.
(6) William, baptized January 1, 1579, died 1657.
(7) Francis, baptized April 23, 1583.

His father, William Perkins, son of George and Katherine Perkins, of

Abbots Salford, in Warwickshire, was baptized there January 1, 1579, and settled in London, where he was a merchant tailor.

<small>WILLIAM PERKINS, OF TOPSFIELD, MASS.</small>

This William Perkins, of London, married three wives. The first was Katherine ———, whom he married May 22, 1603; she died September 18, 1618. The second was Mary, daughter of Mr. George Purchas, of Thaxsted, in Essex, whom he married March 30, 1619; she died October 29, 1639, having been married twenty years and seven months.

His third wife was Jane, widow of ——— Filmer, who then had two unmarried daughters. She survived him; and January 20, 1671, his son William, who was then residing in Topsfield, Essex County, in the colony of Massachusetts Bay, in New England, drew three bills of exchange upon his mother, "Mrs. Jane Perkins, widow, dwelling at the Three Cocks, upon Ludgate Hill, near to the west end of St. Paul's Church, in London."

William Perkins, of London, was possessed of considerable property, and gave £50 to Harvard College, in Boston. He made his will April 18, 1657, and died not long after, for the instrument was proved at the London Registry, November 10th following, by the widow and his son Edward, the executors. In his will (which is recorded in volume "Ruthen," page 450) he directs that he shall be buried in the Parish Church of All Saints, in Bread Street, "where I learnt so much of Jesus' Church, by the ministry of that his faithful servant, Master Richard Stocke."

To his wife he bequeaths £100 and the furniture of his chamber in his dwelling-house; also £10 per annum out of his rents in Bell Yard, to be added to his wife's jointure of £50 per annum, during the time of said lease.

If his wife deceased before the expiration of the Bell Yard lease, then her annuity of £80 per annum for two years was to go to her daughters, Elizabeth and Anne Filmer.

The widow's annuity of £80, her jointure of £50, and the £10 per annum from the Bell Yard rents, make altogether £140, which would be equivalent to about £1,000 a year, present value, so that he must have been a considerably wealthy man for his time.

To his son William he bequeaths £10 per annum out of his Bell Yard rents; also £100 more among his seven children, whose legacies were to be paid at their ages of fourteen and fifteen, probably one-half at each age.

To his daughter Rebecca, who had married Master Martin Cousins, he bequeaths £12 per annum out of his Bell Yard rents, also £100; besides £20, to each of her five children; and to her husband he gives £33 6s. 8d.

Two of his daughters married, respectively, Mr. William Carrington and Mr. Thomas Mead, whom he appoints overseers of his will, and to each of whom he gives £5.

To his daughter, Mrs. Mead, he wills £50; to her six children £10 each; and to her daughter Mary £10 more.

To his daughter, Mrs. Carrington, he bequeaths £100; to each of her three children £20; and to her daughter Mary £10 more.

To his son Edward he bequeaths £10 per annum out of his Bell Yard rents, and appoints him one of the executors of his will. Edward was unmarried probably, and may have been a clergyman, as he is styled "Master Edward Perkins."

WILLIAM PERKINS, OF TOPSFIELD, MASS.

He also bequeaths as follows:

To Master Ashton, £120.

"To Ellen Gomersall, widow, late wife to a minister in Thornecombe, in Devonshire, 100 marks."

The residue of his estate was to be equally divided among all his said children. The legacies were to be raised out of his lands and rents in Rathbury and Kilkiddy, in Ireland.

His children, no doubt, had received their portions before; and, in addition to the legacies mentioned, the residue of his property, stock-in-trade, etc., was probably of considerable value. The fact of his having property in Ireland need not suggest that he was of Irish origin. In 1650 Cromwell subdued Ireland; and land there, no doubt, was to be bought very cheap, and many Englishmen became owners of Irish land.

Since his other children are not mentioned in his will it is probable that they died young and left no families.

The date of the death of his widow, Mrs. Jane Perkins, has not yet been ascertained, but it was after 1671.

The children of William and Katherine Perkins were:

(1) Rebecca, born May 24, 1605; married Master Martin Cousins.
(2) William, born August 25, 1607; emigrated to New England; afterwards of Topsfield, Mass.
(3) John, born January —, 1608; probably died young.
(4) Toby, born March —, 1609; probably died young.
(5) Sarah, born on Low Sunday, April 19, 1612.
(6) Harrington, born March 30, 1615; probably died before 1619.

The children of William and Mary (Purchas) Perkins were:

(7) Harrington, born January 22, 1619; probably died young.
(8) Edward, born January 18, 1622; was living in London in 1657.
(9) Samuel, born June 13, 1624; probably died young.
(10) Elizabeth, born May 15, 1629.

William Perkins sailed for New England in the *William and Francis*, Mr. Thomas, master, leaving London March 9, 1632, and arriving at Boston June 5, following.

In March, 1633, with the illustrious John Winthrop, junior, and twelve others, he began the settlement of Ipswich; was admitted freeman September 3, 1634, and removed to Roxbury, where he married Elizabeth Wootton, August 30, 1636.

October 10, 1638, he was one of the surveyors appointed to survey and run the southerly line of the patent. October 7, 1641, because of his father's gift of £50 to Harvard College, he was granted 400 acres of land by the General Court. In 1642 he removed to Weymouth, and while there was leader of the military band; was also a lieutenant in 1642, and captain in 1644, in which year he represented the town in the General Court.

He was one of the Ancient and Honorable Artillery Company, and was chosen commissioner "to end small controversies in Weymouth." From 1650 to 1655 he was preaching to the inhabitants of Gloucester; in 1651 he gave his testimony in regard to a lost will of Walter Tibbet, of Gloucester, upon which the Court allowed a copy (so called) to be proved.

From Gloucester he went to Topsfield; and after preaching a few years, spent the remainder of his life in the calm pursuits of husbandry.

He was probably one of the most accomplished men among the first settlers of Topsfield; a scholar and a man of business; a clergyman; a soldier and a legislator; and, during the latter part of his life, a farmer.

In each of these relations, so unlike, and, according to present notions, so incompatible, he bore himself, so far as we can learn, with ability and discretion.

He often revisited his native country: was there in February, 1640; in October, 1646; in the spring of 1667; in April, 1670, and during the winter of 1673-4.

January 20, 1671, he mortgaged to Thomas Clark, "late of Plimouth, but now of Boston, merchant," all his house and seven acres of land in Topsfield, on the northerly side of which stood a grist mill, etc., "provided always that if the just and true sum of twenty pounds in lawful money of England be well and truely payed at one entire payment unto the said Thomas Clarke or his assignes in the cittye of London within six weeks space after the arrivall of the good ship called the *Blessing of Boston* above said, whereof is Master William Greenough, in the river of Thames, according to the true intent and meaning of three bills of exchange charged by the above named Wm. Perkins upon his mother, Mrs. Jane Perkins, widow, dwelling at the Three Cocks upon Ludgate Hill, near to the West End of St. Paul's Church in London, which three bills doe beare date with these presents that then this deed is voyd and of none efect, and every clause therein mentioned." (This mortgage was satisfied by Clark February 21, 1676.)

He died at Topsfield May 21, 1682, leaving a widow and nine children surviving. The date of his widow's death has not yet been ascertained.

The children of Rev. William and Katherine (Wootton) Perkins were:

1. William, born October 12, 1639; died December 23, 1639.
2. William, born in Roxbury, February 26, 1640-1; married Elizabeth, daughter of Daniel Clarke, of Topsfield, October 24, 1669; died October 30, 1695, aged 54.
3. Elizabeth, born in Weymouth, June 18, 1643; married John Ramsdell, of Lynn, May 31, 1671.
4. Tobijah, born in Weymouth, October 20, 1646; married Sarah Denison, November 4, 1680; died in Topsfield, April 30, 1723, aged 77.
5. Katherine, born in Weymouth, October 29, 1648; married John Baker, of Ipswich, May 13, 1667.
6. Mary, born in Gloucester, February 17, 1651; married Oliver Purchas, September 17, 1672. His first wife, Sarah, had died October 21, 1671.
7. John, born in Topsfield, April 2, 1655; married Anna Hutchinson, August 29, 1695; settled in Lynnfield and died there January 12, 1712, aged 57. His widow died in 1717.
8. Sarah, born in Topsfield, March 2, 1656-7; married John, son of Governor Simon Bradstreet, June 11, 1677.
9. Timothy, born in Topsfield, August 11, 1658; married Edna Hazen, of Rowley, August 2, 1686.
10. Rebecca, born in Topsfield, May 4, 1662; married Thomas, son of Captain Fiske, of Wenham, November 3, 1678; and died before 1719.

III. William Perkins, of Roxbury, Massachusetts.

WILLIAM PERKINS, OF ROXBURY, MASS.

In 1633 he was sergeant of a military company. September 3, 1634, "Srieant Perkins is chosen ensigne to the company att Rocksbury, & Mr. Pinchon is desired to giue him possession thereof."

March 3, 1635-36. "Ensigne Perkins is discharged of his office of ensigne."

American writers, authorities on the early settlers of New England, do not mention the fact that there were two men of the same name residing in Roxbury at about the same time (1634-43). But there must have been; for it is highly improbable that one, a college-bred, accomplished man, and who was afterwards a minister, could have been the drinking, dissipated man the records prove the other to have been; and it is in support of the theory that there were two, that the following extracts from the records of the General Court are given:

October 1, 1633. "It is ordered that Srieant Perkins shall carry 40 turfes to the ffort, as a punishmt for drunkenes by him comitted."

April 5, 1636. "Ordered, that Willm. Perkins shall (for drunkenes & other misdemeanrs by him comitted) stand att the nexte Genall Courte one houre in publique vewe, with a white sheete of pap on his brest haveing a greate D made vpon it, & shall attend the pleasure of the Court till hee be dismissed."

In the inventory of the estate of Joseph Weld, "late of Roxbury," taken February 12, 1646, the name of "Wm. Pirkines" is mentioned; while the Weymouth records prove the other William Perkins was residing there at that date.

No other facts concerning him have been ascertained.

IV. Isaac Perkins, of Ipswich, Massachusetts.

ISAAC PERKINS, OF IPSWICH, MASS.

He is believed to have been a younger brother of John Perkins, senior, of the same place, and seems to have followed the latter there within a few years after he had settled, and likewise became an inhabitant of the town. He must have settled there some time before 1637, for in that year the town granted him a parcel of land.

He died within a year or two, and the town granted land to his widow, Alice. In 1639 it is recorded that :

"Alice Perkins, widow of Isaac Perkins, is possessed of a parcel of land granted to the said Isaac, lying in Brook Street."

Alice Perkins soon afterwards sold her land, but continued to reside in the town, and is referred to in the will of Joseph Morse, of Ipswich; in which document (dated April 24, 1646) the testator bequeaths to his wife "about six acres bought of Widow Perkins," which indicates she was yet a resident, and known to her neighbours as "Widow Perkins."

The Boston family traces its descent back to an Edmund Perkins, who with his wife had settled in Boston some time before 1675. One family tradition says that he was a son of "Alice Perkins, a widow, and was brought up by John Perkins, of Ipswich"; and another associates him in his early youth with Richard Saltonstall, who was also a resident of the same place from 1635 until 1649.

While no documentary evidence has been discovered that absolutely proves Edmund to have been the son of Isaac Perkins, of Ipswich, authentic records and family traditions clearly indicate, and almost prove, that such was the fact.

Assuming this theory to be true, a tradition in the Boston family supplies the names of the children of Alice Perkins, widow; and also assuming that she was the widow of Isaac Perkins, of Ipswich, the family record is here given:

The children of Isaac and Alice Perkins were:

1. Alice, born about 163-.
2. Ralph, born about 163-.
3. Edmund, born about 1638; married, before 1675, Susannah, widow of John Howlett, and daughter of Francis and Mary Hudson. He died in 1693 (see Edmund Perkins, p. 260).

V. Abraham Perkins, of Hampton, New Hampshire.

He was one of the first settlers of the town, and was there as early as 1638, and was admitted freeman May 13, 1640, at Boston.

He was a man of good education, an excellent penman, and much employed in town business.

Since he and Isaac Perkins (his brother?), also of Hampton, are found in the colony so soon after John Perkins had become an inhabitant of Ipswich, it is probable they were relatives and followed him to New England upon receiving a favourable report of the country. They certainly settled in a town very near to Ipswich, and, although nothing has been discovered that shows any intimacy or communication between them, the frequency of the Scriptural names Abraham, Isaac, Jacob, and Luke, in both families, warrants the conclusion that a relationship existed.

Two children of Abraham Perkins—viz., Humphrey (born 1642), and James (born 1644)—died young; but the names were again given to two other children—viz., James (born 1647), and Humphrey (born 1661)—which proves an evident intention on the part of the parents to perpetuate the names in the family. From the Visitation of Worcestershire, 1569, it appears that a member of the Madresfield branch—viz., James Perkins—had a son Humphrey, who married into Shropshire, and had a son Humphrey, junior. The appearance of these identical names in the Hampton family certainly suggests some sort of a family connection or relationship with this earlier Shropshire family; but as a fact it has not yet been established.

The following is taken from the records of the General Court:

1661. "In ans' to the petition of Abraham Perkins, the Court judgeth it meete to graunt the petitioner's request—*i.e.*, so farr as to revejw his case in the same Court, in case the magistrates of that country are willing thereto, as in his petition is alleadged."

The phrase "of that country" evidently refers to England; and it is possible that the papers in this case may be found among the records of one of the English Courts.

Abraham Perkins is supposed to have been born about 1611; he died in 1683. His will is dated August 22, and was proved September 18 following. His wife was Mary ——, who was born about 1618. She died May 29, 1706.

His old family Bible is still extant, and from it and the town books the family record is compiled.

The children of Abraham and Mary Perkins were:

1. Mary, baptized December 15, 1639; married Giles Fifield, June 7, 1652, and removed to Charlestown, Massachusetts.
2. Abraham, born September 2, and baptized December 15, 1639; married Elizabeth, daughter of Thomas Sleeper, August 27, 1668; killed by the Indians June 13, 1677.
3. Humphrey, born January 22, 1642; died before 1661.
4. James, born April 11, 1644; died before 1647.
5. Timothy, born July , 1646; died young.
6. James, born October 5, 1647; married, first, Mary ———, about 1674; married, second, Leah, daughter of Moses Cox, December 13, 1681. He died before December 9, 1731, upon which date his will was proved. His widow, Leah, died February 19, 1749, aged eighty-eight.
7. Jonathan, born May 26 (or 30), 1650: married Sarah ———, December 20, 1682, at Exeter; died January 20 (or 24), 1689. His widow married, in 1690, Josiah Sanborn; she died at Hampton, September 1, 1748, aged eighty-five.
8. David, born April 28 (or February 2), 1653; was living in 1683.
9. Abigail, born April 2, 1655; married John Foulsham, of Exeter, November 10, 1675.
10. Timothy, born June 29, 1657; died January 27, 1659-60.
11. Sarah, born July 7 (or 26), 1659; was living in 1683.
12. Humphrey, born May 16 (or 17), 1661; married Martha Moulton; died January 7, 1712, aged fifty-one.
13. Luke, born 166- ; was living in 1683.

ISAAC PERKINS, OF HAMPTON, NEW HAMPSHIRE.

VI. Isaac Perkins, of Hampton, New Hampshire.

He is believed to have been a brother of Abraham Perkins, of Hampton, and is supposed to have been born about 1612-13. He settled in Hampton about 1638, and was among the first grantees when the plantation was laid out, and resided in that part of the town called Seabrook.

May 18, 1642, he took the freeman's oath at Boston.

His wife was named Susannah, but her parentage is unknown.

He died November 13, 1685; but the date of his wife's death has not been ascertained.

The children of Isaac and Susannah Perkins were:

1. Lydia, born 163- ; married Eliakim Wardhall, October 17, 1659.
2. Isaac, baptized December 8, 1639; drowned September 10, 1661.
3. Jacob, baptized May 24, 1640; married, December 30, 1669, Mary Philbrick.
4. Rebecca, born 164- ; married John Hussie, September 21, 1659.
5. Daniel, born 164- ; died August 1, 1662.
6. Caleb, born 164 ; married Bethia Philbrick, April 24, 1677.
7. Benjamin, born February 17, 1650; died November 23, 1670.
8. Susan, born August 21, 1652; married, first, Isaac Buzwell, of Salisbury, May 12, 1673; and, second, William Fuller, junior, of Hampton, June 22, 1680.

9. Hannah, born April 24, 1656; married James Philbrick, December 1, 1674; died May 23, 1739, aged eighty three.
10. Mary, born July 23, 1658; married Isaac Chase, of Hampton.
11. Ebenezer, born December 9, 1659; married Mary ——, about 1690.
12. Joseph, born April 9, 1661; married Martha ——, about 1687.

VII. Edward Perkins, of New Haven, Connecticut.   EDWARD PERKINS, OF NEW HAVEN, CONNECTICUT.

He and his three sons were still living as late as 1685, but very little relating to him is known.
He married Elizabeth Butcher, March 20, 1650.
The children of Edward and Elizabeth Perkins were:
1. John, born August 18, 1651.
2. Mehitable, born September 21, 1652.
3. Jonathan, born November 12, 1653.
4. David, born October 3, 1656; and perhaps others.

VIII. William Perkins, of Dover, New Hampshire.   WILLIAM PERKINS, OF DOVER, NEW HAMPSHIRE.

He is said to have been born in the West of England in 1616; was in Dover as early as 1662; took the oath of freeman, June 21, 1669; and died in Newmarket in 1732, at the very great age of 116. Hardly anything is known of him or his family; but he is probably the "William Perkinson" who had a grant of land in Dover in 1694. The names of the members of his family are not known.

IX. Thomas Perkins, of Dover, New Hampshire.   THOMAS PERKINS, OF DOVER, NEW HAMPSHIRE.

He is said to have been born in 1628; was in Dover in 1665; and took the oath of fidelity in 1669. April 25, 1693, he gave land to his son Nathaniel. Nothing more relating to him or his family is known.

X. Luke Perkins, of Charlestown, Massachusetts.   LUKE PERKINS, OF CHARLESTOWN, MASS.

Very little is known concerning him; he was in Charlestown in 1666. His wife's name was Hannah.
The children of Luke and Hannah Perkins were:
1. Henry, baptized January 13, 1667.
2. John, baptized January 13, 1667; died before June 19, 1670.
3. Luke, baptized January 13, 1667; died before March 24, 1667.
4. Luke, baptized March 24, 1667.
5. Elizabeth, baptized March 21, 1669.
6. John, baptized June 19, 1670.
7. Abraham, baptized July 28, 1672.
8. Hannah, baptized December 14, 1673.
9. Mary, baptized April 9, 1676.

XI. Jonathan Perkins, of Norwalk, Connecticut.   JONATHAN PERKINS, OF NORWALK, CONNECTICUT.

Nothing is known of him except that he was in Norwalk from 1671 to 1677.

JACOB PERKINS, OF EDGARTOWN, MASS.

XII. Jacob Perkins, of Edgartown, Massachusetts.

He appears to have been a settler there from 1674 to 1685; nothing further has been learnt concerning him. It is not known whether he had a family.

EDMUND PERKINS, OF BOSTON, MASS.

XIII. Edmund Perkins, of Boston, Massachusetts.

He was established at Boston as a master shipwright some time previous to 1675, when he, Susannah, his wife (late widow of John Howlett), and Andrew Neale petition the court "to confirm their sayle of the house and land of ye late John Howlett," etc.; "but the Court sees no cause to grant thire request."

His wife, Susannah, was the daughter of Francis Hudson and Mary his wife, who was born in England in 1620. She had one daughter by her first husband.

There is strong probability that he was the son of Isaac and Alice Perkins of Ipswich; but no proof of such relationship has yet been found.

The children of Edmund and Susannah Perkins were:

1. Edmund, born May 8, 1678; died September 14, 1682, aged four years.
2. John, born October 14, 1680.
3. Edmund, born September 6, 1683; married, first, Mary Farris, in 1709; and second, Esther Frothingham, March 8, 1722; died in 1762, aged seventy-nine.
4. Jane, born February 25, 1687.

JAMES PERKINS, OF EXETER, NEW HAMPSHIRE.

XIV. James Perkins, of Exeter, New Hampshire.

He was in Exeter as early as 1677. No other facts concerning him are known.

ELEAZAR PERKINS, OF HAMPTON, NEW HAMPSHIRE.

XV. Eleazar Perkins, of Hampton, New Hampshire.

He was a settler in Hampton in 1678. Nothing else is known about him.

DANIEL PERKINS, OF NORWICH, CONNECTICUT.

XVI. Daniel Perkins, of Norwich, Connecticut.

According to Miss Caulkins's "History of Norwich," the first of the family mentioned in the town records, is Daniel Perkins, who in 1682 married Dolinda, daughter of Thomas Bliss, of Norwich. After his marriage he is lost sight of. Nothing else is known about him.

BENJAMIN PERKINS, OF NEWBURY, MASS.

XVII. Benjamin Perkins, of Newbury, Massachusetts.

All that is known of him or his family is that he had a son Daniel, who was born in Newbury, December 18, 1684.

XVIII. William Perkins, of Easthampton, Long Island, New York.

He and his wife, Mary, were living at Easthampton in 1686. On November 19 of that year Governor Dongan, of New York, issued a warrant for the arrest of the minister of Easthampton, because of his having preached "a seditious libel"; and because some of his parishioners upheld him, warrants were issued for the arrest of several of them, and among them was William Perkins; and the warrants directed that they "bee lykewise taken into custody to answ' the same, the same day."

XIX. John Perkins, of New Haven, Connecticut.

There was a John Perkins in New Haven in 1688. Possibly he was a son of Edward of that town; the latter had a son John, who was born August 18, 1651. Nothing further concerning him has been ascertained.

XX. Joseph Perkins, of Norwich, Connecticut.

Miss Caulkins, in her "History of Norwich," says: "The death of a Mr. Joseph Perkins is recorded in 1698." His antecedents are unknown. He must not be confounded with Deacon Joseph, the son of Sergeant Jacob, and grandson of John, senior, of Ipswich, Massachusetts, who settled in Norwich in 1695, where, five years later, he married Martha Morgan. Deacon Joseph Perkins died at Norwich, September 6, 1726.

Besides the above twenty emigrants, there is still another who is found in Dover so early (1703) that he may have been there before the eighteenth century began, which would entitle him to a place in the foregoing list.

His name is Samuel Perkins, and his wife's name is Mary; except the names of their children nothing is known concerning them.

The children of Samuel and Mary Perkins were:
1. Hannah, born December 9, 1703.
2. Francis, born February 11, 1705.
3. Joseph, born August 25, 1714.
4. Abigail, born April 30, 1717.
5. Samuel, born February 13, 1723.

Besides the above emigrants to New England, there were others of the name who sailed for Virginia. The names of several such have been discovered, and we herewith append them:

Edward Perkins, of Virginia.

He was the fourth son of John Perkins, gentleman, of London, who died there in 1665, and who also had nephews and nieces of the name of Boulter or Poulter.

He sailed for Virginia in 1627, and seems to have died young and unmarried. Nothing has been ascertained concerning him after his arrival in Virginia.

James Perkyns.

He sailed from London, January 2, 1634, in the *Bonaventure*, for Virginia.

Robert Perkins.

In 1635, Robert Perkins, aged twenty-five, sailed from London for Virginia.

Martin Perkins.

In 1635, Martin Perkins, aged eighteen, sailed from London for America. These entries can be found in Hotten's "Lists of Emigrants."

32—2

Index.

ABERBURY, MASTER THOMAS, 189
Abbots Salford, 252
Abingdon, Earl of, 20
    ,, Montague, 2nd Earl, 20, 119
Abington, Mr. Thomas, 159
Abor, 17
Achard, Richard, 203
    ,, Robert, 203, 204
    ,, William, 203, 204
Acton, Margaret, 222
    ,, William, 220, 222
Admores, 221
Ailric, 4
Akers, 225
Aldermaston, 44, 46, 47, 48, 51, 52, 74, 91, 102, 106, 109, 119, 127, 131, 155, 170, 171, 172, 175, 179, 180, 203, 204, 221
Aldermaston Church, 46, 132
    ,, House, 138
Aldridge, Elizabeth, 192, 209
    ,, Francis, 212
    ,, Thomas, 110, 192, 209
Aldworth, 24
Aleyn, William, 308
Alianore, wife of Humphry, Duke of Gloucester, 40
Alloway, Francis, 212
Alyng, 95, 201
Amors Court, 17
Amall, Ann, 212
Andrews, Richard, 178
Anna Boleyn, 11
Anne, Queen, 229
Ansculf, William Fitz, 1, 4, 5, 6, 7, 27, 30, 67, 203
Ansley, 245
Anslye, James, 95
Anspach, Margravine of, 233
Apshill, 67

Aragon, Cardinal, 88
Arselet, 96
Ashby de la Zouche, 229, 230
Ashleigh, 37
Ashpoles, 126
Ashton, Master, 254
Astill, Henry, 111
Astlett, Cislye, 79
    ,, Richard, 79
Atherstone, 243
Atkinson, John, 237
Atkynson, William, 204
Attefelde, Roger, 207
Atte-More, Roger, 31
Auberville, 229
Avelin, Robert, 223
Aylen, 96

BABINGTON, 94
Bacon, 180
Baker, John, 255
Ballard, John, 197
Bambridge, 61, 81, 201
Banastre, Alard, 203
    ,, John, 31, 203
    ,, William, 203, 204
Barbour, Richard, 207
Barley, Elizabeth, 228
    ,, Humphrey, 226, 228
Barnoldby le Beck, 237
Barrowby, 239
Bartilmewe, Elizabeth, 46, 53
Bartlet, Edmund, 179
    ,, John, 179
    ,, Richard, 179, 180
Basildon, 111
Bassadona, Joanno, 233
Basset, Gurden, 27
Bath, 132
    ,, Road, 170, 172, 174

Bathampton, Great, 46, 67, 98, 117, 118, 126, 127
Baynham, G. A., 133
Beaconsawe, Peter, 102, 103
Beare, 93
" Agnes, 79
" Thomas, 79
" Wylfe, 92
Beauchamp, Anne, 64
" Henry, 38
" Isabel, 64
" Richard, Earl of Warwick, 38
" Richard, Earl of Worcester, 38
Beaumont, Anthony, 235
Beaurepaire, 195
Becket, Archbishop, 10
Beckford, William, 67
Bedingfield, Sir Henry, 16
Bedworth, 245
Beech Hill, 201
Beeke, or Beke, Dr. Henry, 174, 192, 203
Beenham, 45, 103, 111, 112, 114, 117, 133, 171, 172, 174, 192, 201, 209, 210, 211, 216, 219, 221, 222
Beleth, Sir Michael, 31
Belinda, 125, 160, 163
Bell, Henry, 79
Belson, Augustine, 116, 201, 215
" Katherine, 114, 116
" Leonard, 119
" Maurice, 220
Bely the Great, 241
Benham, Edmund de, 27
Bennet, Henry, 252
Benyon de Beauvoir, Mr., 74
" Mr., 196
Bere Court, 138
Beresford, Aden, 226, 228
Berkshire, Archdeacon of, 188
" Earl of, 20
Berkyn, 226
Berrington family, 159
" John, 118, 119, 127, 128
" Mrs., 133, 212
Bertie, Bridget, 20
" James, 119
" Montague, of Lindsay, 20
Berwick-on-Tweed, 195
Bigge, Christopher, 111
Biggesware, 241
Bigot, Roger, 15
Billimore, William, 194
Bishop, Rev. William, 192, 193, 209, 217
Bisley, 37

Blackwell, Thomas, 245
Blagrave, Anthony, 180
" Sir John, 180
Blancharde, Dorothie, 77
" Henry, 77
" Mary, 77
" Richard, 77
Blande, 102
Blessing of Boston (ship), 253
Bliss, Thomas, 260
Bluet, Father, 88, 89, 90
Blundel, Andrew, 84
Blunt, 112
" William, 201
Bolney, Ann, 221
" Francis, 220
" John, 220
Bolton, Mary, 196
" Robertus, 208
Bonaventure (ship), 261
Bond, George, 241
Boothby Paynell, 239
Borghese, Cardinal, 88
Bosseville, 244
Boston, 239, 255, 256, 258
Boteler, Johannes, 207
Botetourte, Thomas, 22, 24
Bottesford, 237
Boulter, *see* Poulter
Boulton, William, 19
Bowling Alley, 73
Bowyers, 51
Bracey, Johanna, 39
Bradbury, Thomas, 252
Bradfield, or Bradfield, 7, 24, 25, 43, 71, 91, 170, 188, 221
" Nicholas of, 188
Bradmore, 228
Bradstreet, Governor Simon, 255
Bramshaw, 106, 112, 225
Bray, 42
Bresset, Jordan, 176
Brett, Anne, 235
" James, 235
Brewynge, *see* Brunynge
Bridgenorth, 252
Bridges, John, 78
Brightwell family, 43
Brimpton, or Brympton, 52, 61, 62, 170, 221
Bristol, Dean of, 192
Brocas, Bernard, 42, 195
" Mrs., 195
Brockware, 241
Brook, or Brooke, 106, 112
Browise, 241

Index. 265

Brown, Ann, 212
Brunynge, or Brewynge, Elinor, 77, 81
    ,,   Richard, 67, 80, 81
    ,,   Thomas, 80
Brundels, Mary, 211, 212
Brymson, Edmonde, 53
Buckingham, Countess of, 235
    ,,   Duke of, 235
Bucklebury, or Bughulburye, 52, 106, 115, 180, 221
Bullington, 245
Bunney, or Boncy, 228, 229, 230, 231, 235
Burbage, 245
Burdesley, 245
Burfield, or Burghfield, 15, 17, 25, 84, 97, 102, 109
Burford, 37
Burghley, Lord, 17, 231, 233, 234
Burgogne, Bartholomew, 179
    ,,   Robert, 179
    ,,   Thomas, 179
Burr, Mary, 252
Burton, Hastings, 245
Burwell, 239
Buscot, or Borwardescote, 30, 41, 44, 58, 116, 126, 127
Bushey, 245
Buss, Humphrey, 212
    ,,   William, 211, 212
Butcher, Elizabeth, 250
Butler, Edward, 201, 206
Butler, Walter, 183
Butley, 243
Buzwell, Isaac, 258
Byles, Mr., 131

CALCUTTA, Bishopric of, 193
    Caldecott, Johannes, 208
Caldicott, 241
Campanula rapunculus, 217
Carlisle, 236
    ,,   Dean of, 234
Carpenter's lond, 31
Carrington, William, 253
Caryll, John, 124, 125
Caster, Dorothy, 237
Catchmay, Elizabeth, 241
    ,,   George, 241
    ,,   Thomas, 241
Catesby, 69
Cateway, Thomas de, 207
Catherine of Aragon, Queen, 115
Cathorp, 118
Catmore, 108, 112, 176, 201, 222
Caumpeden, Roger de, 208
Cave, Mary, 226

Caversham, 37
Cecil, Secretary, 231
    ,,   Mr. William, 231, 232
    ,,   Sir Robert, 232
Chadlington, 37
Chaloner, Bishop, 133, 211
Chamberlain, John, 231
Chamberleyn, Leonard, 178
Channon Row, 236
Chapel Row, 170
Charles Edward, Prince, 130, 131
Charles I., 108
    ,,   II., 191
Charlestown, Mass., 258
Charlett, 252
Charterhouse, 152
Chase, Isaac, 259
Chawelowe, 203
Child's Manor, 40
Christie, Edward, 213
    ,,   Rev. J. F., 186, 209
    ,,   Thomas, 213
Churchille, William de, 208
Clare, Gilbert de, 37
Clark, Thomas, 253
Clarke, Daniel, 253
Cleconhors, 220
Clement VII., 89
Clerkenwell, 176
Clibburn, William, 200
Cobeham, William de, 189
Codrington, Edward, 112, 201, 206
Coletop, 203
Collee, or Colneye, 228
    ,,   Elizabeth, 41, 204
    ,,   Joan, 204
    ,,   John, 41, 204
    ,,   Margaret, 34, 43, 44, 58, 201, 204, 223
    ,,   Stephen, 204
Collier, Mr. R. P., 152
Collingwood, 69
Cologne, 231
Colsterworth, 239
Compton, 23
    ,,   Basset, 67
    ,,   Lady Warburga, 72
    ,,   Sir William, 72
    ,,   Winyates, 158
Congreve, Mr., 74, 131, 134, 155
    ,,   Ralph, 196
Constance, daughter of Edmund, Duke of York, 38
Cooper, Rev. John, 192, 209
Copenhagen, 232
Corder, Margaret, 95

Corderoy, Mr. Gul., 13
Cornish, Rev. Fraser, 60, 197
" Rev. T. B., 210
Corunna, 19
Couper, Henricus, 208
Cousins, Martin, 253, 254
Coventry, 245
Cowdray, Fulke de, 45
" Jane, 211
" Johana, 212
" Peter, 45
Cowper, William, 70
Cox, Moses, 258
Coylie, 191
Cranfield, Sir Lionel, 234, 235
Crawford, Richard, 110
Cray, Isaac, 99, 102
Cressy, Thomas, 226
Creswell, Mary, 81
" Richard, 81
Crevequer, William de, 15
Crew, Mrs., 13
Cromvale, Henricus, 208
Cromwell, 11
Crondalle, or Crondalles, 28, 119
Crookham Common, 170
Crosse, 95
Crowe, Radulphus, 208
Cuserugge, Baldwin, 27
Cwmcarvan, 241

DANIEL, RICHARD, 211, 212
Deane, Henry, 128
Debra, Bishop of, 133
De Criol, 229
Dee, Dr., 232
De la Beche, Isabella, 29
" John, 29
" Nicholas, 22, 24, 25
De la Hay, Henry, 241
Denbeigh, 195
Denison, Sarah, 255
Depford, or Deptford, 67, 77, 95
Despencer, Alianore, 37
" Edward, 38
" Hugh Le, 24, 34, 35, 36, 37, 38, 64, 201
" Thomas, Earl of Gloucester, 34, 38, 39, 64
Dillingen, 231
Dillingham, Sarah, 251
Doblado's Letters from Spain, 192
" Don Leucalion, 192
Dolman, Humphry, 191
Domesday Book, 1-6, 67, 203
Doncastle, John, 111

Done, Mr., 93
Dongan, Governor, 260
Donnington, 189
Dorchester, 250
Dorking, 116
Douay, 88
Doughty, Mr., 133
Doylye, John, 15
Drake, Sir Francis, 19, 94, 96
Drewrye, Anthony, 77
" Edmonde, 77
" Jane, 77
" Martha, 77
Dudley, Deputy-Governor, 249
Duffield, 102
Duke, Johannes, 209

EAGUST, RICHARD, 191
" Mary, 191
East Barsham, 40
Easthampton, 260
East Rudham, 243
Eddington, 23
Edward the Confessor, King, 1, 2, 5, 203
Edward I., 9
" III., 30
" IV., 68, 70
" VI., 183, 185
" Prince of Wales, 64
Edwards, David, 241
Eglise, Browise, 241
Elibank, Lord, 131
Elizabeth, Queen, 12, 16, 25, 31, 75, 80, 85, 86, 88, 90, 91, 94, 103, 190, 209, 232, 233, 234
" 128
" Baroness Burgesch, 38
" daughter of Earl of Salisbury, 38
" Mistress, 95
Elston, Thomas, 190, 209
Encroys, Walter de, 29
Englefield, or Inglefield, 19, 23, 55, 91, 96, 181
" Elyas de, 27
" Sir Francis, 22, 25, 26, 53, 59, 63, 84, 96
" Francis, 84, 85
" Sir Henry, 127
" House, 95, 170
" Mrs., 84
" Sir Philip, 31
" Sir Thomas, 22, 49
" Thomas, 25, 44
Epilobium angustifolium, 217
Erasmus, Paraphrasis of, 183, 185

Erskine, Rev. Thomas, 60, 186, 193, 210
Essex, Lord, 109
Eton College, 42
Eupatorium rapunculus, 217
Exeter, Lord, 231
Eyston, John, 82, 111, 112, 201, 220, 222
　,,　　Margaret, 109
　,,　　William, 108, 109, 222

FAIRFAX, SIR THOMAS, 230
　Fairford, 37
Farris, Mary, 260
Fawsley, 245
Felhouse, 201
Fenny Bentley, 226, 228
Fermor, Arabella, 114, 119, 120, 125, 126
　,,　　Henry, 114, 119, 201
Fettiplace, Thomas, 44
Ffisher, John, 63
Fieldhouse Farm, 98, 117
Fifield, Giles, 258
Filloughley, 245
Filmer, Ann, 253
　,,　　Elizabeth, 253
Finchampstead, or Fynchampstead, 43, 44, 58, 66, 79, 111, 201, 203, 204, 221, 223
Fingall, Lord, 13
Fishburne, William, 177, 208
Fiske, Captain, 255
Fitten, Francis, 84
Fitzhughe, Lord, 68
Flint, county of, 195
Fogge, of Ashford, 224
Fortescue, 224
　,,　　John, 17
Fosbrooke, 252
Foster, Sir George, 45
　,,　　Sir Humphrey, or Humfrey, 45, 47, 48, 49, 50, 51, 91, 93, 101, 179, 180
　,,　　William, 106, 180
Foulsham, John, 258
Fountell, or Fonthill, 67
　,,　　Gifford, 66
Foxell's Court, 43
Fraser, Dr., 50, 186, 193, 194, 210, 213, 217
Freeman, Sir Ralph, 234
Friswyde, 95
Frodingham, 237
Fuller, William, 258
Fygge, Richard, 207, 208

GALANTHUS NIVALIS, 217
　Galta, John, 79
Gardiner's Ferme, 221
Garnett, Father Henry, 159, 160

Garrett, 99, 160
Gayler, 98, 99, 100
Gentian pneumonanthe, 217
Gerard, Father John, 159, 160
Geranium pratense, 217
Gervace, 234, 235
George III., 131, 195
Ghilo, 1, 5, 7, 203
Gibbet-piece, 194
Gilbert, Sir John, 243
Giles, Johannes, 208
Gipping, 243
Glenfield, 235
Gloucester, 254
　,,　　Humphrey, Duke of, 34, 39, 40, 42, 201
　,,　　Thomas Dispencer, Earl of, 31, 38, 39, 201, 205
Godard Gravenor, 237
Godfrye, John, 79
Gomersall, Ellen, 254
Goode, Marmaduke, 190, 191, 201
　,,　　Robert, 190, 209
Goring, Priory of, 178
Gosling, William, 212
Gould, Phebe, 251
Graves, Alice, 239
Great Marlow, 37
Green, Robert, 153
Greenham, 176
Greenough, William, 253
Gregory XIII., 89
Grendon, Walter, 208
Grenelane, Johannes, 208
Grenville, or Greewill, Sir Richard, 94, 96
Griffith, Christopher, 128, 174, 190
　,,　　Thomas, 241
Grimmer's bank, 175
Grony, The, 241
Groyné (Corunna), 19
Guillym, Richard, 241
Guy, 92

HALDING, ROBERT, 207
　Halifax, Earl of, 129
Hall, Christopher, 241
　,,　　Mr., 93, 96
Halteremmes, 241
Ham, George, 212
　,,　　Lewis, 212
Hampreston, 109
Hampton, 257, 258
Hamstead Marshall, or Hemstede Mareschall, 91, 207
Hanginge Langford, 78, 126, 221
Hanley Castle, 36, 37

33

Hannington, Joseph, 212
Hardwicke, 18, 111
Harle, Widow, 212
Harmswood, Ralph, 110
Harrison, Sir Richard, 204
Harrowe Waye, 171
Hartridge, 23
Hatley, 201
Harvard College, 254
Hawkins, William, 194
Hawkwell, 114
Hawle, Robert, 78
Haws, Richard, 223
  „   Thomas, 223
Hawton, 54
Hayle, 178
Hazen, Edna, 255
Heage, 236
Heandry Skithan, 241
Heckington, 54
Hemstede Mareschall, see Hamstead
Henham, 236
Hennedge, Sir Thomas, 232
Hennison, Monsieur, 232, 233
Henry I., 7, 10, 14, 203
  „   III., 45, 203
  „   IV., 39
  „   V., 40, 42
  „   VI., 40, 41
  „   VII., 64, 69
  „   VIII., 10, 11, 15, 28, 49, 64, 71, 74, 89, 115, 177, 178
Henry, Prince, 229
Herbert, Dr., 235
  „   Richard, 241
Herbyn, Margaret, 77
Herling, 1, 5, 203
Herwardesleia, Simon de, 27
Hethlond, 31
Hide, see Hyde
Higges, Richard, 93, 94
High Meadow, 241
Hildesley, Edward, 171
Hill, Hester, 237
Hind's Head Inn (Aldermaston), 127
Hinlip Hall, 159
Hobson, 201
  „   Elizabeth, 62
  „   Mr., 93
Hoby, 235
Hocley, Mrs., 212
Hodcote, 23
Hoese, de la, Constance, 204
  „   Joan, 204
  „   Peter, 204
  „   Thomas, 204

Holbech Barnaby, 245
Hollo(way), Robert, 80
Holme, 237
Holt, Father, 89
Holwaye, William, 79
Holy Brook, 171
Hopkinson, Henry, 239
Horton, 42
Housebonde, Johannes, 208
Howard, Bernard, 111
  „   Charles, 111
Howlett, John, 257, 260
Hudsfield, 241
Hudson, Francis, 260
Huffinton, see Uffinton
Hugh, Abbot of Reading, 12, 49, 50
Hull, 237
Hulles, William, 208
Humphrey Plantagenet, Duke of Gloucester, 34, 39, 40, 42, 201
Huningham, 245
Hunsdon, Lord, 99
Hunter, Henry Launoy, 196
Huntingdon, Earl of, 230
Hurt, Richard, 229
Husseburne, Master Thomas de, 27
Hussie, John, 258
Hussie's Manor, 41, 43, 44, 45, 46
Hutchinson, Anna, 255
Hutton, 97
Hyde, or Hide, End, 127, 201, 206
  „   James, 116, 163, 201, 210, 215
  „   Jerominus, 209
  „   John, 127, 201

ILLESLEY, ILISLEY, or ILSLEY, 23, 93, 97, 176, 201, 221
Ingepenne, Nicholas de, 8
Inglefield, see Englefield
Inglestadt, 231
Inglewode, Johannes, 207
Ingram, Mr., 132
Inkpen, 23
Ipre, Sir Thomas, 68, 183
Ipswich, 11, 250, 251, 256, 257
Ireland, Mrs., 212
Iris pseudacarous, 217
Isabella, wife of Simon, 7, 8
Isham, Edward, 226, 230
  „   Mary, 229
Ivechurch, 106, 222

JACK OF NEWBURY, 106, 115
James I., 209, 234
James, Elizabeth, 82, 106, 222
  „   Sir Henry, 201, 206, 222

Index.

James, Martin, 106
Jarrett, 99, 160
Jenkins, David, 241
Jennings, 222
Jeyne, William, 241
John, Parson of Uffington, 188
Johnson, Ralph, 237
Jone, Mother, 78
Jones, John, 114, 134, 174, 201
    ,,   Philip, 114, 201
    ,,   Robert, 241
Jubilee, Queen Victoria's, 196

KATHERINE, QUEEN, 11, 64
Kelly, Sir Edward, 232
Kelsall, Henry, 172
Kember, Widdowe, 79
Kemsey, 220, 222
Kenetwode, Nicholas, 31
Kennet, the river, 54, 117, 137, 169, 170, 175
Kennet and Avon Canal, 173
Kenyon, 106, 201, 225
Kilkiddy, 254
Kingston, 23
    ,,   Lord, 127
Kirke, Richard, 237
Knollys, Sir Francis, 12, 99, 100, 101, 102, 103, 221
Kneller, Sir Godfrey, 123
Kydwelle, Peter, 45
Kynedd Awleditt, 241
Kyng, William, 208
Kystland, 52, 221

LADY HOLT, 124
Lambourne, 111
Langford, 67, 127
    ,,   Edward, 22
    ,,   Joan, 173
    ,,   Sir John, 22, 25, 71, 173
    ,,   Sir Thomas, 22, 25
    ,,   William, 22
Lantley John, 245
Lathyrus palustris, 217
La Zouche, William, 37
Leatis, or Leaches, Sara, 212
Lee, William, 209
Leicester, 229, 230
    ,,   Earl of, 90
    ,,   Grange, 245
Leigh, Alice, 55, 66, 81
Lenoir, Mrs., 120
Leyre, William, 40
Libbe, Richard, 180
Lincoln, Countess of, 249

Lincoln, Lord, 69, 70
Lingam, George, 94, 95, 97
Lingar, James, 95
Lingen, Edward, 97
Lister, Michael, 239
Little Wolverton, 220, 222
Littleham, 116
Liverpool, 193
Llanarth, 114, 120, 201
Llanhanog, 241
Llantrishan, 241
London, Bishop of, 88, 89, 235
    ,,   John, 11
Longbridge, 245
Longham, 116
Loughborough, Lord, 230
Lovel, Lord Francis, 68, 69, 70, 71
    ,,   Joan, 68
    ,,   Lord John (of Holland), 68
    ,,   Sir John, 32, 68
    ,,   Sir William, 41
Lovels, the, 142
Lucy, 55
Lycopodium inundatum, 217
    ,,   selago, 217
Lye Farm, 220, 222
Lyfford, John, Lord, 111
Lynnfield, 255
Lynthighte, Hughe, 80
Lyon (ship), 249
Lytilman, Richard, 208

MADEW, FATHER EDWARD, 130, 132, 133, 155, 211, 212, 218
Madresfield or Mattisfelde, 36, 39, 43, 46, 59, 227, 228
Mainwaring, Arthur, 112, 201, 206
Malorie, Robertus, 208
Malvern Chase, 36, 37
    ,,   Court, Little, 159
Mambylad, 241
Manchester, Bishop of, 193, 213, 217
Mapledurham, 125, 133
Maple Durwell, 37
Marchall, Robertus, 207
Margaret, Countess of Salisbury or Sary, 61, 63, 64
Marrige or Marrugge, 20, 170, 176, 188
Marshall, John, 211, 212
    ,,   Thomas, 237
    ,,   William, 239
Marshalsea, the, 94, 97
Martel, Stephen, 27
Martha, Mistress, 95
Martyn, Edward, 80
Marvyn, Marvin, or Mervyn, Lady, 55, 60,

33—2

61, 66, 67, 72, 73, 74, 81, 97, 98, 104, 110,
147, 151, 186, 190, 216, 221
Marvyn, Marvin, or Mervyn, Richard, 78,
95
  ,,   Sir John, 66, 74, 81, 144, 201,
204, 209
  ,,   Sir Walter, 66
  ,,   Edward, 66, 78, 204
  ,,   Elizabeth, 74, 76, 80, 83, 144,
209
  ,,   Jane, 66
Mathewe, Elizabeth, 79
Matilda, Queen, 10
Matthews, Humphrey, 241
Mattisfelde, *see* Madresfield
Maud, Empress, 10, 14
Mauger, Katherine, 237
Mead, Thomas, 253
Measea, or Meysey, or Mesea, 95
  ,,   Mr., 96
  ,,   Thomas, 220
Meere, Mr. Henry, 98
  ,, Thomas de la, 20
Melham, Johannes, 207
Mervyn, *see* Marvyn
Messingham, 237
Michaels, 178
Michell Troy, 241
Micklethwaite, Joseph, Viscount, 245
  ,,   Thomas, 245
Middlesex, Earl of, 235
Mill, Thomas, 245
Mills, William, 110
Milton, 133
Minster, Lovell, 70, 71
Mitchell's Court, 58
  ,,   family, 58
Mitford, Miss, 120
Mompesson, or Mompesonne, Ann, 221
  ,,   Drew, 66, 77, 78
  ,,   Edward, 78
  ,,   Elizabeth, 55, 58, 64, 67, 78, 204
  ,,   L., 77
  ,,   Mary, 66, 78
  ,,   Sir John, 46, 55, 64, 67, 77, 78, 81, 201, 204
  ,,   Susanne, 53, 67, 77, 81, 83
  ,,   Thomas, 76, 77, 78
Montacute, William, Earl of, 36
Montague, Earl of Abingdon, 119
  ,,   Lord, 64, 84
  ,,   Lord John, 10, 42
  ,,   Sir Sydney, 234
Mordaunt, Lord, 66
More, Bernard, 53, 63

More, Dorothy, 34, 44, 46, 50, 58
  ,,   Edward, 44, 46, 201
  ,,   John, 239
  ,,   Richard, 15, 36
  ,,   Thomas, 39
  ,,   William, 48, 50
Morgan, James, 196
  ,,   Roger, 241
  ,,   William, 241
Morley, Edmund, 237
  ,,   Lord, 68
  ,,   Peter, *alias* Perkins, 34, 35, 37, 38, 201
Morse, Joseph, 256
Mortimer, 24, 84, 194
  ,,   Roger, 37
Moulton, Martha, 258
Murray, Alexander, 131
Muston, Joseph, 245
Myddleton, Thomas, 209
Mygeham, 52, 221
Mynshull, Sir Richard, 226, 230

NASH, MARGERY, 220, 222
  ,, Nasenby, 54
Neale, Andrew, 260
Negri Ottario, 233
Nervut, or Neyrvut, John, 8, 9
  ,,   Richard, 7, 8, 29, 119
Nevil, Robert, Bishop of Sarum, 41
Nevile, Anne, 63
Neville, Richard, Earl of Warwick and Salisbury, 38, 42, 63, 64
Newbury, 109, 172
Newent, 250
Newland, 241
Newman, Elizabeth, 212
Newmarket, 259
Newton, Robert, 52
Newtonne, Edmonde, 79
New York, 261
Nicholas, Brother, 159
  ,, IV., Pope, 9
Nicholls, Edward, 241
  ,,   Thomas, 241
Norfolk, fourth Duke of, 111
Norreys, Baron of Rycote, 17, 20
  ,, family of, 119
  ,, Francis, Lord, 104
  ,, Lady, 19
  ,, Margery, 16, 17
  ,, Sir Edward, 18, 19, 20
  ,, Sir Henry, 16
  ,, Sir John, 17, 19, 103
Norton, Elizabeth, 81
  ,, Richard, 81

Index.   271

Norwich, 261
„   Mayor of, 41
Nottingham, 24, 131, 228, 229, 230
Nuneaton, 245
Nunhyde, or Nunhide, 106, 178

OBORNE, WALTER, 244
Offeton, Offetone, Offetune, Offinton,
    or Ofton, *see* Uffinton, etc.
Ogger, son of Ogger, 27
Okefield, or Wokefield, 107, 222
Old Romney, 222
Oriel College, 192, 209
Onge, 249
Osmunda regalis, 217
Ounby, 237
Ovinton, 28
Owen, Brother John, 159, 160
Oxford, 11, 15

PADDINGTON, manor of, 236
    Padworth, 41, 43, 44, 45, 47, 58, 75,
    78, 79, 92, 93, 97, 109, 110, 111, 116,
    117, 128, 147, 172, 174, 175, 201, 203,
    204, 211
Paganel, or Pagnal, or Paynell, Alice, 32
  „   Alicia, 207
  „   Dame Constance, 32
  „   Fulke, 22, 24
  „   Gervase, 22, 24, 25
  „   John, 31
  „   Ralph, 22, 24
  „   Richard, 30, 207
  „   Thomas, 31, 32, 207
  „   William, 30
Pagnel's Manor, 30
Pagenham, or Packenham, Elizabeth,
        204
      „   Sir Edmund, 66, 204
Pam Hall, 44, 128
Pangbourne, 222
Pangbourne's land, 45
Parats, or Parrat, Sarah, 211, 212
Parkyns' arms, 104
Parkins, or Parkyns, Alice, 46, 52, 62
  „   Anna, or Anne, 46, 47, 49, 61,
        81, 97
  „   Christopher, 46, 52, 62, 228, 229,
        231-236
  „   Dorothye, 46, 61
  „   Elizabeth, 46, 48, 51, 52, 53, 63,
        66, 81, 144, 228
  „   Francis, 46, 47, 48, 49, 52, 62, 72,
        73, 74, 75, 77, 78, 79, 80, 81, 91,
        92, 93, 95, 97, 99, 103, 178, 204,
        228, 231

Parkins, or Parkyns, Gertrude, 52, 62
  „   Henry, 52, 53, 62, 75, 76, 78, 80,
        81, 97, 221
  „   Isham, 230
  „   James, 228
  „   John, 34, 36, 38, 39, 43, 44, 58,
        64, 78, 227, 228
  „   Lawrence, 228
  „   Margaret, 41, 46, 58, 76, 78, 81
  „   Mary, 46, 52, 62
  „   Mr., 95, 97
  „   Mrs., 94
  „   Richard, 45, 46, 47, 48, 49, 50,
        51-55, 57, 59, 61, 62, 63, 72, 74,
        79, 81, 83, 96, 97, 102, 103, 105,
        144, 151, 190, 204, 221, 227, 228,
        229, 231, 235
  „   Sir George, 229, 230, 235
  „   Sir Thomas, 231
  „   Theophilus, 230
  „   Thomas, 34, 42, 43, 44, 46, 68,
        78, 102, 103, 204, 227, 228
  „   William, 32, 34, 39-42, 44, 46, 51,
        52, 53, 58, 61-63, 65, 81, 97, 148,
        177, 204, 207, 208, 227, 228, 235
Parkins, or Parkyns, table of descent,
    family of Ashby, parish of Bot-
    tesford, co. Lincoln, 237
  „   of Grantham, co. Lincoln, 239
  „   of Madresfield, co. Worcester,
        and of Notts, 226
  „   of Marston Jabet, co. Warwick, 245
  „   of Norfolk, 243
  „   of Sheffield, 244
Parma, Prince of, 94
Parnell, 124
Parre, John, 181
  „   William, 181
Parry, Thomas, 91, 93
Parsons, Father, 89, 91
Parys, Knighte, 154
Paston Letters, 41
Pattrington, 239
Pavely, Johannes, 208
Paynell, *see* Paganel.
Peace, John, 212
Pegge, George, 245
Peirce, Mr., 249
Penniswick, 126
Penruck, John, 226
Pencraig, 241
Perkins, or Perkyns:
  „   Abraham of Hampton, New
        Hampshire (U.S.A.), 248, 257
  „   Anna, or Anne, 53, 82, 84, 105,
        112, 114, 117, 153, 210, 211, 216

Index.

Perkins, or Perkyns, Arabella, 114, 121, 126, 127, 133
" Arthure, 52
" Barbara, Mrs., 225
" Benjamin, of Newbury, Mass. (U.S.A.), 260
" Charles, 114, 127, 196, 211
" Cristopher, 53
" Daniel, of Norwich, Connecticut (U.S.A.), 260
" Edmond, or Edmund, 82, 106, 111, 112, 180, 210, 225
" Edmund, of Boston, Mass. (U.S.A.), 260
" Edward, 106, 203, 225
" " of New Haven, Connecticut (U.S.A.), 259
" Eleanor, 114, 117, 210
" Eleazar, of Hampton, New Hampshire (U.S.A.), 260
" Elizabeth, 46, 52, 53, 62, 82, 210, 225
" Elusa, 210
" Frances, 82, 115, 210
" Francis, or Franciscus, 21, 28, 46, 52, 53, 82-85, 94, 97, 98, 104-108, 110-119, 121, 127, 133, 139, 151, 152, 180, 185, 186, 190, 205, 206, 209-211, 214-216, 221, 222, 225
" George, 210
" Gertrude, 46
" Henry, 34, 36, 98, 114, 126, 210, 221
" Isaac, of Hampton, New Hampshire (U.S.A.), 248, 258
" Isaac, of Ipswich, Mass. (U.S.A., 248, 256, 257
" Jacob, of Edgartown, Mass. (U.S.A.), 248, 260
" James, of Exeter, New Hampshire (U.S.A.), 248, 260
" Jane, 106, 180, 210
" John, 82, 105, 111, 112, 114, 127, 128, 129, 162, 205, 209-211, 221, 222
" John, of Ipswich, Mass. (U.S.A.), 248-252
" John, of New Haven, Connecticut (U.S.A.), 248, 261
" Jonathan, of Norwalk, Connecticut (U.S.A.), 248, 259
" Joseph, of Norwich, Connecticut (U.S.A.), 248, 261
" Katherine, or Catherine, 46, 82, 110, 114, 210, 211, 215, 222

Perkins, or Perkyns, Luke, of Charlestown, Mass. (U.S.A.), 248, 259
" Margaret, 53, 82, 98, 110, 112, 113, 210, 214, 215
" Maria, or Mary, 82, 114, 116, 128, 210, 211, 215
" Mr., 94, 98, 120, 130, 132, 192, 211
" Ricardus, or Richard, 205, 209, 210, 216, 221, 222
" Samuel, of Dover, New Hampshire (U.S.A.), 261
" Thomas, 100, 205, 208, 209, 221
" Thomas, of Dover, New Hampshire (U.S.A.), 248, 259
" William, 52, 53, 130, 185, 186, 207, 208
" Rev. William, of Topsfield, Mass. (U.S.A.), 248, 252-255
" William, of Roxbury, Mass. (U.S.A.), 248, 256
" William, of Dover, New Hampshire (U.S.A.), 248, 259
" William, of Easthampton, Long Island, New York (U.S.A.), 248, 260
" Winifred, 82, 210
Perkins family, table of descent, of Beenham, co. Berks, 220
" of Pilston, Landogo, co. Monmouth, 241
" of Ufton, co. Berks, 201
" of Winkton, co. Hants, 224
" of Wokingham, co. Berks, 223
" monuments, 184, 185, 214, 215, 216
" Pedigree, of Ufton, Visitation of Berks (1623), 205, (1664 and 1666), 206
Persefield, Walter, 241
Petre, Lord, 124
Philbrick, Bethia, 258
" James, 259
Philip II., 87, 88, 94
Phillip, Thomas, 241
Phipps, James, 191
Piearce, Charles, 212
Pierce, Anne, 245
Pinchbeck, 239
Pinchon, Mr., 256
Pinkney, Pinqueni, or Pinchegni, Ghilo, 6, 7
" Gilbert, 7
" Henry, 7, 8, 9, 29
" Ralph, 7

Pinkney, Pinqueni, or Pinchegni, Robert, 7
  ,, family of, 6
Pinockswick, 116
Pius V., 88, 89, 90
Plantagenet, Edward, 64
  ,, Margaret, Countess of Salisbury, 64
Plimoth, 255
Plowden, 85
  ,, Anna, 82, 84, 107, 214, 225
  ,, Edmonde, 80, 82, 85, 201, 225
  ,, Francis, 84, 105, 106
  ,, Sergeant, of Shiplake, 82, 84, 97
  ,, arms of, 104, 113
Ployden, Mistress Mary, 96, 97
Plumpton, or Plympton, Roger, 91, 92, 93, 94, 95, 98
Plumptre, John, 226, 230
  ,, Henry, 226
Pole Place, 74
  ,, Manor, 67, 68, 69, 71, 72, 73, 74, 83, 142
  ,, Cardinal, 61, 64, 65
  ,, Geoffrey, 226
  ,, Henry, 64
  ,, Richard, 64
Polesworth, 245
Pollard, Mistress, 96
Polygonatum multifloram, 217
Poole Lands, 126
Pope, 124, 125, 126, 129, 164
Potter, James, 191
Poul, Walter, 208
Poulet, Elizabeth, 45
Poulter, or Boulter, 261
Presse, Thomas, 190, 209
Price, Father, 131
Prince of Wales, 196, 225
Prior, Francis, 128, 129
  ,, Mrs., 133, 212
Puckring, Lord Keeper, 97
Pulford, William, 80
Puntsfield, 172
Purcell, or Pursell, Thomas, 84, 107, 222
  ,, Mr., 96, 97
Purchas, George, 253
  ,, Mary, 254
  ,, Oliver, 255
Purefoy, John, 245

QUINCE, JAMES, 212
  ,, John, 211, 212

RADNOR, 195
  Ramsdell, John, 255

Ranfield, 244
Rannulf, Chancellor, 15
Rape of the Lock, 124, 160
Ratcliffe, 69
  ,, Alderman, 232, 233
Rathbury, 254
Rawley, Sir Walter, 98
Rawson, John, 244
Rayner, Edward, 209
Reade, Mr., 192
  ,, Thomas, 209
Reading, 92, 94, 99, 101, 103, 109, 169, 171, 172, 173
  ,, Abbey, 7, 10-15, 27, 38, 43, 45, 119
  ,, Abbot of, 8, 9, 11, 12, 29, 43, 45, 49, 50, 188
  ,, Corporation of, 40
Reasby, 237
Redbrooke, 241
Resum, Robert, 209
Reve, William, 208
Reynes, Robert, 245
Reynolds, Edward, 241
Richard II., 38
  ,, III., 64, 69
Rivington, 224
Roberts, William, 245
Robertson, William, 209
Robinson, Damaris, 252
Rockmore, 28, 119
Rocksbury, 250
Ros, Robertus, 208
Rowley, 255
Roxbury, 254, 256
Rupert, Prince, 109
Russell, James, 183
Russia, Duke of, 232
Rutland, Duke of, 70
Rycote, 16, 17, 18
Rymbaud, John, 9

SAINT CLEMENT DANES, 220, 222
  ,, Fredeswide's College, 11, 15
  ,, Giles, Cripplegate, 245
  ,, George, 112
  ,, John, 201, 206
  ,, James, hand of, 14
  ,, John the Baptist Chapel, 176
  ,, ,, order of, 45, 176, 178
  ,, ,, Chapel, 183, 184
  ,, ,, Gate, 176
  ,, ,, Prior of, 41, 177, 208
  ,, Lawrence Church, 103, 169
  ,, Martin's, Pountney, 222
  ,, Nihill, or Nilsitt, 241

Saint Peter's Church, 176, 182
  ,,   ,, Rectory, 29
  ,,   Saviour's, Southwark, 245
Sagittaria Sagitifolia, 217
Salisbury, Sarum, or Sary, 30, 51, 62, 169, 177, 189, 190, 193, 201, 250
Salisbury, Lord, 231
Salter, John, 53, 63
Saltonstall, Richard, 256
Sanborn, Josiah, 258
Sandeowes, Alice, 78
Sanders, Francis, 245
Sandford, Humphrey, 84
  ,,   Richard, 84, 85
Sargent, William, 252
Sarum, *see* Salisbury
  ,,   Bishop of, 41, 177
Saulf, 1, 5, 203
Savage, Martha, 223
Scobell, 191
Scots, Queen of, 95
Scrope, Lord, 20
Seabrooke, 258
Sear's, or Serry's, Court, 106, 222
Sextus V., 90
Shabourne, or Sheborn, Richard, 207
Shakespeare, 152, 153
Sheffield, 17
  ,,   Reginald, 31
Shilton, Thomas, 245
Shinefield, 13
Shiplake, 84, 105, 201
Shipton, 34, 35, 37, 39, 201
Shootersbrook, 116, 164, 167
Shrynfelde, 52
Simnel, Lambert, 70
Simmons, Thomas, 223
Simon, Bishop of Worcester, 15
  ,,   son of Nicholas, 7, 8, 188
Skithan, 241
Slane, Michael de la, 208
Slater, William, 239
Sleeper, Thomas, 258
Smith, Constance, 111, 185, 214
  ,,   Matthew, 245
  ,,   William, 111, 185, 214, 222
Snowswick, 116, 126
Somerset, Lord Protector, 25
Somery, John de, 22, 24, 29
  ,,   John Ralph de, 22
  ,,   Roger, 22, 29
Southcott, 180
Spalding, 239
Spanish Armada, 90, 96
Sparkeford, 209
Speen, 176

Spencer, 153
Speresholt, 203
Sphagnum, 217
Stafford, Reade, 19, 91, 93
  ,,   Thomas, 23, 45
Standish, Thomas, 62, 63
Stanford, 23, 245
Stapleford, 97, 111
Staunton, Humphrey, 245
Stawell, Lord, 119
Steeple Langford, 75, 98, 117, 126
Stephen, King, 24
Stoke, 70, 226, 228
Stone, Arnold, 245
Stopfountell, 67
Stoteville, 201
Strathfieldsaye, 139
Stubbs, Philip, 153
Sturton, Edward, 239
Sulham, *alias* Nunhyde, 106, 178, 179, 180
Sulhamstead, 17, 84, 93, 104, 172, 174, 178, 188, 203
  ,,   Abbotts, 43, 45, 91
  ,,   Bannister, 203
Sutton Cheyney, 245
  ,,   John de, 22, 24
  ,,   Margaret de, 22, 24
Swinstead, 239

TATTERSALL, Tattershall, Tatershale, Tettersall, or Tottersoll, etc., 204, 223
  ,,   Edward, 96
  ,,   Elizabeth, 111
  ,,   George, 63, 80, 82, 92, 96, 97, 111, 185, 201, 204, 214
  ,,   Mrs., 95, 97
Taylor, 96
  ,,   Agnes, 34, 35, 36, 201, 205
Tal-y-van, 241
Tewkesbury, 37
Thame, Philippus de, 208
Thames Ditton, 245
Thatcham, 171, 172, 220, 222
Thaxsted, 253
Theale, 109, 169, 171, 172
Thomas, son of Alan, 7, 8
Thompson, Anne, 239
Thornecombe, 254
Thorold, Richard, 239
Thorp, Nicholas, 208
Throgmorton, Mr., 249
Tibbet, Walter, 254
Tidmarsh, 22, 25, 26, 44, 45, 104, 221
Tilehurst, 26, 178, 181, 220
Topsfield, 252, 254, 255

Torlaston, 220
Torquay, 192
Tothale, William de, 208
Towne, Thomas, 78
Tull, Abraham, 194
Tusmore, 114, 119, 201
Twynbarrowe, Walter, 226
Tychewell, Hugo de, 207
Tydney, or Tibbeneye, 173
Tyrrel, Thomas, 243
Tysburye, 75

UFFINTON, Uffington, Huffinton, or Ufton, 1, 5, 7, 8, 27, 29, 188, 203
" Laurentius de, 207
" Ralph de, 27, 28
" Richer, 8
" Robert de, 28, 207
" Thomas de, 31
" Walter de, 29, 189, 207
" William de, 29, 30, 189, 207
Ufton Court, 105, 109, 115, 117, 120, 125, 126, 127, 129, 130, 131, 132, 133, 134, 137-167
" Greyshall, 6
" Nervet, see Ufton Richard, or Nervet
" Park, 176
" Pole, or Poole, 6, 73, 104, 109, 111, 116
" Rectory, 192, 194
" Richard, or Nervet, 5-10, 15, 16, 28, 29, 31, 45, 54, 104, 106, 111, 116, 119, 176, 177, 181, 182, 189, 207, 208
" Robert, 6, 22, 39, 41, 43, 44, 45, 47, 51, 52, 54, 59, 61, 62, 67, 68, 73, 74, 83, 104, 109, 111, 116, 119, 176, 177, 178, 189, 204, 207, 208, 221, 227
" Thomas de, 189, 207
Undrewood, John, 32

VACHELL, JOHN, 102
" Mr., 96, 97
" Thomas, 53
Valentia, Jac de, 231
Valladolid, 26, 88
Vanlore, Sir Peter, 22, 30, 32, 72, 104
Vansittart, 192
Vaughan, Captain, 241
" Herbert, 241
Venice, 233
Venour, Joseph, 245
" Peter, 245
Villiers, George, 235
Virginia, 261
Vyenne, 154

WALKLEY, 244
" Wallingford, 176
Wallis, John, 223
Walmer, 226
" Castle, 229
Walpole, 97
Walsingham, Sir Francis, 91, 96, 170, 232
Wantidge, 94
Warde, Katherine, 237
Wardhall, Eliakim, 258
Wareham, William, 117
Warwick, Earl of, 10, 42, 64
Wasing, 176
Waterloo, 196
Watermannes, 79
Watkins, 53
Wayte family, 81, 83
" Anne, 66, 67
" Margaret, 80, 221
" Susan, 221
" William, 66, 80, 201, 221
Webb, Johannes, 208
" Richard, 110
Weedon, 7
Weld, Joseph, 256
Welles family, 83
" Anne, 46
" Gilbert, 81
" Mary, 61, 67, 81
" Richard, 46
" Thomas, 61, 66, 81, 201
Wellhouse, 111
Wells, Thomas, 251
Wenham, 255
Wenman, Sir Richard, 19
West, Thomas, 208
Westminster Abbey, 233
Weston, Dame Anne, 72
" Sir Henry, 72
" Sir Richard, 71, 72, 111
Weymouth, 254
Whately, Archbishop, 193
Wheleton, Johannes, 208
White, Blanco, 192
" John, 242
" Mr, 241
White Knights, 127
Whiten, Thomas, 212
Whitens, 211
Whitmore, Eva de, 28
Whiton, James, 212
Wiatt, George, 239
Wihells, 79
Wichwood, 44, 46, 201
Wickens, John, 191, 212
Wilder, see Wylder

Index.

William and Francis (ship), 254
Williams, Lord of Thame, 16
  „   Mr., 249
  „   Sir John, 15, 28, 119
Wilmore, Thomas, 245
Wilscots, Mr., 95
Wilson, Mary, 128, 129
  „   Thomas, 78, 207
Wimberly, Bevill, 239
Winchcombe, Frances, 82, 115, 201
  „   Francis, 106, 180, 201
Winchcombe, Henry, 82, 115, 201, 215
  „   Jane, 82, 106, 180
Windsor, 42
Winkton, or Winckton, 106, 225
Winthrop, John, 254
Wise, Henry, 245
Witeleia, Turston de, 27
Wokefield Park, 195
Wolkendorf, 232, 233
Wollascott, or Wollaston, Mr., 84
  „   Susan, 81
  „   Thomas, 221
  „   William, 127, 221
Wollscott, 81, 221
Wolsey, 11
Wood, Sampson, 245
Woodiche, John, 79
Woodmenton, 226
Woodstock, 178
Wooley, Sir John, 234

Woolhampton, 44, 52, 127, 138, 171, 172, 221
Wootton, Elizabeth, 254
  „   Katherine, 255
Worgan, 244
Wort, Dorothy, 239
Wray, Edward, 20
  „   Elizabeth, 20
Wronkeshulle, 27, 28
Wright, Abraham, 245
  „   Ann, 239
  „   Jane, 230
  „   John, 190, 209, 245
  „   Nathaniel, 226, 230
  „   Paulet, 174
  „   Robertus, 190, 209
Wyborne, Katherine, 114, 127, 128, 134, 201
Wyborne, John, 114, 201
Wylder, John, 180, 181
  „   Thomas, 180, 181
Wyley, or Wylye, or Wylie, 67, 75, 127
Wymering, 221
Wynnynghtoun, 14
Wyrsall, Johannes, 207
Wytherton, 95

YATTENDEN, 17

ZOUCH, LORD, 233

Elliot Stock, 62, Paternoster Row, London, E.C.

The History of Ufton Court,

Of the Parish of Ufton in the County of Berks, and of the Perkins Family,

Compiled from Ancient Records.

BY A. MARY SHARP

WITH APPENDICES,

CONTAINING PEDIGREES OF VARIOUS FAMILIES OF THE NAME OF PERKINS OR PARKYNS, LIVING IN ENGLAND DURING THE 16TH & 17TH CENTURIES.

ALSO

NOTES CONCERNING THE FAMILIES OF THE SAME NAMES, SETTLED IN AMERICA IN THE 17TH CENTURY.

Rassemblons les faits pour avoir des idées. — *Buffon*

FTON COURT is a picturesque house in Berkshire, which has been standing for more than 300 years. Much that is interesting in English history is connected with it, and as is nearly always the case with such ancestral buildings, much personal and family history also. The parish of Uffetone is mentioned in Domesday, and figures in deeds and documents from that time onwards. The Perkins' of Ufton were an old Catholic family; they had owned the Manor of Ufton since 1411, and the estates remained in their possession till nearly the

end of the last century. The present mansion, Ufton Court, dates from Queen Elizabeth's time, and it still contains many of the curious hiding places used by Catholic recusants during the persecutions of the 16th and 17th centuries. It is also interesting as having been the home of Arabella Fermor, Pope's Belinda of the "Rape of the Lock," during her married life, as the wife of Francis Perkins, of Ufton. The story of such a house and family cannot fail to be of interest to the student of family and local history, and also to those who reside in the County of Berks, or have connections with the locality.

The author has, with much trouble and research, brought together a great deal of interesting information concerning the past of the house and its owners, and presents it in the form of a handsome 4to volume, which it is believed will prove entertaining and curious to the general reader, as well as to the lover of history and antiquity.

Although the book is mainly concerned with Ufton Court itself, much valuable information is given concerning the parish and the neighbouring district, with the ancient families formerly holding property in Berkshire.

The illustrations are very numerous, and are scattered throughout the text. They represent different views of Ufton Court as it now is, and there are also reproductions of original drawings showing the appearance of the house previous to modern alterations. They also comprise views of various ancient buildings and monuments, and of the present Parish Church, and the ruined Church of Ufton Nervet, also many coats of arms, crests, and other objects. Many also represent picturesque nooks and corners and views near the house, which the artist as well as the lover of antiquity will appreciate.

Among the most interesting features may be mentioned:—

An account of Reading Abbey, its possessions in Ufton, and its suppression, also of the persecutions of the recusants and searches of Ufton Court under Queen Elizabeth. A full description of the Architecture of the House and in connection with the History of the Lords of the Manor, many incidents and facts concerning the families of Paganel, Somery, Sutton, Langford of Bradfield, Englefield of Englefield, Foster of Aldermaston Eyston, Wollascott, Tattersall (ancestors of the Dukes of Norfolk), Lovel, Plowden, Norreys, Wylder, Winchcomb and others, with pedigrees of the families of Perkins or Parkyns in Berkshire, Hampshire, Worcestershire and Nottinghamshire, and elsewhere; Also a roll of the 20 pioneers of the name who settled in New England, America, during the 17th Century, with some account of their families. It is believed that this latter section will be found very useful to many American Genealogists.

www.ingramcontent.com/pod-product-compliance
Lightning Source LLC
Chambersburg PA
CBHW022105230426
43672CB00008B/1291